# Evaluating Vehicle Emissions Inspection and Maintenance Programs

Committee
Inspection an

Board on Environme        ._s and Toxicology

Division on Earth and Life Studies

Transportation Research Board

National Research Council

NATIONAL ACADEMY PRESS
Washington, D.C.

**NATIONAL ACADEMY PRESS**     2101 Constitution Ave., N.W.Washington, D.C.     20418

NOTICE: The project that is the subject of this report was approved by the Governing Board of the National Research Council, whose members are drawn from the councils of the National Academy of Sciences, the National Academy of Engineering, and the Institute of Medicine. The members of the committee responsible for the report were chosen for their special competences and with regard for appropriate balance.

This project was supported by Cooperative Agreement CX 827224-01-0, between the National Academy of Sciences and the U.S. Environmental Protection Agency. Any opinions, findings, conclusions, or recommendations expressed in this publication are those of the author(s) and do not necessarily reflect the view of the organizations or agencies that provided support for this project.

Library of Congress Control Number 2001096913

International Standard Book Number 0-309-07446-0

Additional copies of this report are available from:

National Academy Press
2101 Constitution Ave., NW
Box 285
Washington, DC 20055

800-624-6242
202-334-3313 (in the Washington metropolitan area)
http://www.nap.edu

# THE NATIONAL ACADEMIES

National Academy of Sciences
National Academy of Engineering
Institute of Medicine
National Research Council

The **National Academy of Sciences** is a private, nonprofit, self-perpetuating society of distinguished scholars engaged in scientific and engineering research, dedicated to the furtherance of science and technology and to their use for the general welfare. Upon the authority of the charter granted to it by the Congress in 1863, the Academy has a mandate that requires it to advise the federal government on scientific and technical matters. Dr. Bruce M. Alberts is president of the National Academy of Sciences.

The **National Academy of Engineering** was established in 1964, under the charter of the National Academy of Sciences, as a parallel organization of outstanding engineers. It is autonomous in its administration and in the selection of its members, sharing with the National Academy of Sciences the responsibility for advising the federal government. The National Academy of Engineering also sponsors engineering programs aimed at meeting national needs, encourages education and research, and recognizes the superior achievements of engineers. Dr. Wm. A. Wulf is president of the National Academy of Engineering.

The **Institute of Medicine** was established in 1970 by the National Academy of Sciences to secure the services of eminent members of appropriate professions in the examination of policy matters pertaining to the health of the public. The Institute acts under the responsibility given to the National Academy of Sciences by its congressional charter to be an adviser to the federal government and, upon its own initiative, to identify issues of medical care, research, and education. Dr. Kenneth I. Shine is president of the Institute of Medicine.

The **National Research Council** was organized by the National Academy of Sciences in 1916 to associate the broad community of science and technology with the Academy's purposes of furthering knowledge and advising the federal government. Functioning in accordance with general policies determined by the Academy, the Council has become the principal operating agency of both the National Academy of Sciences and the National Academy of Engineering in providing services to the government, the public, and the scientific and engineering communities. The Council is administered jointly by both Academies and the Institute of Medicine. Dr. Bruce M. Alberts and Dr. Wm. A. Wulf are chairman and vice chairman, respectively, of the National Research Council.

# COMMITTEE ON VEHICLE EMISSION INSPECTION AND MAINTENANCE PROGRAMS

*Members*

RALPH J. CICERONE *(Chair)*, University of California, Irvine, California
DAVID T. ALLEN *(Vice Chair)*, University of Texas at Austin, Austin, Texas
MATTHEW J. BARTH, University of California, Riverside, California
HUGH ELLIS, Johns Hopkins University, Baltimore, Maryland
GERALD GALLAGHER, J Gallagher and Associates, Inc., Englewood, Colorado
DEBORAH GORDON, Transportation Consultant, Los Angeles, California
ROBERT HARLEY, University of California, Berkeley, California
HAROLD HASKEW, Harold Haskew and Associates, Inc., Milford, Michigan
DOUGLAS R. LAWSON, National Renewable Energy Laboratory, Golden, Colorado
VIRGINIA MCCONNELL, Resources for the Future, Washington, D.C.
ALISON K. POLLACK, ENVIRON International Corporation, Novato, California
ROBERT SLOTT, Massachusetts Institute of Technology, Cambridge,
    Massachusetts

*Project Staff*

K. JOHN HOLMES, Senior Staff Officer
RAYMOND WASSEL, Senior Program Director for Environmental Sciences and
    Engineering
NANCY HUMPHREY, Senior Staff Officer
CAY BUTLER, Editor
RUTH E. CROSSGROVE, Editor
MIRSADA KARALIC-LONCAREVIC, Information Specialist
RAMYA CHARI, Project Assistant
PAMELA FRIEDMAN, Project Assistant

*Sponsor*

U.S. ENVIRONMENTAL PROTECTION AGENCY

*vi*

Rethinking the Ozone Problem in Urban and Regional Air Pollution (1991)
Decline of the Sea Turtles (1990)

*Copies of these reports may be ordered from*
*the National Academy Press*
*(800) 624-6242*
*(202) 334-3313*
*www.nap.edu*

## ACKNOWLEDGMENT OF REVIEW PARTICIPANTS

This report has been reviewed in draft form by individuals chosen for their diverse perspectives and technical expertise, in accordance with procedures approved by the NRC's Report Review Committee. The purpose of this independent review is to provide candid and critical comments that will assist the institution in making its published report as sound as possible and to ensure that the report meets institutional standards for objectivity, evidence, and responsiveness to the study charge. The review comments and draft manuscript remain confidential to protect the integrity of the deliberative process. We wish to thank the following individuals for their review of this report:

Thomas Austin, Sierra Research, Inc.
Robert Frosch, Harvard University
Jay Gordon, Gordon-Darby, Inc.
Thomas Hubbard, University of Chicago
Roland Hwang, Natural Resources Defense Council
Roberta J. Nichols, Ford Motor Company (retired)
Robert Sawyer, University of California, Berkeley
Joel Schwartz, Reason Public Policy Institute
Donald H. Stedman, University of Denver

Although the reviewers listed above have provided many constructive comments and suggestions, they were not asked to endorse the conclusions or recommendations nor did they see the final draft of the report before its release. The review of this report was overseen by Thomas Graedel, Yale University, and Richard Goody, Harvard University. Appointed by the National Research Council, they were responsible for making certain that an independent examination of this report was carried out in accordance with institutional procedures and that all review comments were carefully considered. Responsibility for the final content of this report rests entirely with the authoring committee and the institution.

# Preface

Controlling motor vehicle emissions is important for improving air quality on urban, regional, and national scales. In response, vehicle emissions standards over the past 35 years have become more stringent in an effort to reduce these emissions. Vehicle emissions inspection and maintenance (I/M) programs have been implemented in areas with air-quality problems to ensure that the emissions-control systems developed in response to these more stringent standards remain operating throughout a vehicle's lifetime.

Studies of I/M programs have shown that these programs have not been as effective as originally thought. Because of I/M's role in reducing emissions from motor vehicles and concerns about its effectiveness, Congress requested the National Academy of Sciences to review these programs. The National Research Council's (NRC) Committee on Vehicle Emission Inspection and Maintenance Programs was formed in response to that request. Specifically, the committee was charged with assessing the effectiveness of I/M programs, identifying criteria and methodologies for their evaluation, recommending improvements to these programs, and identifying research needs.

Many individuals assisted the committee by providing information related to issues addressed in this report. I gratefully acknowledge David Amlin, California Bureau of Automotive Repair; Thomas Austin, Sierra Research, Inc.; Thomas Cackette, California Air Resources Board; Lee Cook, EPA Office of Transportation and Air Quality; Paul Jacobs, California Air Resources Board; Scott Lee, EPA Office of Transportation and Air Quality; James Lindner, EPA Office of Transportation and Air Quality; Michael

Rodgers, Georgia Institute of Technology; Robert Sawyer, University of California, Berkeley; Huel Scherrer, University of Minnesota; Joel Schwartz, Reason Public Policy Institute; Donald Stedman, University of Denver; and Thomas Wenzel, Ernest Orlando Lawrence Berkeley Laboratory.

The committee was ably assisted by K. John Holmes in his role as project director. The committee also acknowledges Raymond Wassel, senior program director of environmental sciences and engineering in the Board on Environmental Studies and Toxicology. We also thank the other staff members who contributed to this report, including Warren Muir, executive director of the Division on Earth and Life Studies; James Reisa, director of the Board on Environmental Studies and Toxicology; Nancy Humphrey, senior staff officer with the Transportation Research Board; Cay Butler, editor; Ruth Crossgrove, managing editor; Mirsada Karalic-Loncarevic, information specialist; and Ramya Chari and Pamela Friedman, project assistants.

Finally, I would like to thank all the members of the committee for their expertise and dedicated effort throughout the study.

Ralph J. Cicerone, Ph.D.
*Chair*, Committee on Vehicle Emission
Inspection and Maintenance Programs

# Contents

Contents

# Evaluating Vehicle Emissions Inspection and Maintenance Programs

# Summary

Motor vehicles are a major source of air pollution on urban, regional, and national scales. Programs to control their emissions have focused on setting emissions standards for new vehicles, resulting in engineering and design improvements in emissions-control systems.

Inspection and maintenance (I/M) programs have been instituted in many jurisdictions to ensure that those controls operate properly throughout the life of a vehicle. These programs are implemented in areas violating federal air-quality standards (nonattainment areas) and in other areas seeking to improve air quality. The inspection typically involves regularly scheduled exhaust tests measuring carbon monoxide (CO), hydrocarbons (HC), and sometimes nitrogen oxides ($NO_x$) emissions. I/M tests also include a visual inspection of the components controlling evaporative and exhaust emissions and may include a functional gas-cap test and a pressure test of the evaporative emissions-control system. The U.S. Environmental Protection Agency (EPA) has oversight and developmental responsibility for I/M programs, which are implemented by state agencies.

Evidence suggests that I/M programs have been less effective than anticipated. This concern prompted Congress to request this study in its fiscal 1998 appropriations to EPA. In response to this request, the National Research Council (NRC) convened the Committee on Vehicle Emission Inspection and Maintenance Programs to conduct this study. Phase 1 of the study, presented in this report, examines the criteria and methodology for evaluating I/M programs and assesses their effectiveness in reducing vehicle emissions. Phase

*1*

2 will evaluate several types of I/M programs in more depth. The study charge also calls for the committee to make recommendations for improving I/M programs. The committee recommends some improvements in this report and will address others in phase 2.

In carrying out its charge for this report, the committee reviewed passenger-car and light-truck emissions (the emissions typically targeted by I/M programs) within the context of overall emissions from mobile sources and other anthropogenic sources. Emissions-control technologies and testing techniques were considered, together with how changes in these factors might affect I/M programs. The committee also reviewed methods to estimate emissions reductions, and it examined previous evaluations of these reductions and other criteria important for evaluating such programs.

## FINDINGS AND RECOMMENDATIONS

The committee found that I/M programs have generally achieved less emissions reductions than originally projected by EPA's Mobile Source Emissions Factor (MOBILE) model and the California Air Resources Board Emissions Factor (EMFAC) model. These model-predicted reductions are important because they serve as part of the formal basis for crediting emissions reductions within state implementation plans (SIPs).[1] Independent and state-sponsored evaluations of ongoing I/M programs have estimated that the emissions reductions attributable to these programs are from zero to about one-half of the reductions predicted by the models.[2] This figure is estimated using in-use vehicle emissions data, such as remote-sensing, random roadside vehicle testing, and I/M emissions testing. The committee concluded that these data provide the best estimate of I/M's effectiveness. Evaluations that rely on model predictions of emissions reductions using few or no in-use data are not accurate. This conclusion is based on a small number of peer-reviewed studies, and the methods used to make these estimates must be improved.

Despite the smaller-than-forecasted benefits from I/M programs, the

---

[1]SIPs describe the strategies that regions in noncompliance with National Ambient Air Quality Standards (NAAQS) use to come into compliance.

[2]The estimated emissions reductions are dependent on the pollutant and version of the model used for comparison. They are lowest for test-and-repair idle test programs and highest for hybrid or centralized transient test programs.

committee still sees a great need for programs that repair or eliminate high-emissions vehicles (commonly called high-emitting vehicles or high emitters) from the fleet, given the major influence of this small fraction of the fleet on total emissions and air quality. However, I/M programs should improve the way they identify vehicles in need of repair and verify repairs. Improvements are also needed in the methods used to evaluate the impacts of these programs.

The use of the MOBILE and EMFAC models to predict emissions-reduction benefits from I/M programs in the development of air-quality-attainment plans indicates a flaw in the SIP process. EPA has granted states substantial emissions-reduction credits for I/M programs without the need to verify the extent to which the predicted emissions reductions are actually occurring. That situation creates a regulatory disincentive for states to evaluate the actual emissions-reduction benefits from I/M programs. Such an evaluation might reveal a shortfall in a state's emissions-reduction benefits and trigger requirements for SIP revisions.

The committee recommends that the crediting of emissions-reduction benefits for I/M programs, as with other emissions-control strategies, should be tied to the actual emissions reductions produced by these programs. Emphasis on observational data and empirical evidence has been inadequate in most aspects of I/M program evaluations. Rigorous scientific and technical analyses have been lacking in supporting decisions related to program implementation. EPA should expand its use of outside experts and publication of analyses in peer-reviewed literature to address that deficiency. Improvements are especially needed in the quantification of I/M program impacts based on more data-intensive approaches. These evaluation methods and their applications to estimate emissions benefits of state I/M programs should be reviewed independently and be disseminated to policy makers and the public.

## Prospective Estimates of Emissions Reductions from I/M Programs

### Findings

*On the basis of evaluations by states and by independent researchers, the committee found that I/M programs provide much lower benefits than estimated by the models.* The MOBILE model estimates that a fully implemented enhanced I/M program[3] would produce overall emissions reductions of 28% for HC, 31% for CO, and 9% for $NO_x$.[4] Reasons for overstating emissions reductions include the following:

- Overestimation of the deterioration of vehicle-emissions performance (which overestimates potential benefits from I/M-induced emissions repairs).
- Inadequate representation of the behavior of motorists and mechanics.
- Overestimation of compliance with the program and the effectiveness of repairs.
- Overestimation of the ability to identify high-emitting vehicles.
- Incomplete implementation of some components of I/M programs (e.g., effective evaporation tests and inclusion of all older vehicles).

## Recommendations

*EPA and states should expect lower emissions-reduction benefits from I/M programs as currently configured.* In general, models projecting emissions reductions from I/M programs should be improved to reflect actual reductions more accurately. States should perform periodic on-road sampling and evaluations of emissions reductions and compare those observations with modeled forecasts used in SIPs. To the extent that states are allowed to use default parameters in emissions models to forecast I/M emissions reductions for SIP credit, the default values of key parameters (e.g., compliance rates and repair effectiveness) should be more pessimistic (i.e., forecast lower emissions reductions) than those currently used. That might help to create an incentive for states to provide evidence that their programs achieve greater emissions reductions than specified by the default settings in the model.

## High-Emitting Vehicles

### Findings

*A small, malfunctioning fraction of the fleet contributes a substantial proportion of overall vehicle emissions. Typically, less than 10% of the*

---

[3]Enhanced I/M programs are required in areas classified in "serious," "severe," or "extreme" nonattainment of National Ambient Air Quality Standards.

[4]The discussion here refers to analysis that was performed in 1992 using the version of the model known as MOBILE4.1.

*fleet contributes more than 50% of the emissions for any given pollutant.* Emissions reductions are skewed; a relatively small share of the vehicles failing an I/M test contributes a large proportion of total excess emissions (emissions above the standard for failing a vehicle), while vehicles with emissions just above the threshold for test failure (so-called "marginal emitters") often have only a small reduction in overall emissions after repairs or, in some cases, actually have an increase in emissions after repairs. Thus, the largest potential reductions in emissions from I/M programs are associated with a small number of high-emitting vehicles.

Studies that combine data for vehicle ownership, high-emitter frequency, and income levels suggest a strong link between low household income and the likelihood of owning a high-emitting vehicle. Studies also show that between 10% and 27% of vehicles that fail an I/M test never pass the test. Their exact fate has not been well characterized, although some have been found to be still in operation in I/M areas in some states more than a year after their last test. More study of this issue is needed to determine how serious this problem is and what policies will improve it.

## Recommendations

*I/M programs should focus primarily on identification, diagnosis, and repair of the highest-emitting vehicles along with verification of those repairs.* A number of testing or identification regimes can identify high-emitting vehicles, including traditional I/M programs testing all vehicles, programs targeting certain vehicles for more or less frequent testing, and remote sensing. States should be given flexibility to choose a regime that meets their emissions-reduction goals at the lowest cost to the public.

The focus on high-emitting vehicles should extend to promoting policies that seek effective repair or removal of all such vehicles. However, any program designed to repair high-emitting vehicles might raise serious fairness concerns, because high emitters are more likely to be owned by persons of limited economic means. The committee recommends that policies be explored to provide financial or other incentives for motorists of high-emitting vehicles to seek repairs or vehicle replacement. Clearly, further research is needed to design the means to reduce high emitters in ways that are effective as well as socially and politically acceptable. States would have to evaluate which policies are the most cost-effective and acceptable ways of obtaining emissions reductions from high-emitting vehicles.

The committee is aware that identification of high-emitting vehicles is problematic and that the designation is relative. The sense of the committee is that more needs to be known about the cost-effectiveness of setting different emissions cutpoints,[5] including the value of repairing vehicles with emissions only marginally higher than current cutpoints, to determine optimal cutpoints for vehicle tests.

## Evaluating I/M Emissions Reductions

### Findings

*Official biennial evaluations of enhanced I/M programs required by the Clean Air Act Amendments of 1990 have not been completed by the majority of states required to perform them.* The guidelines developed by EPA for performing these evaluations are limited to a single method, which compares an I/M program with a benchmark I/M program. These guidelines are being revised and expanded. Most past evaluations have been performed by state agencies in response to state requirements for estimates of emissions-reductions benefits or by independent researchers interested in the same issue.

The primary data sources for evaluation of emissions-reduction benefits are test data from I/M programs, remote sensing of on-road vehicles, and roadside testing of on-road vehicles. Vehicle registration data are also important for estimating changes in the fleet over time. There are three approaches for using those data to determine emissions-reduction benefits. The "reference method" compares vehicle emissions in the program area with those in some reference area, which can be a benchmark I/M program or a non-I/M area. The "step method" compares emissions of vehicles tested under a newly instituted I/M program with emissions of vehicles in the same area that have yet to be tested under the new program. The "comprehensive method" tracks changes in emissions for vehicles that pass the test, those that initially fail and then pass, and those that fail and never pass.

Each data source and evaluation method has inherent advantages and disadvantages. For example, simple comparison of emissions data in one area with those in a reference area needs to correct for physical and socioeconomic

---

[5]The emissions levels that define whether a vehicle passes or fails are called cutpoints.

differences between regions in which emissions would be expected to vary regardless of the presence or absence of an I/M program. In addition, using data on repaired vehicles collected as part of the I/M program to estimate the emissions-reduction benefits might not account fully for noncompliance with the program or for repairs made in anticipation of the I/M test.

## Recommendations

*EPA should provide additional guidance for carrying out I/M evaluations.* The agency is commended for beginning this work, and the committee recommends that it be expanded to include additional methods of evaluation. EPA's guidance should be based on sound measurement and statistical evaluation methods and be peer reviewed. The agency should address comments gathered during the review of these evaluation methods. In addition, EPA should publish aspects of these evaluations in professional journals so that they can be reviewed further and disseminated.

*The committee recommends that EPA and states ensure that some programs undergo comprehensive, long-term evaluations using multiple data sources and analytic techniques.* I/M programs that undergo repeated, in-depth evaluations using multiple data sources and methods can potentially help improve the design of I/M programs and evaluation process nationally. Questions about the fate of vehicles that fail their I/M test, the durability of vehicle repairs, or the impact of I/M programs on vehicle registration and ownership patterns can be answered only through well-designed, comprehensive evaluations using a number of data sources.

Independent researchers should perform parts of these comprehensive evaluations. As stated previously, these full evaluations should be peer reviewed independently by experienced researchers, and EPA should pursue publishing some aspects of these evaluations in professional journals. Because such evaluations are resource-intensive, EPA should select several programs for such treatment and should support a portion of this work.

*The committee recognizes that not all jurisdictions will be able to devote the resources needed to perform comprehensive evaluations using multiple sources of primary data. The committee recommends that guidelines for a shortened evaluation method also be developed and peer reviewed.* The method should not rely on the MOBILE model but should be based on the best evidence from ongoing full evaluations and should include estimates of all components of emissions reductions achieved by I/M programs. These shortened evaluations will likely have to rely primarily on I/M program data and other local data for primary data sources, although on-road data would be valuable. States should be urged to collect at least the amount of on-road data required under the rules for implementing enhanced I/M (0.1% of the fleet). Evidence from full evaluations done in other locations might have to be incorporated to account for factors such as repair deterioration; ineffective, incomplete, or fraudulent repairs; pretest repairs; and program avoidance by changing vehicle registration.

A review committee should be established to advise EPA in the selection of shortened evaluation methods and in the selection of what information can be drawn from full evaluations to inform the shortened evaluation. The committee is concerned about the need for states to complete overdue evaluations and urges EPA to continue to develop these evaluation methods in a timely manner. Assumptions used in the shortened evaluation can then be continually improved as more evidence becomes available.

*Both the comprehensive and the shortened program evaluations should include a consistent set of performance indicators, such as the number of high-emitting vehicles driven in an I/M program area that are avoiding testing.* Although such indicators do not incorporate direct estimation of emissions reductions, they can help track the performance of a program over time and provide relatively concise indicators of program success. These performance indicators could include the following:

- An estimate of the total number of vehicles driven in the I/M region, the share of those vehicles that are eligible for inspection, and the share of those that are inspected.
- Estimates of the actual number of high emitters on the road.
- Failure rates by model year at the program cutpoints.
- Estimates of the average emissions of vehicles that pass and that fail inspections.
- Share of failing vehicles that actually get repaired to below program cutpoints and their average emissions rates before and after repair.
- Share of failing vehicles that do not ever pass the I/M test, their average emissions rates, and estimates of the number of those still driven in the area.
- The rate of repeat failures from one I/M cycle to the next.

## Research Issues in I/M Evaluation

### Findings

*Many critical factors that have large effects on the emissions-reduction benefits from I/M programs are still unknown.* An example is the length of time that repairs remain effective for a vehicle initially failing an I/M test. Estimates of the average effective duration for such repairs range from most of the benefits disappearing in less than 6 months to remaining for 2 years or more. Without better understanding of repair duration and other unknown factors, the full effect of I/M programs on vehicle emissions will remain uncertain. Full evaluations of at least a few I/M programs would shed light on many such issues.

### Recommendations

*Comprehensive evaluations of I/M programs should be used to research aspects thought to have major impacts on the emissions-reduction benefits from I/M programs.* These include the following aspects:

- The distribution of the duration of repairs for vehicles that fail an initial I/M test.
- The extent of pre-inspection repairs.
- The extent to which temporary repairs and test fraud result in vehicles registering low emissions only for the purpose of passing an I/M test (the "clean for a day" phenomenon).
- The fate of vehicles that fail their initial I/M test and never pass (unresolved failures).
- Consequences of I/M programs for nontailpipe HC reductions.

In addition, many of these unresolved issues relate to human responses to I/M programs, but only a few studies have attempted to examine those aspects. Comprehensive evaluations can shed light on the type and magnitude of behavioral responses, but separate behavioral studies are likely to be needed to provide additional important insight.

## $NO_X$ and Particulate Matter (PM) Emissions

**Findings**

*Future air-quality improvement programs are likely to place greater emphasis on controlling $NO_x$ and PM emissions.* I/M programs traditionally have focused on inspecting vehicles for high CO or HC emissions or both. Loaded-mode emissions testing procedures[6] that are needed to measure $NO_x$ emissions have been introduced widely in only the past 5 years. Apart from smoking-vehicle complaint programs and some testing of heavy-duty diesel-truck smoke opacity, little effort has been made to identify and repair vehicles with high emissions of exhaust PM.

Currently, there are few assessments of I/M program effectiveness in reducing emissions of $NO_x$ and PM pollutants. Although diesel engines are a minor source of CO and HC, they are significant contributors to mobile-source $NO_x$ and PM emissions.

**Recommendations**

*I/M programs should clearly state which pollutants they are seeking to reduce. Different types of repair actions and different mechanic training programs are needed for I/M programs that focus on reducing $NO_x$ and PM emissions. Because heavy-duty diesel vehicles are a significant source of $NO_x$ and PM, I/M programs that target these pollutants might have to incorporate heavy-duty diesel vehicles to a greater extent.*

## Remote Sensing

**Findings**

*Remote-sensing measurements are an excellent source of fleet-average CO and HC emissions data. Remote sensing can also be a useful screening tool to identify vehicles likely to pass or fail conventional I/M*

---

[6]A loaded-mode test involves testing vehicle emissions while the vehicle is on a dynamometer that simulates the load a vehicle is under during on-road driving.

*program tests. Although use of remote sensing is increasing, its capabilities remain underutilized in I/M programs.* Combined remote-sensing and roadside pullover studies have shown that a high proportion of vehicles identified by remote sensing as high emitters of CO, HC, or both also failed roadside tests given immediately after the remote-sensing test. However, the fraction of high-emitting vehicles that escaped detection by remote sensing in these studies and the number that do not participate in conventional I/M programs are unknown.

## Recommendations

*Remote sensing should have an increased role in assessing motor vehicle emissions and I/M program effectiveness, determining the extent of pre-inspection repairs, and estimating the extent of certain types of noncompliance.* Remote sensing is also effective for identifying high emitters; however, its implementation into an I/M testing program should be an area of further research.

Greater attention must be paid to site selection and quality-assurance and quality-control issues in remote-sensing studies. Some prior studies have focused too heavily on the number of vehicles and sites sampled and have sacrificed quality in seeking large quantities of data.

To determine the ability of remote sensing to identify vehicles with high $NO_x$ emissions, combined remote-sensing and roadside pullover studies that focus on this pollutant should be conducted. An intercomparison of the ability of different remote sensors to measure $NO_x$ emissions accurately should also be performed.

An important research priority is the development and evaluation of remote-sensing capabilities for exhaust PM emissions. Further research is also needed to increase the number and types of roadside sampling sites where remote-sensing equipment can be deployed.

## On-Board Diagnostics

### Findings

*The committee found that the current data set for evaluating the effectiveness of OBDII for I/M testing is inadequate.* Contemporary on-board diagnostic (OBD) equipment, included on 1996 and newer model-year vehicles, represents a technological innovation for monitoring the performance of emissions-control equipment on light-duty vehicles. Current OBD technology, known as OBDII, provides rapid verification of the operation of both exhaust and evaporative emissions-control components but does not measure emissions. It alerts motorists to potential problems by illuminating a malfunction indicator light (MIL) and provides mechanics with diagnostic information about the source of malfunctions, including malfunctions that are intermittent in nature (e.g., a misfire). OBDII also represents a potentially improved method for assessing evaporative emissions-control components. Given its current specifications for MIL warnings however, it is not clear whether OBDII can fulfill both objectives of alerting vehicle owners to potential vehicle malfunctions and serving as a testing device in I/M programs. In addition, it is not known how motorists will react to MIL illumination, especially when the vehicles are no longer under warranty.

The OBDII system could operate as designed by automobile manufacturers and still indicate OBD I/M test failures on vehicles with low emissions. The current specification is that the MIL will illuminate if a problem is detected that results in or could potentially result in emissions higher than 1.5 times the vehicle's emissions certification standard. Studies have shown that if OBDII were used to decide whether vehicles passed or failed an inspection, most OBDII failing vehicles would have emissions less than 1.5 times the standard. Current I/M programs typically have much higher cutpoints than 1.5 times the vehicle's certification standard. The OBDII failure point might be too stringent for a cost-effective and publicly acceptable I/M program especially for older OBDII vehicles. An alternative approach, such as tailpipe testing, might be needed for those vehicles.

## Recommendations

*An independent evaluation should be established, with appropriate funding, using researchers outside the agencies to review the effectiveness and cost-effectiveness of OBDII testing programs before moving forward with full implementation of OBDII rule requirements.* The rule allows states up to 3 years to phase in OBD I/M, which is required to begin January 2002. The recommended evaluation should study the issues of intermittent failures and the value of repairing vehicles with low emissions to prevent an increase of emissions in the future. Failing a large number of vehicles with emissions below 1.5 times the certification standards could undermine the commitment to find high-emitting vehicles and ensure that they are repaired. An alternative to using OBDII as a failure criterion in I/M testing is to use it as an advisory tool to inform motorists of potential emissions problems. This option can be used while phasing in an OBDII I/M program. It may also be considered for OBDII vehicles when they become older. No matter how OBDII is used, a substantial effort by EPA is needed to help the public thoroughly understand this system. Besides the issues of intermittent failures and the value of failing marginal-emitting vehicles with malfunctioning sensors or monitors, studies of other issues related to OBDII should be done. Such issues include the following:

- The fraction of vehicles appearing in I/M lanes with MILs illuminated.
- The fraction of vehicles with MILs illuminated that do not fail the exhaust test or any evaporative test.
- The fraction of vehicles without MILs illuminated that fail the I/M test.

- The response rates of consumers to MIL illumination in both the absence and the presence of an I/M program and in the absence of a warranty.
- The use of OBDII diagnostic information to identify vehicle repairs that have a high-emissions-reduction potential and repairs that have only a marginal impact on emissions.
- The possibility for changes in the cutpoint settings on OBDII systems to allow OBDII to focus on high-emitting vehicles.
- In the long-term, the promotion of actual emissions readings in future OBD systems.
- Methods for measuring actual emissions-reduction benefits from OBDII.

## Use of the MOBILE Model

**Findings**

*The SIP process mandated by the Clean Air Act and its amendments requires that modeling be used to predict emissions inventories and estimate benefits from I/M programs in future years. Based on comparisons with I/M program evaluations, predictions from the current version of the*

*MOBILE model have greatly overestimated the emissions benefits from I/M programs.*[7]

These findings and the 2000 report *Modeling Mobile-Source Emissions* by the National Research Council suggest that there has been inadequate emphasis on data and empirical evidence in modeling I/M benefits.

## Recommendations

*The methodology used in MOBILE for estimating I/M benefits should be reevaluated.* MOBILE should allow its users to readily incorporate data from current I/M program evaluations into assessments for future years. Key parameters (e.g., compliance rates, repair effectiveness, and OBDII I/M benefits) used to forecast I/M emissions-reduction benefits should have pessimistic default estimates resulting in lower expected reductions. States might then have an incentive to demonstrate, through evaluation, that their programs are better than the default. Further, embedded assumptions in the model should be simplified as much as possible so that assumed parameter values are transparent to users, and users can incorporate the latest available data into parameters.[8] In the long-term, the overall I/M estimation methodology in MOBILE should be substantially revised. Empirical data show that the underlying I/M modeling approach is flawed.

The committee recognizes the need to continue using models to estimate I/M program benefits in future years. It is important, however, to reiterate that evaluations of current program performance should rely as extensively as possible on empirical data (e.g., on-road vehicle-emissions measurements) rather than on models such as MOBILE.

### Importance of Cost-Effectiveness and Public Response to I/M

### Findings

*Although emissions reductions are central to any evaluation of I/M programs, costs are inextricably linked to emissions reductions, making*

---

[7]EPA is currently working on MOBILE6, which is expected to be less optimistic in its I/M benefit predictions.

[8]Naturally, these input data should undergo some type of evaluation and approval process so that the resulting emissions estimates are credible.

*cost-effectiveness a critical evaluation criterion.* For example, costs influence the behavior of vehicle owners and repair technicians, thereby affecting the emissions reductions achieved. Both the emissions reductions and the associated costs must be considered in the design and improvement of I/M programs, and in the determination of whether effort is best directed at I/M or at alternative ways of reducing emissions.

Another important consideration is public concern about new technologies, such as OBDII or remote sensing, that are increasingly used in I/M programs. For example, confusion about what the MIL is conveying to drivers could impede the use of OBDII in I/M tests. Confusion about new technologies could reduce public and political support for their introduction into I/M programs and/or reduce their effectiveness.

## Recommendations

*I/M programs can be improved by identifying ways to make them more cost-effective and more readily understood and by easing the testing burden for vehicle owners.* States should be encouraged to develop and implement cost-effective means for finding and repairing high-emitting vehicles. Analysis of cost-effective measures, however, must take account of the effect of I/M program requirements on owners' behavior. Some of the issues that deserve further research include the following:

• The roles of repair cost waivers in I/M programs. I/M programs typically devote considerable money and effort to finding failing vehicles. Once a vehicle is identified as a very-high-emitting vehicle, that vehicle should be repaired, sold out of the area, or scrapped. Vehicle scrappage programs and repair assistance programs are examples of policies that could be used to accomplish such a goal. The most cost-effective policies may differ by region.

• *The use of emissions profiles for determining testing frequency.* There is already growing evidence that reducing the frequency of testing vehicles with a low probability of failure, including exemption of recent model-year vehicles from regular testing, is very cost-effective. On the other hand, increasing the inspection frequency of vehicles with a high probability of failure and/or those with high repair deterioration should be investigated to determine its cost-effectiveness for identifying high emitters.

• *The durability of emissions-control systems.* Encouraging the production of vehicles with more robust emissions-control systems through the use of extended warranties and new-vehicle compliance programs may be an alternative approach to maintaining low emissions throughout a vehicle's lifetime.

- *Understanding and quantifying owners' responses to I/M regulations.* For example, not enough is known about the extent of old-vehicle scrapping in response to I/M or of program avoidance and other types of noncompliance among different socioeconomic groups.

- *The cost and emissions consequences of enforcement efforts.* Greater enforcement of existing regulations may be a cost-effective way to improve program performance.

- *More effective means of public outreach and education.* New approaches to providing information to the public about new technologies that may be incorporated in I/M programs should be developed and studied. Priority should be given to concerns regarding remote sensing and OBDII.

# 1

# Motor Vehicle Emissions and Regulation

Motor vehicle emissions are a major source of air pollutants, and significant efforts over the past 35 years have been directed at reducing these emissions. As required by the Clean Air Act Amendments of 1990 (CAAA90), regulatory agencies, particularly the U.S. Environmental Protection Agency (EPA), are pursuing multiple strategies to reduce emissions from mobile sources. These strategies include implementing vehicle-emissions inspection and maintenance (I/M) programs, setting tighter new vehicle tailpipe and evaporative emissions standards, and promoting alternative and reformulated fuels. This report focuses on vehicle-emissions I/M programs, which are designed to identify vehicles that have higher than allowable emissions and to try to ensure that they are repaired or removed from the fleet. I/M programs attempt to control emissions throughout a vehicle's lifetime by ensuring that the emissions-control system is maintained and repaired when needed. As such, I/M programs can improve overall air quality.

## THE COMMITTEE'S CHARGE AND HOW IT ORIGINATED

In its fiscal 1998 appropriations for EPA, the U.S. Congress called for the National Research Council (NRC) to assess the effectiveness of I/M programs for reducing mobile-source emissions. The study is funded in two phases. The first phase, which is the subject of this report, was charged to use available information to assess general relationships between motor vehicle emissions characterized through I/M programs and emissions estimated by other methods. Also in phase 1, the study is charged to develop criteria and methodologies for evaluating the design, implementation, and effectiveness of specific federal and state I/M programs. Phase 2 will evaluate several types of I/M programs.

Specifically, phase 1 of the study, the subject of this report, is charged with the following:

1.  Describe the significance of emissions from motor vehicles subject to I/M programs relative to other emissions sources. The committee will assess the magnitude of emissions of carbon monoxide (CO), volatile organic compounds (VOC), oxides of nitrogen ($NO_x$), and particulate matter (PM) from motor vehicles that exceed certified levels.

2.  Compare motor vehicle emissions in areas with and without I/M programs. The committee will compare motor vehicle emissions estimated from I/M programs with emissions estimated from other sources of data. (This will address the validity of using I/M program data to characterize fleet emissions levels.) The analysis will consider the merits and limitations of various approaches used to estimate fleet emissions.

3.  Identify criteria for the evaluation of I/M programs, including equipment needs, program costs, repair effectiveness, program effectiveness for vehicle categories, and effects of human behavior (such as vehicle tampering and I/M avoidance due to cost, inconvenience, program perceptions, and nonresponse to on-board diagnostic (OBD) indicator lights).

4.  Develop methodologies for evaluating I/M programs based on the work described in items 1-3. The methodologies should be applicable to existing programs as well as programs to be implemented in the near future that will use OBD checks.

5.  Make recommendations for improving I/M programs.

6.  Identify research needs.

## COMMITTEE'S RESPONSE TO THE CHARGE—REPORT CONTENTS

This report documents the committee's response to the charge described above. The report consists of seven chapters and a summary. The committee found it useful to review passenger-car and light-truck emissions, the emissions typically targeted by I/M programs, within the context of overall mobile-source and anthropogenic emissions. We also found it useful to review regulations covering motor vehicle emissions, especially those pertaining to I/M programs. These topics are discussed in Chapter 1 of the report. We considered it important to further describe vehicle emissions control technologies and I/M testing techniques and to discuss how I/M has affected vehicle emissions. Chapters 2 and 3 examine these subjects. Chapter 4 discusses emerging testing techniques that may be incorporated into future I/M programs. Chapter 5 examines the modeling used for simulating and predicting emissions reductions from I/M programs. Chapters 6 and 7 examine criteria and methods for evaluating I/M programs. Chapter 6 discusses evaluation methods for estimating emissions-reduction benefits due to I/M programs. Chapter 7 covers other criteria important for evaluating I/M programs, including costs and enforcement issues. The committee's findings and recommendations are presented in the Summary of the report. We begin with discussions of vehicle emissions and regulations pertaining to emissions standards and I/M programs.

## AIR POLLUTANTS EMITTED BY MOBILE SOURCES

The air pollutants that are directly associated with mobile sources include CO, PM, VOCs or hydrocarbons (HC),[1] and $NO_x$ (the sum of NO and $NO_2$). Mobile sources also contribute to ground-level ozone as HC, CO, and $NO_x$ emitted by vehicles react in the presence of sunlight to form ozone.

Figures 1-1 through 1-3 present estimates of the contribution of mobile sources to national annual emissions of CO, $NO_x$, and VOCs based on modeling results (EPA 2000a). Although these data give a general indication of the magnitude of mobile emissions compared with other major sources (fuel combustion in the figures refers to stationary sources), these emissions inventory estimates are lower than those estimated from on-road vehicle studies and

---

[1]The terms VOCs and HC are used in this report to denote organic compounds that are emitted as vapors under typical atmospheric conditions. Unless quoting an emissions inventory source or a regulation that uses another term, the report uses the term HC exclusively. Appendix B describes the differences among the terms used to refer to HC.

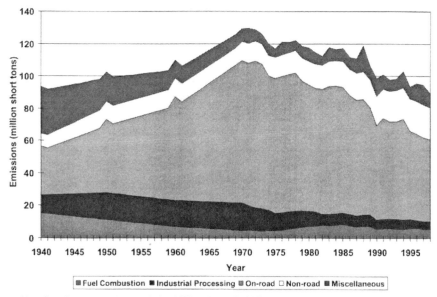

Note: Some fluctuations in the years before 1970 are the result of different methodologies.

**FIGURE 1-1** Trends in nationwide CO emissions, 1940-1998. Some fluctuations in the years before 1970 result from the use of different methods. Source: EPA 2000a.

ambient measurements in urban areas, especially for HC and CO (Ingalls et al. 1989; Pierson et al. 1990; Fujita et al. 1992; Singer and Harley 1996; Gertler et al. 1997; Watson et al. 2001).

The mobile emissions reported in Figures 1-1 through 1-3 are categorized into on-road and non-road emissions; on-road emissions refer to both light-duty vehicles (LDVs) and heavy-duty vehicles (HDVs). The differentiation between LDVs and HDVs historically has been 8,500 pounds gross vehicle weight (the weight of the vehicle plus the weight of the rated load-hauling capacity). LDVs are fueled primarily by gasoline, and HDVs use both diesel fuel and gasoline. The heavier HDVs, however (those with gross vehicle weights greater than 26,000 pounds), are fueled almost exclusively with diesel fuel. Although these heavy HDVs make up about 1% of the total number of vehicles, they represent about 5% of total vehicle miles traveled (VMT) and about 14% of total fuel consumption (Davis 1999). Heavy HDVs are also an important source of PM and $NO_x$ emissions (EPA 1998a). Non-road emissions come from a wide variety of vehicles, including construction, logging,

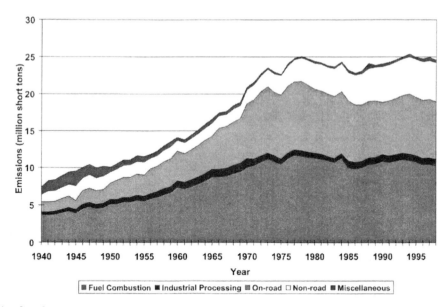

Note: Some fluctuations in the years before 1970 are the result of different methodologies.

**FIGURE 1-2** Trends in nationwide NO$_x$ emissions, 1940-1998. Some fluctuations in the years before 1970 result from the use of different methods. Source: EPA 2000a.

mining, and farm equipment; lawn and garden equipment; marine vessels; recreational vehicles; industrial, light commercial, and airport services; locomotives; and aircraft.

In 1998, on-road and non-road mobile sources were estimated to contribute over 75% of CO emissions nationwide (about 70,000 thousand short tons), about 50% of the NO$_x$ (about 13,000 thousand short tons), and 40% of the VOCs (about 7,800 thousand short tons) (EPA 2000a).[2] The remaining emissions came primarily from stationary source fuel combustion and industrial processes. The role of mobile-source emissions as a source of PM is not well understood. Emissions inventories indicate that mobile-source exhaust is a

---

[2]Mobile-source emissions are estimated with the MOBILE and NONROAD models, which are reviewed in NRC (2000). To the extent that these emissions are projected using these models, they are subject to the types of uncertainties discussed in that report.

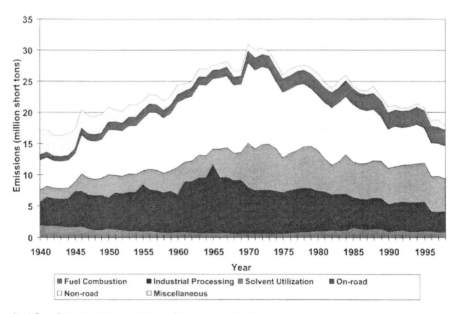

Note: Some fluctuations in the years before 1970 are the result of different methodologies.

**FIGURE 1-3**  Trends in nationwide VOC emissions, 1940-1998. Some fluctuations in the years before 1970 result from the use of different methods. Source: EPA 2000a. Source: EPA 2000a.

relatively minor source of $PM_{10}$ (atmospheric PM < 10 μm in aerodynamic diameter) and sulfur dioxide. Mobile-source contribution to fine particles (<2.5 μm in aerodynamic diameter and referred to as $PM_{2.5}$) is an area of continuing study. Recent studies reported higher than expected $PM_{2.5}$ emissions from LDVs at higher elevations (Fujita et al. 1998; Lawson and Smith 1998; Watson et al. 1998; Cadle et al. 1999a,b; Yanowitz et al. 1999). Understanding these contributions is important as increased emphasis is now being placed on fine PM ($PM_{2.5}$) because of its potential effect on human health (Dockery et al. 1993). A substantial fraction of $PM_{2.5}$ consists of secondary particles converted from gaseous pollutants by atmospheric processes (NRC 1998).

Within urban areas, mobile sources contribute an even greater fraction of air pollutant emissions than suggested by the national data shown in Figures 1-1 through 1-3. For example, emissions from mobile sources (both on-road and non-road) contribute 50% of total HC, 89% of $NO_x$, and 94% of CO emissions in the South Coast Air Basin (which encompasses Los Angeles and Orange

Counties and the urbanized portions of Riverside and San Bernardino Counties in California) (IMRC 2000). On the basis of its models, EPA suggests that vehicles typically contribute between 35% and 70% of HC and NO$_x$ emissions, and 90% or more of CO emissions in cities with high levels of air pollution (EPA 1993a). However, as described previously and in NRC (2000), on-road vehicle emissions studies and comparisons of ambient data with emissions inventories have shown that mobile-source emissions are significantly higher than estimated by the models.

## VEHICLE TYPES AND STANDARDS

### Vehicle Types

Mobile-source emissions can be categorized by the type of vehicle and engine system generating the emissions and by the type of fuel used. Table 1-1 (Sawyer et al. 2000) summarizes vehicle types, engines, and fuels that are commonly used. A single vehicle type may use any of several engines (e.g., a light-duty on-road vehicle might use a spark-ignition or compression-ignition engine, hybrid gasoline-electric, or electric engine) and any of several fuel types (e.g., gasoline, diesel, or liquefied petroleum gas). Most vehicle usage is associated with gasoline-powered, spark-ignition, light-duty on-road vehicles. Of the approximately 200 million vehicles registered in the United States, about two-thirds are light-duty, gasoline-powered passenger cars. There are also approximately 57 million light-duty trucks and 9 million heavy-duty trucks and buses in the current vehicle fleet (Sawyer et al. 2000).

As a rough guide to the significance of these vehicle categories, national emissions inventories for 1998 indicate that gasoline-powered vehicles accounted for 65% and 95% of on-road NO$_x$ and VOC emissions, respectively, with diesel trucks and buses contributing the remaining 35% of NO$_x$ and 5% of VOCs (EPA 2000a). Figure 1-4 presents estimates of emissions by fuel type for on-road vehicles. Gasoline-powered vehicles dominate VOC and CO emissions, and vehicles that operate on diesel fuel represent a significant fraction of NO$_x$ and direct PM emissions. As noted previously, however, mobile-source emissions have been underestimated and are subject to considerable uncertainty.

I/M programs in the United States have been designed primarily for gasoline-powered, spark-ignition, light-duty on-road vehicles, although smaller

**TABLE 1-1** Mobile-Source Vehicles, Engines, and Fuels

| |
|---|
| **Vehicles** |
| Light-duty on-road |
| Heavy-duty on-road |
| Heavy-duty off-road |
| Light-duty off-road |
| Aircraft |
| Ships |
| Locomotives |
| |
| **Engines** |
| Spark ignition |
| Compression ignition |
| Gas turbine |
| Electric |
| Steam turbine (marine) |
| |
| **Fuels** |
| Gasoline |
| Diesel |
| Jet fuel |
| Residual fuel oil |
| Liquefied petroleum gas |
| Natural gas |
| Electricity |
| Alcohols |

Note: These sources are listed in approximate order of their use; boldface indicates the most important sources of HC and $NO_x$.
Source: Adapted from Sawyer et al. 2000.

and newer programs have been introduced for HDVs in a few areas, such as California, Colorado, and several East Coast states. Therefore, most of this report focuses on LDV emissions, even though they are not the only important category of mobile-source emissions.

I/M programs for HDVs represent an issue of increasing interest. Because these vehicles are significant sources of PM and $NO_x$ emissions and they have not been subjected to extensive I/M programs, significant emissions reduction opportunities may exist. Currently, 11 states have testing programs for assessing smoke emissions from heavy-duty diesel vehicles.

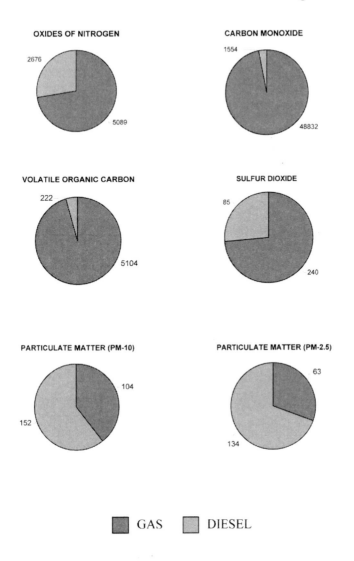

FIGURE 1-4 Estimated emissions by fuel type from the on-road motor vehicle fleet in the United States. Emissions are shown in thousands of tons. Source: EPA 2000a.

## Vehicle Exhaust Emissions Standards

Over the past 3 decades, efforts to reduce emissions from mobile sources have focused on reducing exhaust and non-tailpipe emissions from on-road vehicles, specifically passenger cars and light-duty trucks. Passenger cars, as the name implies, refer to personal vehicles used primarily to transport people. For a given model year, a single set of emissions standards applies to all passenger cars (except for California, which has separate standards) regardless of size, passenger occupancy, or use. Except for the first 2 years of regulation (1968-1969), emissions have been regulated on a grams per mile basis. For 1968-1969, the standards were specified on a concentration basis, 275 parts per million (ppm) for total HC and 1.5% for CO. This form of the standard allowed larger vehicles (with higher exhaust flow) to produce more emissions by mass than smaller models. The test procedure and the standards were revised for 1970-1972 to include an estimate for the exhaust volumetric flow based on the weight of the vehicle and a calculation of the mass of emissions produced per mile traveled. The test procedure and standards were modified again for model year 1972 and later vehicles to utilize a constant volume sampler (CVS) technique, which allowed a more accurate estimate of the vehicle mass emissions. New vehicles are certified by a chassis dynamometer test, such as the Federal Test Procedure (FTP).[3]

Table 1-2 displays historical categories of standards (in grams per mile) for passenger cars for up to 50,000 miles and from 50,001 to 100,000 miles.[4] Table 1-3 summarizes some of the major milestones for these standards. The first federal emissions standards began with 1968 model-year vehicles and controlled engine ("crankcase") and tailpipe emissions of HC and CO. The 1970 Clean Air Act Amendments required that HC, CO, and $NO_x$ be lowered as soon as possible by at least 90%. Originally, the emissions standards were set at 0.41, 3.4, and 0.4 grams per mile (g/mi) for HC, CO, and $NO_x$ respectively, to be implemented starting with the 1975 model year. These standards were slightly modified and delayed, however, and were not fully implemented until the Clean Air Act Amendments of 1990 (CAAA90), which produced the Tier 1 emissions standards beginning with the 1994 model year. The final fed-

---

[3]In a chassis dynamometer test, the whole vehicle is mounted on a dynamometer for testing. In contrast, in an engine dynamometer test only the engine, not the whole vehicle, is mounted on a dynamometer. The FTP was designed as a standardized test for measuring the emissions from new vehicles.

[4]Manufacturers are allowed to certify compliance using low-mileage cars and an agreed-upon deterioration assumption. They are not required to recall and test in-service vehicles. (Vehicles may be recalled if emissions control systems are found to be faulty.)

**TABLE 1-2**  Passenger-Car Exhaust Gaseous Emissions Standards (all values in grams per mile except as noted)

| | 50,000 miles | | | 100,000 miles | | |
|---|---|---|---|---|---|---|
| | HC | CO | NO$_x$ | NMHC[a] | CO | NO$_x$ |
| *Model Year* | | | | | | |
| Precontrol[b] | 10.6 | 84.0 | 4.1 | | | |
| 1968-1969 | 275 ppm | 1.5% | — | — | — | — |
| 1970-1971[b] | 4.1 | 34.0 | — | — | — | — |
| 1972 | 3.4 | 39.0 | — | — | — | — |
| 1973 | 3.4 | 39.0 | 3.0 | — | — | — |
| 1975-1976 | 1.5 | 15.0 | 3.1 | — | — | — |
| 1977-1979 | 1.5 | 15.0 | 2.0 | — | — | — |
| 1980 | 0.41 | 7.0 | 2.0 | — | — | — |
| *Category* | | | | | | |
| Tier 0 (1981-1993) | 0.41 | 3.4 | 1.0 | — | — | — |
| Tier 1 (beginning with model year 1994) | 0.41 (0.25)[a] | 3.4 | 0.4 | 0.31 | 4.2 | 0.6 |
| NLEV (beginning with model year 1999) | — | — | — | 0.09 | 4.2 | 0.3 |
| Tier 2—Default set in CAAA90 (beginning with model year 2004) | — | — | — | 0.125 | 1.7 | 0.2 |
| Tier 2—Current proposed standards (beginning with model year 2004) | — | — | — | >0.09[c] | >4.2[c] | 0.07 |

[a]Emissions standards were originally written for total HC and later for nonmethane HC (NMHC, shown in parentheses in the second column).  Appendix B describes the differences among the terms used to refer to gaseous organic compounds.  This report, unless otherwise noted, refers to the general class of gaseous organic compounds as HC.
[b]Standards adjusted to current test procedure methods.
[c]The proposed Tier 2 standards are a corporate average standard with a focus on NO$_x$ emissions.  This allows NMHC and CO emissions standards to "float," in that fleet emissions rates depend on the mix of vehicles used to meet the NO$_x$ standard.  The emissions standards shown for NMHC and CO are those that would result given the mix assumed in the Notice of Final Rulemaking (EPA 1999a) to meet the NO$_x$ standard.
Sources:  Chrysler Corporation 1998; EPA 1998b, 1999a; Davis 2000.

**TABLE 1-3** Significant Milestones in the Evolution of U.S. Vehicle Emissions Control Regulations[a]

**Crankcase Emissions**
1968    Control of crankcase emissions

**Exhaust Emissions**
1968    HC and CO control—Concentration based
1972    Mass-based HC and CO control (CVS technique—FTP driving)
1973    $NO_x$ control added
1975    Lower standards forcing catalytic converters and lead-free fuel
1976    High-altitude emissions requirements
1981    Lower standards forcing three-way catalysts (closed-loop systems)
1994    Lower "Tier 1" standards (EPA 1991)
2000    Control of emissions from aggressive driving and A/C operation (supplemental federal test procedure) (EPA 1996)
2004    Lower "Tier 2" standards (EPA 1999a)

**Evaporative Emissions**
1971    Carbon trap-based requirements (diurnal + hot soak)
1978    Enclosure-based (SHED)[b] requirements—6.0 g (EPA 1976)
1981    Enclosure-based (SHED) requirements—2.0 g (EPA 1978)
1996    Enhanced evaporative emissions regulations (multiday diurnal and running loss) (EPA 1993b)
1998    On-board refueling emissions controls (EPA 1994)

[a]The model year that the regulation first affected is listed in the left column. Many rules are phased in over 3 or more years.
[b]The Sealed Housing Evaporative Determination (SHED) test involves placing the vehicle in a sealed enclosure and monitoring HC concentrations over time.

eral Tier 1 emissions standards were set at 0.25, 3.4, and 0.4 g/mi for non-methane HC, CO, and $NO_x$, respectively.

The emissions standards for vehicles sold in California differed from the federal standards; typically they are more stringent with regard to $NO_x$ and less stringent for CO. Furthermore, California introduced additional tighter standards that would be phased in based on estimated vehicle sales. These standards were identified as transition low-emissions vehicles, low-emissions vehicles, ultra-low-emissions vehicles, and zero-emissions vehicles. The California Air Resources Board (CARB) required automobile companies to produce these vehicles through a set of financial incentives and penalties (CARB

1998). Following California's lead, the national lower-emissions vehicle (NLEV) program was set up as a voluntary agreement between the federal government and automobile makers to put cleaner vehicles onto the market before that would be mandated under the Clean Air Act. The first NLEV cars were available in New England in 1999 and in the rest of the country in 2001.

In 1998, EPA concluded that more stringent vehicle standards, known as Tier 2 standards, were needed to meet the National Ambient Air Quality Standard (NAAQS) for ozone and that the technology to meet these vehicle emissions standards was available and cost-effective. The Tier 2 motor vehicle emissions standards (EPA 1999a) take effect in 2004. The final rule for the Tier 2/sulfur gasoline program also requires that gasoline produced by refiners or sold by importers meet an average sulfur content of ≤30 ppm by 2007. California is planning on tightening its already stringent emissions standards with its LEV-II program (CARB 2000a).

The light-duty truck (LDT) category originally described vehicles designed for load hauling rather than for passenger transportation and was divided into weight categories. These different weight categories had different emissions standards. Some of these LDTs, and some passenger cars, have evolved into vans and sport-utility vehicles. As a result, size and function among passenger cars, LDTs, vans, and sport-utility vehicles have become more similar. As a consequence, EPA in its Tier 2 emissions standards proposes to apply the same emissions standards to passenger cars and LDTs by 2007. The boundary between LDVs and HDVs will again be 8,500 pounds gross vehicle weight. As with passenger cars, pollutant emissions limits for LDTs are expressed in grams of pollutant per mile and vehicles are certified on a chassis dynamometer.

For HDVs, different exhaust emissions standards apply to two broad categories: trucks and buses. Emissions are regulated on grams of pollutant per brake-horsepower-hour because of the difficulty of devising reasonable gram-per-mile limits for the broad range of vehicles covered. Engines are certified on an engine dynamometer. Different emissions standards are applied to gasoline and heavy-duty diesel engines.

**Vehicle Evaporative Emissions Standards**

Non-tailpipe emissions from motor vehicles can be defined as all the HC emissions from a vehicle that do not come from the engine's exhaust (Pierson et al. 1999). Non-tailpipe emissions, including those resulting from leaks of liquid fuel, can be classified into five categories: diurnal, resting loss, hot soak, running loss, and refueling loss. Diurnal losses involve HC evaporation, primarily from the fuel tank of the vehicle as temperature rises during the day. Resting losses occur when the vehicle is not running and represent the permeation of fuel through the tank, lines, and fittings and liquid leaks that are not the result of temperature variation. Running losses refer to HC evaporation from any part of the vehicle containing gasoline when the vehicle is in operation. Hot-soak emissions represent temporary emissions of HC for the first hour after the vehicle is turned off. Finally, refueling HC emissions occur when gasoline vapors escape from the fuel tank. As shown in Table 1-3, originally only diurnal and hot-soak evaporative emissions were regulated. In recent years, a separate limit was placed on the running loss. The first refueling-loss standard began with a 3-year phase-in period on passenger cars in 1998. For model years 1998 and newer, an on-board vapor canister controls refueling emissions.

Figure 1-5 shows the EMFAC2000 emissions model's projections of the relative proportions of total HC emissions from tailpipe (running exhaust and starting exhaust) and evaporative losses (diurnal, hot soak, running loss, and resting loss) for all LDVs. This plot is for the South Coast Air Basin for an average summer day in the year 2000 and projected for 2010, and it shows that non-tailpipe sources are significant for HC emissions. The most recent version of California's mobile-source emissions model, EMFAC2000, was used to develop these estimates.[5] The general trend shown in this figure is that evaporative emissions will become a relatively larger proportion of vehicle HC emissions from 2000 to 2010. The accuracy and reliability of these results are not known.

## DISTRIBUTION OF VEHICLE EMISSIONS

Numerous studies conducted over the past 2 decades have produced a fairly comprehensive characterization of mobile-source emissions and the

---

[5]The EMFAC model is used to estimate vehicle emissions and the effectiveness of control strategies such as I/M, reformulated fuels, and emissions standards. It is similar to EPA's MOBILE model, which is discussed in detail in Chapter 5 and in the NRC (2000) report. The current version of the MOBILE model, MOBILE5b, is thought to underestimate emissions from projected evaporative sources (NRC 2000). MOBILE6 is expected to significantly increase evaporative emissions estimates.

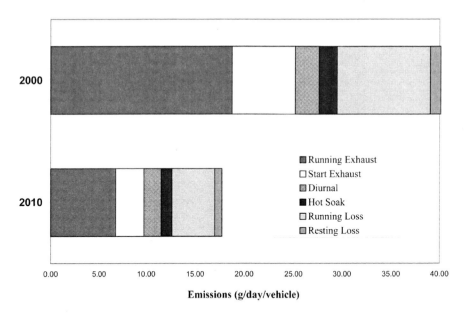

**FIGURE 1-5** Estimated proportion of total HC emissions for the South Coast Air Basin from exhaust and evaporative sources for all light-duty vehicles developed using EMFAC2000 Version 1.99h. Note that evaporative emissions are the total of diurnal, hot-soak, running, and resting emissions.

variability in emissions as functions of vehicle age, operating condition, and other factors. Certainly not all aspects of this complicated issue are fully understood, but some consistent and generally agreed upon findings have emerged. The most important one for the application of I/M is that a relatively small fraction of on-road vehicles are responsible for a relatively large fraction of emissions. Identifying and repairing these high-emissions vehicles (referred to as high-emitting vehicles or high emitters) to regulated levels or below is one of the core functions of I/M programs.

High-emitting vehicles are generally identified based on air-pollutant emissions rates in grams per mile; however, no precise definition exists. The 1992 Air Quality Improvement Research Program, for example, classified a high emitter as having CO emissions greater than 15 g/mi and/or HC emissions greater than 1.1 g/mi (Knepper et al. 1993). Lawson (1995) defined high emitters as vehicles that can emit as much as or more than 0.25 pound of CO or 1 ounce of HC per mile (113 and 28 g/mi, respectively). Slott (1994) defines a super emitter as a vehicle that emits CO at 150 g/mi or HC at 10 g/mi.

These definitions typically involve emissions an order of magnitude greater than the emissions standards shown in Table 1-2. By contrast, the OBD system available on all vehicles built after 1996, known as OBDII, implicitly defines a vehicle emitting 1.5 times the standard as a high emitter.[6] EPA recently defined high-emitting vehicles as those having emissions 2 or 3 times the emissions standards for vehicles when they were new but notes that "other reasonable boundary levels could also have been chosen." No formal analysis was done to prove that these levels were optimum (EPA 1999b). However, EPA asserts that these definitions "have generally been shown in the past to be a good dividing point between high-emitting broken vehicles and lower-emitting vehicles which are not broken."

However high-emitting vehicles are defined, substantial evidence indicates that most LDV emissions are caused by a relatively small percentage of vehicles.[7] Typical numbers reported in the literature (usually obtained from measurements of in-use vehicles) show that 50-60% of on-road LDV exhaust emissions are produced by about 10% of the dirtiest LDVs. The pronounced skewness of LDV emissions has been known since 1983, when Wayne and Horie (1983) reported to CARB that 47% of the CO emissions generated in FTP measurements were produced by only 12% of vehicles tested. Since that time, remote sensing, I/M data, and roadside pullover studies have supported those initial observations (Stedman 1989; Lawson et al. 1990; Ashbaugh and Lawson 1991; Stephens and Cadle 1991).

Data from the California I/M pilot study, conducted by CARB and California Bureau of Automotive Repair (CARB 1996), provide another example of the skewness of exhaust emissions. In this study, 643 vehicles that were due for their biennial I/M (Smog Check) test were recruited for extensive emissions testing and repairs. The data from the study are shown in Figure 1-6,

---

[6]The OBDII system illuminates a malfunction indicator light (MIL) if a problem is detected that might cause emissions to exceed 1.5 times the emissions standards, thus implicitly defining such vehicles as ones with high emissions. OBD is discussed more in later chapters.

[7]This evidence can be thought of as an example of Zipf's law, which says that the probability (or intensity) $P_n$ of an event in a series depends on the rank order (n) of the event in the form of a power-law function $P_n \sim 1/n^a$, where the exponent a is approximately 1. The law has been applied to a variety of data sets, including the frequencies of use of English words (Zipf was a linguist), and the populations of cites. See http://linkage.rockefeller.edu/wli/zipf.

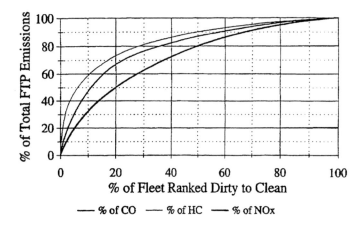

FIGURE 1-6 Total FTP emissions from the California I/M pilot study for CO, HC, and NO$_x$, rank-ordered from highest to lowest emitters.

where FTP emissions for CO, HC, and NO$_x$ for 618 vehicles[8] are rank-ordered for each pollutant from highest to lowest (the highest emitters for one pollutant are not necessarily the highest for another). Figure 1-6 shows that the highest emitting 10% of the recruited fleet produce 47%, 59%, and 33% of the CO, HC, and NO$_x$ FTP emissions, respectively.

Recent studies (Bishop et al. 1999, 2000a; Popp et al. 1999a; Pokharel et al. 2000) using remote sensing of automobile emissions indicate that the skewness of vehicle emissions might have increased in recent years. Figure 1-7 shows the results of one of the studies. In studies of vehicle emissions in Denver, Chicago, and Los Angeles in 1999 and Phoenix in 1998, the ranges of contributions from the dirtiest 10% of the vehicles are 63-71% for CO, 47-66% for HC, and 45-56% for NO$_x$. These studies showed that CO is more skewed than the other pollutants, but all three are skewed. As the vehicle fleet gets cleaner on average, the skewness of the emissions distribution will increase and the probability of randomly finding a high emitter in a program that tests all vehicles will decrease.

---

[8]Although 643 vehicles entered the study, emissions tests for all pollutants and several test types were completed for only 618 vehicles. For the 618 vehicles with emissions tests, almost 400 were given both FTP and IM240 tests, which are described in Chapter 3. The remainder were given only an IM240 emissions test. A correlation between the FTP and IM240 emissions tests was developed to estimate an FTP emissions estimate for those vehicles given only the IM240 test.

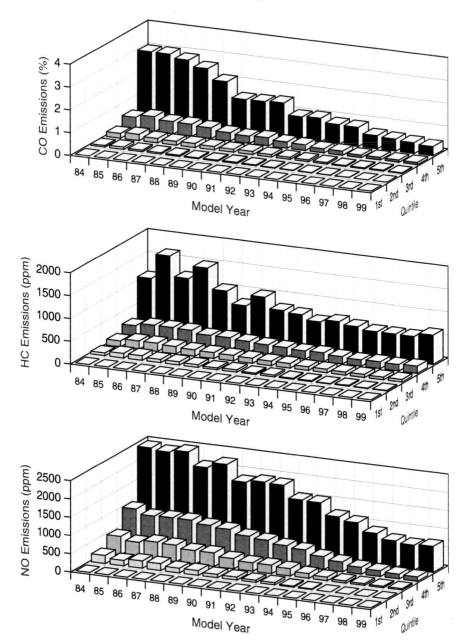

**FIGURE 1-7** Vehicle emissions by model year, gathered using remote sensing and divided into quintiles for Phoenix, Arizona. Source: Bishop et al. 1999. Reprinted by permission; copyright 1999, Coordinating Research Council, Alpharetta, GA.

Although a small population of vehicles is responsible for a large fraction of each category of exhaust emissions, the same vehicles are not necessarily super emitters in all emissions categories. Sawyer et al. (2000) conclude that although "there is significant overlap in the subset of the vehicle fleet that are high emitters of CO and HC...the $NO_x$ high emitters comprise a different, mostly disjoint set of vehicles from the CO and HC gross polluters." Figure 1-8 shows this relationship developed from roadside pullover tests in California.

An important implication of the skewness of emissions distributions is that emissions targeted by I/M programs (those above the I/M cutpoints[9]) are concentrated in a small group of vehicles. For example, in the California I/M pilot study cited above, the data in Figure 1-9 have been used to demonstrate that about 75% of the excess aggregated CO, HC, and $NO_x$ emissions were produced by only 10% of the fleet. Excess emissions are defined here as the difference between a vehicle's current emissions rate and two times its certification standard. Aggregate excess emissions are determined by summing $(1/7(CO) + NO_x + HC)$. This equation for aggregating excess emissions from multiple pollutants is described by the California Inspection and Maintenance Review Committee (IMRC 1993). It should be noted that there is no standard definition of excess emissions or of how excess emissions relate to the amount of emissions that are "repairable."

This concentration of excess emissions is also shown in the data from the 1999 California roadside survey, which pulled over 8,443 vehicles. The rank-ordered excess CO, HC, and $NO_x$ emissions are shown in Figure 1-10, which indicates that only 5% of the fleet produces 76%, 83%, and 85% of the excess CO, HC, and $NO_x$ emissions, respectively. These results, however, might have been influenced by the methodology used to gather the test data. In an attempt to determine acceleration-simulation-mode fleet emissions rates with 95% confidence and a relatively small variance, a sampling method was used to ensure that a large proportion of the data collected are from older-model-year vehicles. Older vehicles have higher emissions and thus were selected more frequently for testing in this study. If new vehicles were adequately represented in this data set, the degree of skewness would be even larger.

Skewness is not limited to exhaust emissions. Liquid gasoline leaks are present in a small, but significant, fraction of current in-use vehicles. Recent investigations have indicated that although the frequency of liquid leaks is low,

---

[9]Cutpoints are emissions levels that are used in an I/M program to determine whether a vehicle passes or fails.

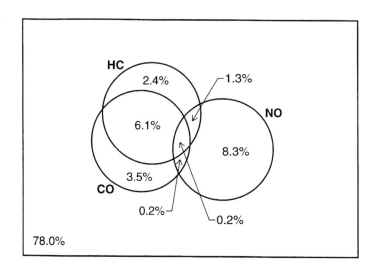

**FIGURE 1-8** Degree of overlap among the highest 10% of emitters of CO, HC, and NO$_x$ in the LDV fleet. This figure shows the number of vehicles in each category. The figure is based on results of ASM 2525 emissions tests (controlled load) administered on 12,977 vehicles in California random roadside inspections tested June 9, 1998, until October 29, 1999. Sizes of the smaller overlapping areas are not drawn to scale. Of the vehicles tested, 78% did not fall in the top 10% for CO, HC, or NO$_x$. Source: Diagram prepared by Gregory S. Noblet, University of California, Berkeley.

the gasoline lost becomes a significant contributor to the HC emissions inventory. A recent Coordinating Research Council/American Petroleum Institute leak study (McClement et al. 1997) examined 1,000 vehicles—500 in Arizona and 500 in Ohio during the fall of 1997. Half the vehicles selected were 1991 and older; the other half were 1992 and newer. Vehicles were recruited from I/M lanes and given a physical inspection next to the I/M lane. Twenty-two significant leaks were found in the older sample (4.4%). No significant leaks were found in the newer vehicles. Significant leaks were defined as expected to have "immediate, measurable reduction in whole gasoline emissions if repaired." Another study recruited 151 vehicles (1971-1991 model year) from an Arizona I/M lane during the summer of 1996 and measured the 24-hour diurnal emissions (Haskew and Liberty 1999). This study included only vehicles from model-year 1991 and older. Liquid leaks were identified in 32 of the vehicles tested (21%); 5 of them had significant leaks of greater than 50 g/day. The skewness of non-tailpipe emissions is also described by Pierson et al. (1999).

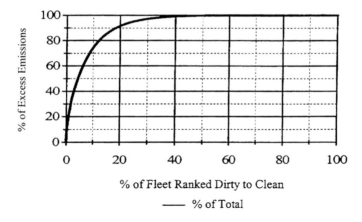

% of Fleet Ranked Dirty to Clean

—— % of Total

**FIGURE 1-9** Aggregated excess FTP CO, HC $NO_x$ emissions from the California I/M pilot study rank-ordered from hightest to lowest emitters. Excess emissions for each pollutant are aggregated using the equation $(1/7(CO) + NO_x + HC)$.

## OVERVIEW OF VEHICLE I/M PROGRAMS

Over the past 30 years, a range of I/M programs have been created to reduce vehicle emissions. Vehicle I/M programs were identified as an option for improving air quality in the 1970 Clean Air Act, and the first I/M program was implemented in New Jersey in 1974. In that program, exhaust emissions at idle conditions were tested for light-duty, gasoline-powered vehicles manufactured during or after 1968. The 1977 Clean Air Act Amendments mandated the use of I/M for areas with long-term air-quality problems, and, in

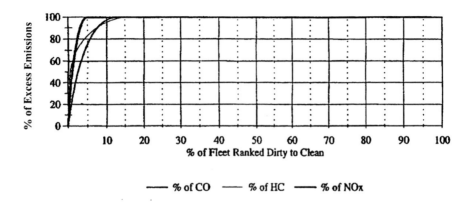

% of Fleet Ranked Dirty to Clean

—— % of CO    —— % of HC    —— % of NOx

**FIGURE 1-10** Excess emissions based on the California roadside pullover study.

1978, EPA issued guidance for I/M programs, including minimum emissions reduction requirements, administrative requirements, and implementation schedules. This guidance was broad, and, consequently, a variety of state programs emerged.

The CAAA90 was much more prescriptive about I/M, and EPA was required to develop enforceable guidance for "basic" and "enhanced" I/M programs. Basic programs were required for areas in moderate nonattainment of NAAQS, and enhanced programs were required for serious, severe, and extreme nonattainment regions.[10] The CAAA90 further mandated that enhanced I/M programs be annual (unless biennial programs were proven to be equally effective), centralized (unless decentralized was shown to be equally effective),[11] and enforced through registration denial (unless a preexisting enforcement mechanism was shown to be more effective). The CAAA90 also required the use of on-road testing and the biennial assessment of I/M program effectiveness. However, the assessment requirement has not been enforced.

In 1992, EPA published its rule (EPA 1992a) requiring enhanced I/M programs in response to the CAAA90. The rule required specific tailpipe, evaporative, and visual inspections of vehicles, including use of the IM240 emissions test for model-years 1986 and newer. The IM240 test, which is described in Chapter 3, is a 240-second test simulating actual driving with the engine in gear. The 1992 I/M rule also specified guidelines that required enhanced I/M programs to collect IM240 emissions tests on a random sample of 0.1% of the fleet. In addition, programs were supposed to perform on-road testing of an additional 0.5% of the fleet using either remote sensing or roadside pull-overs. It should be noted that EPA never described how these data would be used, and the agency has not enforced these requirements.

Implementation of the model I/M program was projected to achieve reductions of 28% in HC, 31% in CO, and 9% in $NO_x$ for enhanced I/M regions, compared with emissions in the absence of an I/M program, by the year 2000

---

[10]Nonattainment areas are areas violating federal air-quality standards for the criteria pollutants: sulfur dioxide, particulate matter, nitrogen dioxide, carbon monoxide, ozone, and lead.

[11]A centralized network consists of a relatively small number of stations that perform emissions tests only. A decentralized testing network consists of a larger number of low-volume stations that do both emissions testing and vehicle repairs. These networks are described in more detail in Chapter 3.

(EPA 2000b). Basic I/M programs were projected to give emissions reductions of 5% in HC and 16% in CO (EPA 2000b). These estimates were made based on emissions simulations for average national conditions using EPA's Mobile Source Emissions Factor (MOBILE) model.[12] Chapter 5 contains a discussion of the use of MOBILE for estimating I/M emissions reductions.

The enhanced I/M rule included a 50% credit discount for I/M programs with decentralized vehicle testing, based on EPA's observations of the degree of improper testing found in such programs (EPA 1993c). This discount was incorporated into the 1992 rule and addressed the implicit requirement in the CAAA90 that EPA distinguish between the relative effectiveness of centralized versus decentralized programs. The discount for decentralized programs evolved into a major area of contention between EPA and states, including California (IMRC 1995a,b).

The National Highway Systems Designation Act of 1995 included a provision allowing decentralized I/M programs to claim 100% of the emissions-reduction credits afforded a similar centralized program. States were required to provide a good faith estimate of program effectiveness, which was to be substantiated with an evaluation using program data 18 months after program approval. This 18-month demonstration is based on criteria developed by the Environmental Council of States and is separate from the biennial evaluation requirement.

Recent regulations have provided for more flexibility in I/M program design and evaluation from those set out by the CAAA90 and the 1992 rule. EPA (1998c) removed the requirement that evaluation be based on IM240 or other mass emissions transient test data. It called for evaluation to be based on "sound" methodologies; some of which have been discussed in further guidance memoranda (EPA 1998d, 2000b). EPA (1999c) proposed rule revisions to the motor vehicle I/M program requirements to incorporate recent policy decisions and statutory requirements. This proposed rule would provide states additional flexibility to tailor their I/M programs to better meet current and future needs. Among these is the need to maximize program efficiency

---

[12]The MOBILE model is used to estimate vehicle emissions and the effectiveness of control strategies such as I/M, reformulated fuels, and emissions standards. The MOBILE estimates are critical as they quantify the emissions-reduction benefits that a state can claim for their I/M program. The benefit estimated in the 1992 rule were made using version 4.1 of MOBILE using 1992 national default assumptions for vehicle fleet characteristics and other factors.

and customer convenience by capitalizing on newer vehicle testing options, such as OBD system testing and remote sensing. EPA (2000c) recently released a notice of proposed rule-making concerning the use of OBD in I/M. It proposes to provide states the flexibility to replace traditional I/M tests with OBD checks for cars equipped with OBDII (1996 model year and newer). This rule was finalized April 5, 2001 (EPA 2001).

More than 30 states now operate I/M programs. Table 1-4 summarizes some of these programs. Each program has distinct rules, test types, and frequencies of operation. Program effectiveness data, collected in response to the mandate for biennial evaluations, are beginning to emerge. Chapter 3 discusses a selection of state-sponsored and independent evaluations. As data on program effectiveness have become available, comparisons have been made between the emissions reductions initially projected for I/M programs and the emissions reductions suggested by the program evaluation data. These comparisons are critically important, given the significant role of I/M programs in developing state implementation plans (SIPs).[13] Moreover, evidence thus far suggests that actual emissions reductions attributable to I/M programs are considerably less, at least for exhaust emissions, than those credited to states on the basis of modeling using EPA's mobile-source emissions model MO-BILE.[14]

## EVOLVING ISSUES AFFECTING I/M IN THE FUTURE

Surrounding all these issues is yet another consideration involving the nature of current testing protocols and improvements in late-model vehicle emissions-control technologies. For the late-model vehicle fleet, current testing programs are not *inspection* and *maintenance* programs but rather *inspection* and *repair* programs. The distinction is substantive and points out a very important technological development. With regard to emissions characteristics, the emissions controls in current cars (including those dating back to the intro-duction of computer-controlled fuel injection and emissions control—most of

---

[13]Regions in nonattainment of NAAQS must develop a SIP detailing how they will come into compliance. Included in SIPs are estimates of the emissions benefits from an array of control programs, including I/M programs.

[14]Emissions-reduction credits in SIPs are developed from modeling using MOBILE, not measurements. In California, the EMFAC model is used for SIP devel-opment.

**TABLE 1-4** Major Elements and Status of Biennial Evaluations of Selected I/M Programs

| State | Network Type | Test Type | Cutpoints[a] | Visual Checks | Evaporative Tests | Tech Training | Frequency | Vehicle Types | Model Years | Estimated Start Date | Biennial Program Evaluation Due Date |
|---|---|---|---|---|---|---|---|---|---|---|---|
| Alaska | Test & Repair (85% Test Only credit) | 2-speed idle | 220/0.5 | Catalyst, air pump, EGR, PCV, evap. disable | None | | Biennial | LDGVs LDGTs | Anchorage 1968+ Fairbanks 1975+ | 7/85 | 1/97 (overdue) |
| Arizona (Phoenix) | Test Only | 81+: IM147 <81: Idle and cruise | 2/12/3 220/1.2 | Catalyst, air pump, PCV, evap. disable | Pressure, gas cap | | Annual | All | 1967+ <5 exempt | 1/75 | 1/97 (overdue) |
| Arizona (Tucson) | Test Only | 80+: Idle and cruise <80: Idle | 220/1.2 | Catalyst, air pump | Gas cap | | Biennial | All | 1967+ <5 exempt | 1/75 | |
| California (basic) | Test & Repair | 2-speed idle | 220/1.2 | Catalyst, air pump, EGR, fuel inlet | Gas cap | 100% TTC | Biennial | LDGVs, LDGTs, HDGVs | 1974+ <4 exempt | 1995 | 6/00 |
| California (enhanced) | Hybrid | ASM | 120/1.0 | Catalyst, air pump, EGR, PCV, evap. disable | Gas cap | 100% TTC | Biennial | LDGVs, LDGTs, HDGVs | 1974+ <4 exempt | 7/98 | |
| Colorado (Denver and Boulder) | Test Only | 82+: IM240 <82: Idle OBD MIL check | 5/25/8 300/3.0 | O₂ sensor, catalyst, air pump, fuel inlet | Gas cap | | 82+: Biennial <82: Annual | LDGVs, LDGTs, HDGVs | All except <4 exempt | 1/95 | 1/97 (overdue) |

*(Continued)*

TABLE 1-4 (Continued)

| State | Network Type | Test Type | Cutpoints[a] | Visual Checks | Evaporative Tests | Tech Training | Frequency | Vehicle Types | Model Years | Estimated Start Date | Biennial Program Evaluation Due Date |
|---|---|---|---|---|---|---|---|---|---|---|---|
| Colorado (Colorado Springs, Greeley, and Fort Collins) | Test & Repair (50% Test Only credit) | 81+: 2-speed idle <81: Idle OBD MIL check | 400/1.5 | $O_2$ sensor, catalyst, air pump, fuel inlet | Gas cap | | 82+: Biennial <82: Annual | LDGVs, LDGTs, HDGVs | All except <4 exempt | 1/95 | |
| Delaware | Test Only | Idle 81+: 2-speed idle | 220/1.2 | Catalyst, fuel inlet | Gas cap, pressure | | Biennial | LDGVs LDGTs | 1968+ | ongoing | 1/97 (overdue) |
| Georgia | Hybrid (100% Test Only credit) | 2-speed idle for <5 years old, ASM or older | 220/1.2 | Catalyst, Gas cap | Gas cap | | Biennial | LDGVs LDGTs | 1975+ <2 exempt | 10/98 | 10/00 (overdue) |

[a]Cutpoints are for HC in ppm and CO in percent for ASM and idle test, and for HC, CO, and $NO_x$ in grams per mile for IM240 and IM147 tests.

Source: EPA (1999d). Available at www.epa.gov/oms/epg/state.htm, except for status of biennial evaluation. The status of evaporative emissions tests for the I/M programs in Arizona and Delaware was updated April 2001.

the fleet) are relatively maintenance-free. If a late-model car has excessive emissions, it is often the result of a system component failure. The component would have to be replaced, as opposed to undergoing maintenance in the traditional sense of carburetor or other engine function adjustments.

An increase in vehicle durability, including durability of emissions-control components, has accompanied these and other technological improvements. According to Davis (2000) the average age of in-use passenger cars has increased from a mean age of 5.6 years in 1970 to 8.8 years in 1998. Additionally, the average lifetime of a 1990 model-year passenger car is 2.7 years longer (14.0 years) than that of a 1970 model-year car. These trends have resulted in a large change in the percentage of older vehicles in the fleet. In 1970, the percentage of vehicles 15 years and older was only 2.9%; in 1998, the percentage had risen to 13.2%.

These changes in the nature of vehicle technology, durability, and vehicle lifetimes have implications for future I/M programs. The increased durability and lack of need for periodic maintenance in the sense of engine "tuning" should allow for reducing the testing burden through an increased use of clean screening of vehicles or increases in model-year exemptions.[15] Technological innovations in OBD systems might greatly speed up the inspection process, and eventually make the remote monitoring and reporting of vehicle emissions a reality. Indications are that the new technology vehicles are cleaner, and capable of remaining cleaner for a longer period of time. The possible need for high-cost repairs towards the end of vehicle life remains. Older vehicles probably will still tend to be owned by people in lower-income groups who are least able to afford repairs. Thus, behavioral and economic issues might continue to play important roles in maintaining low emissions throughout vehicle lifetimes.

Emerging air-quality issues also have implications for the future of emissions testing programs. For example, the South Coast Air Quality Management District (2000) recently reported that mobile-source emissions are the most significant contributor to human exposure to air toxics. Increased understanding of the effects of air toxics and PM, as well as the implementation of stricter standards for ozone and PM, might place new demands on future vehicle I/M programs.

---

[15]Clean screening is a method for exempting vehicles from regularly scheduled inspections through low-emitter profiles or remote sensing. Both are discussed in Chapter 4.

## SUMMARY

Chapter 1 of this report began with a statement of the committee's charge, how the charge originated, and the committee's response to the charge. It then describes the air pollutants associated with motor vehicle use and characteristics of these pollutant emissions. This includes a categorization of emissions by vehicle type, exhaust standards, evaporative standards, emissions distributions, a brief overview of existing I/M programs, and an assessment of future I/M issues.

Motor vehicles represent a significant fraction of overall emissions, especially in urban areas, and a relatively small fraction of on-road vehicles are responsible for a large fraction of the emissions. Typical numbers reported in the literature (usually obtained from measurements of in-use vehicles) suggest that for any given pollutant, 50-60% of LDV exhaust emissions are produced by about 10% of the highest-polluting LDVs. The skewness of excess emissions is even greater, with 5% of vehicles producing 75% or greater of excess emissions. Identifying and repairing high-emitting vehicles clearly has the potential to reduce mobile-source emissions. Vehicle I/M programs provide the primary method for obtaining these reductions.

Despite their widespread use in air-quality management, a number of concerns are associated with I/M programs. As data on program effectiveness have become available, comparisons have been made between the emissions reductions initially projected with MOBILE and those estimated by program evaluation data. These comparisons are critically important given I/M programs' significant role in SIPs. Evidence thus far suggests that actual emissions reductions attributable to I/M programs are considerably less than those credited to states on the basis of simulations using MOBILE (emissions-reduction credits in SIPs are developed from simulations using MOBILE, not measurements). This evidence has raised questions about the effectiveness of I/M as a strategy for improving air quality. Additionally, the proposed rule for implementing the enhanced I/M program also created controversy by mandating the use of the IM240 test at centralized facilities and discounting by 50% the emissions-reduction benefits for programs that relied on decentralized tests. These issues were at the forefront during a 1995 hearing of the House Subcommittee on Oversight and Investigation on the effectiveness of vehicle I/M programs and how the MOBILE model credits these programs (U.S. Congress 1995). They also prompted Congress to request the NRC study reported here.

An important consideration for the late model vehicle fleet discussed in this chapter is that current testing programs are not I/M programs but rather inspection and repair programs. With regard to emissions characteristics, current cars (including those dating back to the introduction of computer-controlled fuel injection and emissions control, as discussed in Chapter 2) are essentially maintenance-free. If a late-model car has excessive emissions, then a system component has failed and must be replaced. Maintenance in the traditional sense of carburetor or other engine function adjustment, for example, no longer applies.

Changes in the nature of vehicle technology, durability, and lifetimes have serious implications for future I/M programs. These implications are discussed throughout this report and are a focus of the second phase of this study. Increased durability and the lack of need for periodic maintenance should reduce the testing burden through increased use of clean screening of vehicles. Technological innovations in OBD systems might speed up the inspection process and perhaps eventually make the remote monitoring or reporting of vehicle emissions characteristics a reality. New technology vehicles are cleaner and capable of remaining cleaner for a longer period of time; however, the technology is so new that it remains to be seen what their emissions and repair requirements will be at the end of their useful lives.

# 2

# Vehicle Emissions-Control Technologies

Inspection and maintenance (I/M) PROGRAMS were created to ensure that motor vehicle emissions-control systems operate properly throughout the lifetime of the vehicle. They do so by identifying vehicles with higher than allowable emissions and requiring them to be repaired or removed from the fleet. Therefore, it is important to understand the functions of the basic components of motor vehicle emissions-control systems. As outlined in Chapter 1, emissions-control hardware has changed over time to reflect changing emissions standards as well as changes in vehicle design, fuel efficiency standards, and technological capabilities. Emissions controls can be grouped into three basic types: engine, evaporative, and diagnostics. Each of these can be further divided as follows (years of introduction in parentheses):

*Engine Emission Controls*
- Engine Adjustments (1968 to 1974)
  Primary control consisted of modifications to mixture strength and spark timing.
- Oxidizing Catalysts (1975 to 1980)
  Lean mixtures and oxidization catalysts were used for hydrocarbons (HC) and carbon monoxide (CO) control. Exhaust gas recirculation (EGR) was used to control nitrogen oxides ($NO_x$).
- Closed-Loop Three-Way Catalysts (1981 to current)
  Precise mixture control and three-way catalysts control HC, CO, and $NO_x$.

*Evaporative Emission Controls*

- Early Trap Test Technology (1971 to 1977)
  Tank and carburetor bowl were vented to a small carbon canister.
- Early sealed housing for evaporative determination (SHED) Test Technology (1978 to 1995)
  Material in the detail seals on the carburetor are claimed for reduced permeation and increased purge.
- Enhanced Evaporative Emissions Controls (1996 to 2003)
  Three-day diurnals, measuring running losses, high-temperature hot soaks, and 10-year life required larger canisters and more permeation control. Refueling controls were added to cars starting in 1998.

*On-Board Diagnostic Systems (OBD)*

- Preregulatory Systems (1981 to 1987)
  GM and Ford had OBD systems starting on 1981 models.
- OBDI (1988 to 1995)
- OBDII (1996 and beyond)

These are described in greater detail below.

## OVERVIEW

The first emissions-reduction requirements were mandated nationwide for model-year 1968, and they consisted of crankcase and engine controls. The emissions regulations were written as performance-based standards (as opposed to technology-based) but resulted in the application of certain classes of hardware for compliance. First-generation catalytic converters (two-way catalytic converters) were added in 1975 to provide significant after-treatment reductions of HC and CO. The enablers were the development of catalyst technology and the nationwide availability of lead-free fuel.

The next major innovation, which enabled improved emissions and performance, was the development of computer controls on vehicles. On-board computers permitted the adoption of closed-loop fuel control and three-way catalytic converters (able to provide after-treatment control of $NO_x$ in addition to CO and HC) in model-year 1981. Closed-loop fuel control consists of the addition of an air-to-fuel ratio[1] sensor in the exhaust and fuel rate adjustment capability in the carburetor or fuel injection system. The air/fuel sensor provides system feedback and allows the air/fuel ratio to be adjusted to very precise values. The ability to simultaneously reduce $NO_x$, CO, and HC in a three-way catalyst depends on accurate control of the air/fuel ratio. In contrast, earlier open-loop systems did not have these feedback mechanisms and depended on the initial calibration and adjustment of the carburetor or fuel injection settings. Open-loop systems are sensitive to atmospheric pressure, temperature, fuel properties, and wear and, therefore, suffer from variable emissions during use.

Evaporative emissions were first controlled nationwide[2] in model-year 1971. Carburetor and fuel-tank vapors were routed to a small (about 1 liter) container of activated carbon for temporary storage and eventual use by the engine. Basic evaporative control hardware has not changed much since then, but control effectiveness has increased greatly as materials, understanding, and measurement techniques have improved.

OBD hardware and software do not directly control emissions but are a vital part of contemporary emissions-control systems. OBD systems monitor and control various engine functions, including the emissions-control system, and help to diagnose emissions-control problems so that repairs will be more timely and effective. Some manufacturers incorporated OBD on a voluntary basis in model-year 1981. The most recent version of OBD, known as OBDII, is required on all model-year 1996 and newer vehicles.

## ENGINE CONTROLS

The control of engine emissions can be segregated into crankcase controls, combustion controls, and exhaust after-treatment. Crankcase controls contain

---

[1]The air/fuel ratio is the ratio by weight of air to gasoline entering the intake in a gasoline engine. The ideal ratio for complete combustion is 14.7 parts of air to 1 part fuel. Air/fuel ratios less than 14.7 are termed rich and contain excess fuel for complete combustion; air/fuel ratios greater than 14.7 are termed lean and contain more air than is required for complete combustion.

[2]California typically has required controls 1 or more years before the federal requirement.

the "blow-by" gases[3] within the engine and use the engine's vacuum to recycle them back into the combustion process. Combustion controls modify engine hardware and engine settings to reduce the amount of unburned combustion gases and thus lower emissions. Examples include EGR and variable spark-timing. Exhaust after-treatment (i.e., catalytic converters) reduces atmospheric emissions by treating the exhaust stream to eliminate pollutants before they exit the tailpipe.

## Crankcase Emissions Controls

Crankcase emissions controls are an important part of the emissions-control system intended to eliminate blow-by emissions. Positive crankcase ventilation (PCV) was the first emissions-control system used on cars. It was introduced first on some California models in 1961 and nationally on a large number of models in 1963. PCV was required by California on 1964 and later vehicles. Uncontrolled blow-by emissions have been estimated to be 4.1 g of HC per mile, which is 100 times the tailpipe HC emissions allowed under the California ultralow-emissions vehicles requirements.

Figure 2-1 illustrates the operation of the PCV. A small fraction of combustion gases leak past the piston rings and collect in the crankcase. Precontrol vehicles vented these gases directly to the atmosphere. The PCV system uses the engine's intake vacuum to draw these gases back into the combustion process. All the pipes and hoses must be present for this system to work.

## Combustion Emissions Controls

The combustion emission controls, used on the precatalyst vehicles in 1968 through 1974, involved proper engine mechanical operation, lean (excess air) air/fuel combustion ratios, spark modifications, and external exhaust gas recirculation. Good engine condition is required for emissions control. Poor engine condition that has excessive blow-by gases, inadequate spark for combustion, and vacuum leaks can defeat all other attempts at emissions reductions

---

[3]Blow-by gases are hydrocarbons that leak past the piston rings into the crankcase during the combustion and exhaust process.

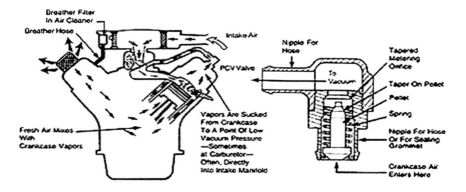

**FIGURE-2-1** Operation of positive crankcase ventilation. Source: NAPA Echlin 2001a. Reprinted by permission; copyright 2001, Dana Engine Controls.

and create permanent damage to catalytic converters. A lean air/fuel mixture minimizes emissions of CO and HC. Air/fuel ratios with excess fuel produce more power at the expense of fuel economy and increased CO and HC emissions. External spark control devices, such as the spark advance control solenoid, were added to reduce HC and $NO_x$ emissions during the 1970s and early 1980s. These parts were used to optimize the spark timing during the combustion cycle to simultaneously reduce HC and $NO_x$ emissions. EGR, shown in Figure 2-2, was a primary $NO_x$ control measure and has been used on the great majority of engines from 1973 to today. Higher combustion temperatures result in greater $NO_x$ formation. Exhaust gas is recirculated in controlled amounts to dilute the combustion charge and lower the peak combustion temperature. In general, emissions-control systems used on the precatalyst vehicles in 1968-1974 relied completely on combustion controls and usually compromised the performance of the engine, resulting in degraded driveability and fuel economy, and promoting the practice of tampering with, or defeating, the emissions-control system. Engine design modifications coupled with exhaust after-treatment devices represent the best method for meeting current and future emissions standards. It is difficult for engine design modifications alone to reduce simultaneously HC and $NO_x$ emissions.

## Exhaust After-Treatment

After-treatment devices consist of catalytic converters and air-injection systems. The early catalytic converters promoted the oxidation of HC and

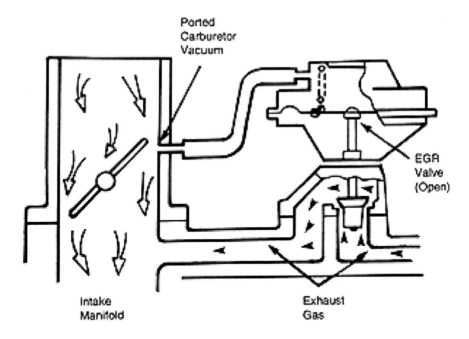

**FIGURE 2-2** Process of exhaust gas recirculation. Source: NAPA Echlin 2001b. Reprinted by permission; copyright 2001, Dana Engine Controls.

CO by passing the exhaust over a bed containing small amounts of precious metals (platinum, palladium, and rhodium). Catalysts were typically mounted under the floor, at about the front seat position, although some were positioned in the engine compartment. Faster warm-up and, therefore, quicker catalytic converter operation were achieved with a location closer to the engine. A location further back in the vehicle gave better protection to the catalyst from damage due to high temperatures.

The three-way catalytic converter introduced in 1981 and later model years looked very much like the previous oxidizing models but included $NO_x$ control. Figure 2-3 illustrates that if a 14.7:1 (stoichiometric) air/fuel ratio were maintained, the catalysts could effectively promote both the oxidation of HC and CO and the reduction of $NO_x$. Simultaneous efficiencies of over 80% were possible under warmed-up operation. Closed-loop fuel control was required for effective operation.

Catalysts can be damaged by several mechanisms (Ihara et al. 1987). They can be poisoned through an accumulation of deactivating materials due to excessive oil consumption or the use of leaded fuel over a long period. They

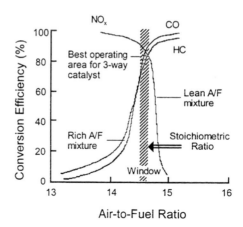

Air-to-Fuel Ratio

**FIGURE 2-3** Catalyst conversion efficiency as a function of air/fuel (A/F) mixture ratio. Source: Adapted from Canale et al. (1978).

suffer thermal damage from high-load misfire, when the mass rate of air/fuel mixture is high enough to produce a damaging temperature rise. The substrate can melt or fracture and pass out the tailpipe. Thermal damage can occur suddenly or over a long period.

Air injection was and, to some extent, still is used both to promote HC and CO oxidation after the engine by adding air to the hot gases as they exit the exhaust port to augment the effectiveness of the catalytic converter. Engine-driven air pumps were common, with valves to supply or divert air as required. Another type of air injection system, the pulse air system, was sometimes used on four-cylinder engines. Check valves and appropriate plumbing allowed the normal pulsations of the exhaust system to supply excess air to the exhaust. Electric air pumps are becoming common on new applications, operating only for a brief period at start-up, while the catalyst is cold and not fully operational.

## EVAPORATIVE CONTROLS

Evaporative emissions are the HCs that escape from the vehicle that do not come from the tailpipe. These emissions include fuel and vapor leaks from the tank and plumbing, refrigerant from the air-conditioning system, coolant leaks, tire emissions, and solvents in the vinyls and adhesives of the vehicle. Such sources contribute significantly to overall HC emissions. Evaporative

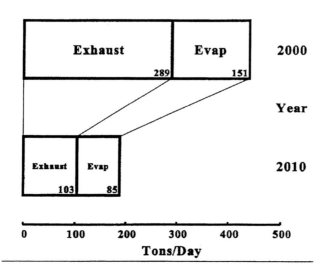

FIGURE 2-4 Exhaust and evaporative emissions for the South Coast Air Basin (SCAB) in 2000 and 2010 using EMFAC2000 Version 1.99h.

emissions have become increasingly important as other sources have been controlled. Figure 2-4 shows model projections for the aggregate exhaust and evaporative emissions for the South Coast Air Basin for an average summer day in 2000 and 2010. The most recent version of California's mobile-source emissions model, EMFAC2000, was used to develop those estimates. The uncertainties in those projections are not reported by the model but are likely to be large. Evaporative emissions are estimated to be about one-third of the daily light-duty vehicle (LDV) HC in the South Coast Air Basin in 2000 and are estimated to be 45% of the total in 2010.

Evaporative emissions can escape from a wide variety of places on the vehicle. The purpose of this section is to define some terms and illustrate where they might occur. The materials used and, to some extent, the design of the later fuel injection systems have resulted in a more durable system less prone to leaks than the carburetor models that they replaced. Fuel injection systems are first discussed, followed by the differences found in the older carburetor-equipped models.

The fuel tank is usually located at the rear of the vehicle. A vapor volume is provided above the liquid, even when the tank is full, to allow for expansion and to help separate the liquid from the vapor. The fill neck (the pipe between the gas cap and the tank) can be a separate component connected to the tank in one or more places with rubber hoses and clamps. The gas cap is a critical component—one that is removed and replaced repeatedly over the lifetime of the vehicle. A cap not replaced or one with a cracked seal results in uncontrolled evaporative emissions of up to 20 g of HC in a single day.

Fuel-injection vehicles typically have a fuel supply pump that is mounted in the tank. The chassis fuel line, typically an 8- or 9-millimeter-diameter tube, carries the pressurized fuel forward to the engine. The chassis line typically is made of steel and rigidly mounted to the underbody of the vehicle. Nylon has also been used for a number of years; it offers superior corrosion resistance and reduces the potential for fuel leaks. A serviceable fuel filter is usually fitted in the supply line. The chassis line is connected to the fuel tank with a flexible hose for assembly, service, and isolation. A similar flexible connection is made to the engine at the front of the vehicle. Many engine fuel systems use an engine-mounted pressure regulator and return excess fuel back to the tank through a duplicate chassis line. The return line is not at the supply pressure, but it is still pressurized. These fuel lines and connectors might be sources of liquid fuel leaks.

Vapors from the fuel tank are routed through a tank vent tube to a carbon canister for storage. The canister is required for the late 1990s models with on-board control of refueling vapors and may be close to the tank or located in the engine compartment. Vehicle motion can produce "slosh" in the tank, and liquid can be trapped in the vent unless provisions have been made to separate it. Some applications use special liquid/vapor separators to ensure that only vapor is routed to the carbon canister. The canister is rejuvenated or "purged" during engine operation by using the engine's vacuum to draw air through the carbon bed and to the engine. The canister has at least three connections: a tank vapor vent, a purge line, and an air-supply port.

Engines with carburetors have all the above features and one more—a line venting the carburetor to the carbon canister. The carburetor includes a reservoir or "bowl" where fuel is stored before it is drawn through the carburetor metering systems into the combustion chamber. A carburetor typically has approximately 50 milliliters (38 g) of fuel in the bowl. After engine shutdown, residual engine heat rises into the bowl, creating vapors and, under severe summer conditions, boiling away the fuel. Unless the carburetor bowl is properly vented, these vapors can find their way into the environment.

## OBD SYSTEMS

The exhaust emissions standards (HC, 0.41 g/mi; CO, 3.4 g/mi; $NO_x$, 1.0 g/mi) that were required in the 1981 model year forced the adoption of computer-based closed-loop control systems. The digital computers used for these applications were able to monitor and actuate many vehicle system functions and signal the driver and repair technician if system problems were present. Computer-controlled cars are able to maintain near optimal air/fuel ratios, enabling the adoption of durable three-way catalytic converters. Many manufacturers used OBD systems to help with the service and reliability of their vehicles (Grimm et al. 1980; Gumbleton and Bowler 1982). The OBD system is made up of the sensors and actuators used to monitor and modify specific components as well as the diagnostic software in the on-board computer. Such a system can communicate its findings to a service technician using diagnostic trouble codes stored in the computer's memory. California regulators recognized the potential of the OBD system, expanded the scope, and required it on new vehicles starting with a 1988 model year phase-in. California and the U.S. Environmental Protection Agency expanded the scope and coverage of diagnostics with the OBDII regulations, which were phased in beginning with the model-year 1994 vehicles.

All LDVs built after 1996 (with a few exceptions) are equipped with the OBDII system. OBDII periodically checks many emissions-control functions. The check includes monitoring the following emissions-control components: catalysts, oxygen sensors, evaporative canister purge system, fuel tank leak check, misfire detection, and on-board computers. If a problem is detected that could cause emissions to exceed 1.5 times the emissions standards, the OBDII system illuminates a malfunction indicator light (MIL), also known as the "check engine" light, on vehicle dashboards. Note that the MIL illuminates if emissions *could* exceed 1.5 times the certification standard and that OBDII does not actually measure emissions. Some vehicles with illuminated MILs might not have emissions at that level yet, and some may have an intermittent problem. An issue with intermittent problems is that the MIL might illuminate once a problem is detected but remain on for a significant period of time before the light is extinguished, and the stored code erased. Besides notifying the operator of a malfunction, the objective of the OBDII system is to protect the catalytic converter from permanent damage from exposure to excessive emissions. Further developments of OBD technology, such as remote monitoring or reporting, can provide alternatives to the traditional tailpipe tests used now to monitor vehicle emissions-control systems. OBDII systems that can report vehicle status through remote monitoring or reporting are referred to as OBDIII systems. The I/M aspects of the OBD system are discussed later in this report.

## SUMMARY

Emissions-control systems have grown more comprehensive and have matured over the years as the technology and the public commitment to air quality have grown. The earliest tailpipe controls (1968-1974) required frequent adjustments and benefited only certain modes of vehicle operation. The need for periodic inspection and adjustments for the life of the vehicle was critical to maintaining emissions performance. Oxidation catalytic converter after-treatment systems (1975-1980) allowed major reductions in CO and HC emissions levels but still relied on engine adjustments and periodic inspections to ensure good performance. An important aspect of the periodic inspection was to ensure that the vehicle still had a functional, nontampered emissions-control system. Introduction of the computer-controlled exhaust feedback systems in 1981 created a new generation of self-adjusting systems. The three-way catalyst controlled $NO_x$, but required stoichiometric operation to have sufficient CO for $NO_x$ reduction to occur. OBD systems were added later (by regulation in 1994) to signal the driver that there was a system problem and to help the service technician make the correct diagnosis and repair. OBD technology has the potential to change the role of I/M for new-technology vehicles.

# 3

# Vehicle Inspection and Maintenance Programs

This chapter describes the basic components of the inspection and maintenance (I/M) program, the components that attempt to identify, diagnose, repair, and verify repairs for vehicles with high emissions. The following sections describe the various network types, testing methods, and other elements of an I/M program. Also discussed are results from some previous evaluations of the effectiveness of existing programs.

## I/M PROGRAM NETWORK TYPES

The implementation structure of an I/M program, also known as "network type," can have a major impact on its operation. Three basic network types that are currently in operation are

- Centralized.
- Decentralized.
- Hybrid.

Remote sensing establishes yet another testing type.[1] Each program type

---

[1]States are now beginning to evaluate the feasibility of incorporating remote sensing as an integral part of their I/M programs. For example, the Denver Regional Air Quality Council has recommended beginning a "clean screen" program in January 2002, where on-road remote-sensing measurements would be used to exempt vehicles from scheduled testing (Regional Air Quality Council 2000). Missouri has been operating a remote-sensing clean screen program since early 2000.

has its strengths and weaknesses in terms of effectiveness, cost, and acceptance by the public, the repair industry, and politicians. The following sections further describe the characteristics of the centralized, decentralized, and hybrid network types.

## Centralized Network

A centralized network consists of a relatively small number (relative to a decentralized network) of stations that perform only emissions tests. Vehicles that fail the inspection must be repaired elsewhere. This network typically is operated by a government entity or by a contractor with government administration.

This system performs a high volume of emissions tests at low operating costs. The centralized network can achieve an economy of scale in terms of the investment in equipment, inspector training, quality control, data collection, and reporting. Program management, consisting of administrative and operational controls, is also more effective because there is better direct communication with the testing stations. The smaller number of stations associated with a centralized testing network also simplifies program management.

Disadvantages of a centralized network include the need to make inspection stations convenient for the public while controlling costs for construction and operation. Property conveniently located for the motoring public is often difficult to find and/or very expensive. The centralized network might be more inconvenient to the public because of fewer testing stations and longer travel times to reach them. The centralized network also might be more inconvenient to the public when a facility is experiencing high demand due to test expiration deadlines or lane closures due to equipment problems.

An additional disadvantage of the centralized network is the "ping-pong" effect. This happens when a vehicle fails the I/M test, obtains repairs at a separate location, and returns to the I/M centralized network but fails again. Some centralized networks have implemented measures such as the "repair effectiveness index," which rates the effectiveness of repair stations to minimize the ping-pong effect. Motorists can use this information to select a repair station to minimize the need to go back and forth between testing and repairs. Technicians in the repair industry might think they need to purchase emissions analyzers to verify that the emissions repairs they perform allow the vehicles to pass the test after repair. However, in a centralized network, this equipment would be purchased without the opportunity to collect a fee for the emissions test verification.

## Decentralized Network

A decentralized testing network consists of a larger number of low-volume stations that do both emissions testing and vehicle repairs. This type of network links testing to the repair process and is operated by private sector stations.

An advantage of the decentralized network is that it provides a revenue stream from testing fees, which in turn may enable the repair industry to acquire the training and skills needed to perform emissions-related vehicle repairs. In addition, the repair technician can use the emissions analyzer to verify the effectiveness of the repairs performed and eliminate the ping-pong effect that can occur for some vehicles in the centralized network.

Program enforcement and quality control are more difficult in a decentralized network than in a centralized program because of the larger number of stations in the network.[2] There can be more instances of fraud because of the difficulty of overseeing all test stations. Test-and-repair stations have additional economic incentives not present in centralized test programs to fix vehicles to pass (to please the customer),[3] or to fail (to get more repair business).[4]

---

[2]There is no recent comprehensive study, however, to indicate that there are more fraudulently passed vehicles occurring in decentralized programs. Testing fraud has been reported in both decentralized and centralized programs. Since there are many more stations performing inspections in the decentralized network, the number of stations cited for testing fraud will likely be higher compared to a centralized program. However, the number of inspections an individual station may be performing could be low whereas testing fraud at a high-volume centralized testing facility may impact a large number of tests. The committee could not find a rigorous comparison of these program types to state definitively that the number of vehicles impacted by testing fraud is greater in a decentralized program.

[3]Hubbard (1998) found that test-and-repair stations have an incentive to help vehicles pass inspections to increase the long-term demand for their inspections, even though they could increase short-term demand for emissions-related repairs by helping vehicles fail.

[4]Both test-and-repair and repair-only stations may provide more repairs than are actually needed (to make more money for the shop). Thus, some of the issues concerning repairs will happen in centralized testing as well.

However, advances in the design of emissions analyzers are thought to have made decentralized programs more effective by incorporating built-in quality control, making analyzers less prone to tampering, and linking station data to central data collection facilities.

## Hybrid Program

A hybrid network is one that incorporates elements of both decentralized and centralized programs. One type of hybrid program incorporates both high-volume "test-only" stations and low-volume "repair-and-retest" stations. This approach achieves economy in enforcement, data and program management, and quality control for the initial test, which has the largest volume of testing. It also provides an incentive to the repair industry by allowing them to perform the official retest and eliminates the problem of repaired vehicles having to return to a centralized facility for the retest.

Another type of hybrid program sends a fraction of vehicles, such as those fitting the profile of a vehicle having high emissions, to a test-only station and allows others to choose to go to either a centralized station or a decentralized test-and-repair station. Such a program attempts to ensure that vehicles most likely to fail will undergo testing at facilities with the highest quality control. It also provides fairly convenient testing for most vehicle owners at the decentralized testing locations.

## VEHICLE-EMISSIONS TESTING

Vehicle emissions tests vary in terms of the complexity of driving conditions represented. An important issue is the need for the test to obtain an accurate measurement of emissions while keeping equipment costs low and test duration short.

### Mass Emissions versus Concentration Measurements

The two principal methods of measuring exhaust emissions are (1) directly measuring the mass of emitted pollutants, and (2) measuring the concentrations of pollutants in exhaust emissions. These methods are known as mass emissions tests and concentration tests, respectively.

Mass emissions tests quantify vehicle exhaust emissions by measuring the mass of various pollutants that are emitted. Generally, these emissions are expressed as the mass of pollutant emitted divided by the distance the vehicle is driven on a simulated driving cycle. In this type of testing, a vehicle is driven on a dynamometer and the results are expressed in terms of grams of pollutant emitted per mile traveled.

Concentration tests, on the other hand, measure the relative pollutant concentrations in a vehicle's exhaust. Because the measurement is a concentration measurement (generally expressed in terms of percentage or parts per million of total exhaust volume) little is known about the absolute amount of pollution generated. For a given exhaust concentration, vehicles with larger engines and higher fuel consumption will have higher mass emissions. To understand the magnitude of actual emissions, both pollutant concentrations and the volume of exhaust must be known. The exhaust volume is measured in some, but not all, of the emissions tests used in I/M programs. By knowing the volume of emissions and airflow, it is possible to determine an average mass emissions rate. Converting concentration test results to mass emissions introduces uncertainty in the estimates (Haskew et al. 1987).

## Steady-State Versus Transient Testing

Another way to differentiate vehicle emissions tests is by describing the conditions under which emissions are measured. Emissions can be measured under static or dynamic conditions, which are referred to as steady-state or transient tests, respectively.

Steady-state tests measure vehicle emissions under one stable operating condition. Typically, a vehicle is tested at idle, when no dynamometer is used, or under steady speed with a simulated load when tested on a dynamometer. Dynamometer-based tests, such as the acceleration simulation mode (ASM) tests, are steady-state tests because they run the engine under a constant load instead of varying the load throughout the test, as is done in transient tests. Although steady-state tests do not simulate the range of driving conditions that are included in transient tests, they require smaller expenditures for testing equipment and may be performed in less time.

Transient tests require a vehicle to operate under varying speeds and loads. They represent on-road driving conditions much better than steady-state tests, and they are transitory in nature. In emissions testing, typically the speed and acceleration of the vehicle are varied. By testing a vehicle under different speeds and engine loads, a broader range of emissions results is measured. To obtain a measurement that is more representative of emissions when vehicles are driven on the road, test cycles have been developed that seek to replicate actual driving conditions.

## Exhaust Emissions Test Types

A number of tests are commonly used to measure vehicle exhaust emissions. These range from unloaded idle tests to sophisticated transient-cycle mass emissions tests, such as the Federal Test Procedure (FTP). Some of the more common tests are described below.

## Mass Emissions Tests

• FTP—City Driving Test—This is a loaded-mode laboratory grade mass emissions test with transient (stop-and-go) driving conditions that is used by vehicle manufacturers to certify the emissions of prototype vehicles before they can sell the vehicle for the first time in the United States. It is usually considered the benchmark emissions test by which all other light-duty vehicle tests are measured. The FTP has extensive protocols, including specifying fuel parameters and environmental conditions and requires large expenditures of time, personnel, and capital. The test is split into various phases designed to measure the emissions from cold-start, urban driving, and hot-start operating conditions. To perform the City Driving Test (also known as the Urban Dynamometer Driving Schedule) and all other elements of the FTP (including preparing the vehicle for testing), at least 2 days per vehicle are usually required. A problem with the FTP has been that the test does not measure emissions that occur during heavy acceleration or high-load operating conditions that are sometimes observed in on-road driving (Kelly and Groblicki 1993; St. Denis et al. 1994; Cicero-Fernandez et al. 1997). The Supplemental Federal Test Procedure (SFTP) was proposed in 1996 (EPA 1996) to control emissions at high speed, at high load, and with the air conditioning operating.

• IM240—This test is a shortened version of the FTP, in which the vehicle is given minimal conditioning, and is assumed to be tested when fully warm. Thus, it can be conducted outside the laboratory in a well-equipped inspection station. It is a loaded-mode transient dynamometer test, which measures the mass of emissions collected over a 240-second, 2-mile driving cycle that corresponds to the first 240 seconds of the City Driving Test of the FTP (see Figure 3-1). Many states that utilize the IM240 test have implemented a "fast/pass" or a "fast/fail" procedure or both. This shortened version can reduce the testing time by several minutes.

• BAR31—This is a short, loaded-mode dynamometer test utilizing similar equipment as the IM240. The driving cycle has been truncated to 31 seconds, with the vehicle sharply accelerating and then decelerating through the test. A vehicle has three chances to pass the test.

• IM93/CT93—Connecticut 93—This test is a short version of the IM240 test cycle, utilizing the first "hill" or phase of the IM240. It consists of the first 93 seconds of the IM240.

• IM147—This is also a shortened version of the IM240, specifically the second phase (final 147 seconds). A major difference is the application of a retest algorithm that determines whether a failing vehicle needs preconditioning before a final failure determination is made.[5] A vehicle may be given up to three consecutive IM147 drive cycles before it fails.

• VMASS—The VMASS flowmeter system converts a concentration measurement to a mass measurement. The test methodology could use any transient I/M test cycle, such as the BAR31, CT93, or IM147. In this system, BAR97 type equipment (see below) is coupled to a transient dynamometer.

**Concentration Tests**

• Idle test—This steady-state unloaded test uses a tailpipe probe to measure directly the concentrations of CO, HC, and carbon dioxide ($CO_2$) in exhaust emissions from idling vehicles. A high-idle test, in which engine speed is manually increased to ~2,500 revolutions per minute (rpm), is sometimes performed in addition to the natural or "low-idle" test; in all cases, there is no

---

[5]Preconditioning refers to a vehicle that is fully warmed up so that it can give a valid result from an I/M emission test. Cutpoints, which determine passing or failing for such a vehicle, are based on testing a fully warmed-up vehicle in which the emissions control equipment, including the catalytic converter, are fully functional. If an owner drives a short distance to the test station or if the vehicle has to wait in the test station for a long time, the vehicle might not be fully warmed up, resulting in a false reading; a car that would have passed if fully warmed (i.e., fully preconditioned) would fail.

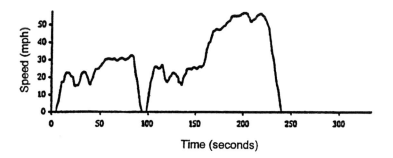

**FIGURE 3-1** IM240 driving cycle.

load applied to the engine. $NO_x$ concentrations are not usually measured as part of idle tests because $NO_x$ emissions are low if the engine is not under a load. The idle test is less expensive than loaded-mode testing because no dynamometer is required. Although idle tests measure and report pollutant concentrations, Marr et al. (1998) describes how mass emissions rates (i.e., grams of pollutant emitted per minute at idle) can be calculated from engine displacement volume, engine speed at idle, and measured tailpipe concentrations from the idle test.

• ASM—This series of loaded-mode steady-state emissions tests measures exhaust concentrations from motor vehicles operated on a dynamometer. The test series measures vehicle emissions under a loaded condition that simulates an acceleration event. The ASM steady-state test measures vehicle emissions at 15 (ASM 5015) and 25 (ASM 2525) mph. The tests subject the vehicle to load conditions that are based on the maximum acceleration events in the FTP. The ASM 5015 subjects a vehicle to 50% of the maximum load conditions in the FTP test, and the ASM 2525 subjects a vehicle to 25% of the maximum load conditions in the FTP.

• BAR97—This refers to emissions testing equipment and software that meet the 1997 California Bureau of Automotive Repair's specifications for use in their I/M programs. The same test equipment may be used to perform either the ASM or the idle tests described above. This test equipment is normally used for concentration measurements. When a BAR97 test analyzer is used in conjunction with a VMASS flow meter, it is then used to measure mass emissions. Earlier versions of the BAR analyzer specifications were issued in 1984, 1990, and 1994. Analyzers that met pre-1997 specifications were usually used to perform idle tests only.

• Remote sensing—This is a nonintrusive method of measuring emissions from individual vehicles as they drive by a sensor deployed at a roadside location. In normal operation, a beam of light is projected across a single lane of traffic at tailpipe height, and light absorbed by pollutants is measured, usually at specific infrared wavelengths (ultraviolet light absorption is used in some systems to measure NO emissions). Remote-sensing measurements are typically coupled to a video image of the vehicle license plate, which can be used to obtain vehicle make, model year, and other relevant information from a central database.

## Comparison of Exhaust Emissions-Test Types

The California I/M pilot study (CARB 1996) provided the opportunity to compare emissions results from several candidate exhaust test types: the FTP, IM240, ASM5015, ASM2525, and low- and high-speed idle tests. In this program, 380 vehicles due for their biennial inspection were given all six emissions tests. As a result, this sample was probably enriched in high emitters relative to the whole vehicle fleet. The data were analyzed to compare different emissions tests for measuring tailpipe CO and HC emissions. Figures 3-2 and 3-3 present the results, which are described further by Lawson and Koracin (1996). In Figure 3-2, the CO emissions from the 380 vehicles were rank-ordered from dirtiest to cleanest according to their FTP, IM240, ASM, and idle-test results. For the ASM and idle tests, the maximum value from either of the two ASM or idle tests was used. Figure 3-3 shows the results for HC plotted in the same manner. The correlation among the different test types is shown in Table 3-1. The statistic used is the Spearman rank-order correlation,[6] which is a statistical method that measures the correlation between ranks of two sets of variables, rather than their absolute values. The data from the California I/M pilot study illustrate that there is considerable correlation among different test types for measuring exhaust CO and HC. A similar comparison of test types has not been done for $NO_x$, which is typically not in an idle test.

---

[6]A correlation coefficient measures the degree to which two variables are related. For perfect positive correlation, the value of the correlation coefficient is +1; for perfect negative correlation, the value is -1. A correlation coefficient of 0 means there is no relationship between the variables. The Spearman rank correlation coefficient is a nonparametric (distribution-free) statistic measuring the strength of the associations between two variables when the variables are rank ordered.

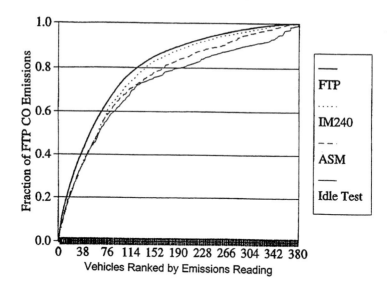

FIGURE 3-2 Comparison of FTP, IM240, ASM, and idle-test results for CO.

Replicate emissions tests were not performed for the 380 vehicles. Correlation of readings from two sets of tests with the same set of vehicles is far from perfect; Lawson (1995) reported an r-squared value of only 0.66 for IM240 test results between I/M lane data and laboratory data for the same vehicles.

Another comparison of different test types can be done with results of the Colorado's IM240 and idle-test programs.[7] Colorado's Automobile Inspection and Readjustment (AIR) program operates an IM240 program for 1982 and newer cars in the Denver metropolitan area, and a two-speed idle-test program in three other counties in Colorado. Vehicles older than 1981 in the Denver metropolitan area are also tested with the two-speed idle test. A recent audit of this program (Air Improvement Resource 1999) using data for calendar year 1998 reported that the idle-test program given outside the Denver metropolitan area had a higher failure rate than the IM240 tests given in the Denver

---

[7]Additional comparison of test types could and should be done, including comparing an annual idle test program for HC and CO with a biennial IM240 test program. Emissions-reduction benefits of a biennial idle-test program could be compared with a biennial IM240 test program in which both had approximately the same failure rates.

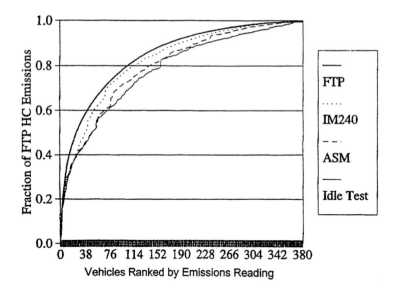

**FIGURE 3-3** Comparison of FTP, IM240, ASM, and idle-test results for HC.

area (16.7% versus 5.1%), a smaller emissions-reduction benefit per repaired vehicle (23% versus 58%), and a similar overall emissions reduction (6.5% versus 6.1%) compared with vehicles tested with the IM240 test. Average repair costs for the idle-tested vehicles were $95 per repair versus $211 for the IM240 tested vehicles. Both achieved about the same level of CO benefit in 1998. However, the idle test does not measure $NO_x$, and while it fails more vehicles, average emissions reductions and costs per repair are less. No attempt was made to determine whether differences between the vehicle fleets in the Denver metropolitan area and the nonmetropolitan Denver counties caused any of these differences.

## Evaporative Emissions Tests

Exhaust emissions are relatively easy to sample for routine inspection—the exhaust exits from the tailpipe and a collection hose is attached to the tailpipe for testing. Evaporative emissions can occur from many places on the vehicle. The fuel tank, filler neck, and gas cap are typically at the rear of a vehicle. The engine's fuel components are at the front, perhaps 12 feet away. If one tries to detect the presence of leaks from the system, the entire vehicle must

**TABLE 3-1**  Spearman Rank-Order Correlations for Different Emissions Test Types for CO and HC

| Test Type | FTP CO (HC) | IM240 CO (HC) | ASM5015/2525 CO (HC) | Idle Tests CO (HC) |
|---|---|---|---|---|
| FTP | — | 0.89 (0.90) | 0.73 (0.80) | 0.68 (0.72) |
| IM240 | 0.89 (0.90) | — | 0.75 (0.79) | 0.65 (0.68) |
| ASM5015/2525 | 0.73 (0.80) | 0.75 (0.79) | — | 0.63 (0.63) |
| Idle tests | 0.68 (0.72) | 0.65 (0.68) | 0.63 (0.63) | — |

be enclosed, and an increase in HC concentration in the trapped volume must be detected. Therefore, it is nearly impossible to envision a comprehensive but quick technique for inspecting vehicles for evaporative emissions.

A partial solution is a targeted inspection, such as a gas-cap check. Typically, the gas cap is screwed onto a test cavity and put under pressure. The supply is removed and the system is monitored to identify whether the pressure decays, indicating a leak in the cap. This functional check can be part of a routine vehicle inspection. The failure rate of in-use caps is substantial (12.4% in the California test) and the consequences of a failed cap are significant (Klausmeier et al. 2000). In Colorado's centralized IM240 program in 2000, 0.1% of the vehicles tested had a missing gas cap, and 3.3% failed the gas-cap pressure test (J. Sidebottom, CO Dept. of Public Health and Environment, personal commun. January 12, 2001). A gas cap check can be a cost-effective control measure.

Another evaporative emissions test is a fuel-tank vapor-system pressure check. Air or nitrogen is introduced at the canister's connection to the tank, and the tank is pressurized to a slightly positive pressure. The pressure source is removed and the pressure is monitored for a brief time. If a major vapor leak is present, the system cannot be pressurized at all. Minor leaks result in a pressure loss over the observation period. Drawbacks to this approach are that (1) not all vehicles have accessible canisters—some cannot be tested or are difficult to locate; (2) removal of the tank vent connection at the canister can break the nipple and requires replacement of the canister; and (3) the canister tank vent connection might not be replaced properly, creating a leak and evaporative emissions where none existed before. Several states are performing a simpler fill-pipe test, which involves pressurizing the fill-pipe and monitoring for the loss of pressure.

A third evaporative emissions test is a purge check. The activated carbon in the canister stores the fuel-tank HC vapors over the course of 1 day or more, but it requires periodic rejuvenation for proper function. The engine's vacuum is used to draw air through the carbon bed during vehicle operation, drawing the HC vapors off the carbon, and regenerating storage capacity. These fuel vapors are burned by the engine and result in a small increase in fuel economy. If the engine is not allowed to purge the canister, the carbon bed fills to capacity, and then the daily emissions are uncontrolled. Purge checks can be made in several ways but typically involve interrupting the line between the canister and the engine and sensing the presence or absence of flow during engine operation. The drawbacks are the same as outlined above for the pressure check. EPA has acknowledged problems with the current purge test. Therefore, states that have indicated they will perform a purge test when one is available may continue to take 100% of the emissions-reduction credit for the purge test, without actually performing such testing, until EPA develops an effective purge-test procedure.

A critical shortcoming in the current I/M testing programs is the lack of a method for identifying liquid leaks. Liquid leaks as high as 777 g/day have been reported (Haskew and Liberty 1999). That amount is similar to the amount of exhaust HC that would be emitted in 1 day by 60 Tier 1 vehicles being driven an average of 30 miles (using the 50,000-mile standard for Tier 1 vehicles of 0.41 g/mi). Even a small liquid leak can be significant because liquid fuel is so much denser than fuel vapor.

## OTHER PROGRAM ELEMENTS ADDRESSING TESTING AND REPAIRS

A wide variety of other elements constitute an I/M program. Table 1-4 shows some of the variations in currently implemented programs. Some of the additional elements that affect the emissions-reduction potential of an I/M program are

- Technician training.
- Test-cycle interval (time between required I/M tests).
- Waivers or repair cost limits.
- Cutpoints.
- Compliance and enforcement.

The following sections briefly discuss each of these program elements.

Many of these elements focus on improving the repair aspect of I/M programs. The repair component of I/M programs consists of identifying vehicles that need repairs, diagnosing the repairs they need, doing the repairs, and verifying that the repairs have occurred. In shorthand, it is IDRV for identify, diagnose, repair, and verify. As discussed in Chapter 1, the evolving nature of the vehicle fleet puts additional emphasis on the repairs as opposed to the maintenance aspect of I/M programs.

## Technician Training

To ensure air-quality benefits from an I/M program, proper emissions-related repairs must be made. If improper or unnecessary repairs are made, unwarranted costs are imposed on the motorist with little or no air-quality benefit. A program must be implemented to provide training to technicians who perform emissions-related repairs. These programs may be offered through the technical educational system or by a private contractor. Certification of completion of such programs should be required for all technicians who do emissions-related repairs.

Although repairs can be performed by anyone, states encourage motorists who need emissions repairs to use technicians with some specialized training. California requires repair technicians to pass the Smog Tech certification to legally make Smog Check repairs. Most states offer certification programs for repair technicians. These states also offer information about facilities where technicians can obtain training or technical advice. In addition, some states provide performance ratings for repair facilities that take into account such factors as the training of the technicians and the retest passing rates of vehicles that they repaired. The effects of technician training have not been measured and should be evaluated.

In addition, adequate technician training is important because all states will have new vehicle fleets that reflect more stringent emissions standards. Improvements in new vehicle standards will introduce advanced vehicle emissions-control technology, which may consist of

- Fuel injectors.
- Feedback fuel management systems.
- Advanced catalytic converters and/or traps.

- Air injection systems.
- Exhaust gas recirculation (EGR) systems.
- Computer controls.
- On-board diagnostics (OBD).
- Evaporative fuel controls.
- Turbocharged diesel engines.

With the introduction of these and other vehicle emissions-control technologies, emissions-related repairs will require that the automobile repair industry remain up to date on emissions-control repair protocols.

## Test-Cycle Interval

Another element of the I/M program is its frequency of testing. Most centralized programs, including all those using the IM240 test, inspect vehicles once every 2 years. Many of the decentralized I/M programs inspect vehicles once a year. Annual testing provides additional income to the inspection stations. This income helps cover the expense of the decentralized inspection equipment, which can range from $35,000 to $45,000 per station. Some states vary the test cycle by vehicle age and emissions technology. Colorado inspects 1981 and older vehicles every year and 1982 and newer vehicles every 2 years. In addition, many states require vehicle inspection upon change of ownership.

The emissions benefit derived from more frequent inspections is based on the effectiveness and duration of repairs performed. If the repair starts to deteriorate before the next inspection, then a more frequent inspection is warranted. The duration of the emissions-reduction benefit, as it relates to repairs, is not well documented in any I/M program. Limited data suggest that if correct repairs are performed, up to 70% of the emissions-related benefit can be maintained during a 2-year test cycle (ENVIRON 1998; Regional Air Quality Council 2000). However, other on-road data suggest that emissions reductions from the centralized IM240 program might be about half the amount calculated from inspection data (Wenzel 1999a; McClintock 1999a). The level of emissions reduction obtained from repairs and the length of time these repairs last will have a large impact on the emissions benefit of an I/M program. The issue of the durability of repair is discussed again in Chapter 6.

## Waiver Limits

Many states have established a repair-cost waiver limit for repairing vehicles that fail the I/M test. If repair costs exceed this waiver limit, the vehicle owner may be granted a waiver of the requirement to pass the test. Before the 1990 Clean Air Act Amendments (CAAA90) which requires a minimum waiver limit of $450 for repairs (in 1989 dollars) that is adjusted for inflation for enhanced I/M areas, many states had repair-cost limits as low as $75 to $100. Often the repair industry performs only partial repairs on a high-emitting vehicle because the motorist exercises the repair cost waiver or the motorist is unwilling or unable to spend money on proper, long-lasting repairs. This situation is discussed further in Chapter 7, which describes the higher repair expenditures found in studies in which repairs are made under laboratory conditions with little regard to cost compared with repair expenditures reported in I/M programs. States that are required under the CAAA90 to adjust their repair-cost limits beyond the $450 by the consumer price index (CPI) to account for inflation have not done so. Adjusting for the CPI means that waiver limits should be $620 in 2000. Not adjusting for the CPI limits repair effectiveness.

## Cutpoints

Cutpoints are individual emissions standards that are used in an I/M program to determine whether a vehicle passes or fails the emissions test. Cutpoints vary among programs, depending on the pollutant of concern and the severity of the air-quality problem. For example, Colorado is concerned with CO emissions, so its I/M program cutpoints are relatively more stringent for CO than for HC and $NO_x$. Areas that need to control ambient ozone are most likely to have tighter standards for HC and $NO_x$ than for CO. It should be noted that in places where ozone production is HC limited, such as the South Coast Air Basin and Chicago (Blanchard and Tanenbaum 2000; Fujita et al. 2000; Pun et al. 2000), $NO_x$ controls might increase ambient ozone levels in the urban center. However, such controls might help abate average ozone levels on regional scales (NARSTO Synthesis Team 2000).

Cutpoints are set much higher than the EPA's new vehicle certification standards, shown in Table 1-2. In addition, the I/M cutpoints are set according to age and technology of the vehicle fleet within the I/M program. These cutpoints may be in units of pollutant concentration (percentage of exhaust gas) or mass (grams per mile), depending on the test type. At the start-up of an I/M program, the cutpoints or standards are set at a phase-in level, which is designed to fail fewer vehicles than in an established I/M program. The reasons for the phase-in are to prevent very high failure rates for some engine families or model-year vehicles and to increase public acceptance of the program. For example, under the original cutpoint envisioned by EPA for enhanced I/M, over 60% of early 1980s vehicles would fail the test. It was hoped that technicians would learn to make more effective repairs over time and that cutpoints could then be tightened. However, very little is known about how much emissions reduction will result from tightening cutpoints, especially since it will increase the number of failing marginal emitters,[8] which are often very difficult to repair.

The California I/M pilot study provides an example of failure rates and emissions reductions that could result from tightening I/M cutpoints. In this data set, the FTP CO, HC, and $NO_x$ emissions of 618 vehicles due for their biennial inspection were examined. Failure rates were established for this fleet, using multiples of those vehicles' certification standards for CO, HC, and $NO_x$. The total emissions above the certification standards for each vehicle (the sum of $1/7(CO) + NO_x + HC$)[9] was calculated as the difference between a vehicle's current emissions rate and its certification standard for each pollutant. Finally, the percentage of total emissions above the certification standards that could be "captured" by each set of cutpoints was calculated. The results are shown in Table 3-2.

The data from the California I/M pilot-study fleet show that if the I/M cutpoints were set at 1.5 times the certification standard, 68% of that fleet would fail the I/M emissions test. At that cutpoint, 81% of the total emissions above the certification standards would be identified, and that would account for 48% of the fleet's total FTP emissions ($1/7(CO) + NO_x + HC$). Because of the skewness of the fleet's emissions, an emissions cutpoint of 10 times the certification standards would fail only 6% of the fleet but would still capture 20% of the total emissions above the certification standards and 12% of the

---

[8]Marginal emitters are those vehicles that fail emissions tests by only a small amount (Lawson 1995).

[9]A discussion of weighting multiple pollutants is contained in Chapter 7. This pollutant weighting is described in IMRC (1993).

**TABLE 3-2** Impact of Cutpoints on Failure Rates and Emissions

| I/M Emissions Cutpoint | Failure Rate, % | % of Total Emissions Above Certification Standards | % of Total Fleet Emissions |
|---|---|---|---|
| 1 | 85 | 100 | 59 |
| 1.5 | 68 | 81 | 48 |
| 2 | 52 | 68 | 41 |
| 4 | 22 | 44 | 26 |
| 10 | 6 | 20 | 12 |

Notes: The I/M emissions cutpoint is a multiple of the new-vehicle certification standards for CO, HC, or $NO_x$. A cutpoint of 1 means that vehicles fail the test when emissions are the same value as the certification standard or greater; a cutpoint of 1.5 means 1.5 times the standard. Emissions above the certification standard were calculated as the difference between a vehicle's current emissions and its certification standard. The percentage of total fleet emissions is the percentage of total emissions above those given by each cutpoint. Excess and total fleet emissions are calculated using the formula $(1/7(CO) + NO_x + HC)$.

fleet's total FTP emissions. The data suggest that changing I/M cutpoints will have diminishing returns as the cutpoints are made increasingly stringent.

## Compliance and Enforcement

Other critical components are mechanisms put in place to ensure program compliance. These components include the measures to ensure that vehicle owners have their vehicles inspected and, if necessary, obtain needed repairs. Measures used to ensure that testing is properly performed and that certifications of compliance are not mishandled are also included. Because of its importance in judging how well an I/M program is performing, this topic is discussed along with other criteria for evaluating I/M programs in Chapter 7.

## EFFECT OF CURRENT I/M PROGRAMS
## ON VEHICLE EMISSIONS

One method of evaluating the effectiveness of I/M programs is to measure their ability to reduce emissions. Federal and state mandates that require estimates of I/M emissions benefits have prompted a portion of the previous state evaluation work. Independent investigators interested in the same issue have produced additional evaluations. Although the methods and results of these evaluation studies varied, in general, they found that I/M programs provide lower emissions benefits than were originally predicted by the MOBILE and EMFAC models. This section describes some of these evaluations. The methodological issues associated with evaluating emissions benefits as well as other criteria for evaluating I/M programs are discussed in Chapters 6 and 7.

Federal regulations include two requirements for evaluating the performance of enhanced I/M programs. First, states that have adopted decentralized enhanced I/M programs are given 18 months from the time of their interim approval to submit information showing that their program meets the EPA standards set for centralized enhanced I/M programs. If the standards are met, then these states can claim emissions-reduction benefits given for centralized programs. The Environmental Council of States developed the evaluation methodology. States receive a list of 12 evaluation criteria from which they must select to evaluate their programs. These criteria include performing mass emissions testing on vehicles before and after repairs, and comparing results with MOBILE; conducting random audits of inspection stations to ensure that all aspects of the I/M test were being performed correctly; and comparing I/M test data with remote-sensing measurements made before and after testing. The results of this evaluation are then used to decide whether the program can receive all or a fraction of the emissions-reduction credits afforded a centralized program (ECOS/STAPPA/EPA 1998).

The second requirement mandates that each state submit an evaluation of the emissions reduction achieved by its enhanced I/M program within 2 years after its start date and biennially thereafter. The data collection requirements and two evaluation methods have been outlined by EPA. The first evaluation method compares fleet-average emissions of vehicles in Phoenix, Arizona, with emissions of vehicles in another I/M area in need of evaluation (Sierra Research 1997). The fleet-average emissions relative to the benchmark Phoenix program are then used to determine whether the I/M program is meeting the EPA performance standard for an enhanced I/M program. This method has been approved for use by states conducting their biennial evaluations (EPA 1998d). Presumably, the reason for using a reference method, comparing with Arizona's I/M program, is because EPA believes that the Phoenix, Arizona I/M program is represented by MOBILE. However, the effectiveness of the benchmark Phoenix program has not been clearly established. If the benchmark obtains an actual benefit lower than that estimated by the model, comparisons with other programs will provide higher-than-realized emissions benefits. The second method uses remote sensing to measure I/M emissions reductions. Although EPA has not yet approved this method, it has recently developed a draft document providing guidance on the use of remote sensing in evaluating I/M programs (EPA 2000b).

Of the 18 states with biennial evaluations due, only two (California and Texas) have submitted evaluations. Although the lack of formal guidance on other evaluation methods may be one reason for the overdue evaluations, other factors must not be overlooked. In particular, states may fear undermining their own state implementation plans (SIPs) and therefore are wary of producing evaluations that show smaller emissions reductions than originally predicted. The California evaluation (CARB 2000b) has recently found that its program was not producing the emissions benefits predicted in their SIP, which might necessitate SIP modifications.

## Recent Official Evaluations of State I/M Programs

In addition to federal requirements, states also require that I/M programs be evaluated to estimate their effectiveness. For example, California is required by state law to evaluate its program against the emissions reductions required under its SIP. Colorado is required by state law to audit its program for its impact on air quality and on the emissions reductions that are needed to comply with federal air-quality standards. The California and Colorado programs have undergone state-sponsored evaluations using multiple quantitative techniques and thus serve as examples of emissions-reduction estimates for I/M programs.

## Evaluations of California Smog Check Program

The California Smog Check program requires most vehicles in California to have a biennial emissions test. The Smog Check program began in 1984 with idle tests administered at privately owned inspection stations. In 1998, the program was modified in response to the Clean Air Act Amendments of 1990 (CAAA90) requirement for areas with the most serious air-quality problems to implement loaded-mode testing. Three types of programs currently operate in the state: the Enhanced Smog Check program, a Basic Smog Check program, and a change-of-ownership program. The Enhanced Smog Check test subjects vehicles in southern and part of central California to an ASM test for HC, CO, and $NO_x$. The Basic Smog Check operates in most of the rest of the state and subjects vehicles to a two-speed idle test for HC and CO. Vehicles anywhere in the state are also subjected to emissions tests upon change of ownership.

The California Air Resources Board (CARB), along with the Bureau of Automotive Repair (BAR), recently released an evaluation of the state's Enhanced Smog Check program based on test data from vehicles randomly pulled over and given a roadside ASM test (CARB 2000b). The objectives of this evaluation were to estimate total program emissions reductions, compare these reductions with California's obligations under its SIP, and assess the emissions impacts of charges to the program. The evaluation measured emissions of two random, on-road fleets consisting of vehicles that had undergone enhanced testing and those that had gone through only the idle-test program. The "before" fleet consisted of 5,200 vehicles, and the "after" fleet was 4,200 vehicles. Both groups underwent ASM testing—the same exhaust test as found in the I/M lanes. To convert to mass emissions, ASM test results were first converted to equivalent FTP values using equations developed by Eastern Research Group and Radian International (1999). These values provided the current mass reductions in exhaust emissions resulting from moving from the original idle test program to the enhanced program. The EMFAC2000 model was then used to forecast the benefits gained from the tightening $NO_x$ cutpoints, implemented in October 1999, and to account for the benefits from reducing evaporative emissions. Neither the forecasted benefits from tightening $NO_x$ cutpoints nor the evaporative emissions-reduction benefits have been evaluated with in-use data.

Table 3-3 shows the estimated total emissions reductions by the CARB/BAR study (exhaust plus evaporative emissions reductions for HC) from the Smog Check enhanced program in tons per day. Emissions were estimated to be reduced by 28 tons/day for HC and by 12 tons/day for $NO_x$ for the lenient $NO_x$ cutpoints and by 34 tons/day for HC and by 32 tons/day for $NO_x$ for the more stringent $NO_x$ cutpoints.

It is important that the CARB/BAR evaluation shows smaller emissions reductions from California's Enhanced Smog Check program than the reductions required in the SIP. The emissions reductions estimated for the SIP were made with the EMFAC model. (Version EMFAC7F was used to develop the SIP estimates.) Using the tighter $NO_x$ cutpoints, HC emissions reductions are

**TABLE 3-3** Estimates of Emissions Reductions from the CARB/BAR Evaluations of California's Enhanced I/M Program

|  | HC (tons per day) | $NO_x$ (tons per day) |
|---|---|---|
| CARB/BAR evaluation using original $NO_x$ cutpoints | 28 | 12 |
| CARB/BAR evaluation using tightened $NO_x$ cutpoints | 33 | 32 |
| Emissions reductions from enhanced I/M contained in California's SIP | 55 | 55 |

Source: CARB 2000b.

60% and $NO_x$ emissions are 59% of those called for in the SIP. Some reasons for the decreased effectiveness of the program, recognized by the CARB/ BAR evaluation, include legislative changes to the program (exemptions for vehicles less than 4 years old and those manufactured before 1973); reductions in the number of vehicles subject to testing at test-only facilities; and elimination of the requirement for annual inspections for vehicles identified as gross polluters.

The California I/M Review Committee (IMRC) released a separate evaluation of the Enhanced Smog Check program (IMRC 2000). The IMRC evaluation focused on underlying factors that influence the effectiveness of the Enhanced Smog Check program. Data were collected on the outcomes of vehicles that initially failed an I/M program and then passed a retest (fail-pass vehicles). The IMRC evaluation also used registration data, roadside pullovers, and some remote-sensing measurements. This information was used to assess emissions reductions and their duration. Reductions were assumed to come from two sources. One is from repairs to vehicles that stay on the road, and the other is from vehicles that leave the region as a result of the I/M program. Estimates of the duration of repairs were made possible by California's change-of-ownership emissions-test requirement that allowed multiple tests for a sample of vehicles.

The IMRC report provides two separate emissions-reduction estimates: one based on in-program data and one based on roadside pullover data. Emissions reductions based on in-program data are 39-116 tons/day for HC and 59- 93 tons/day for $NO_x$. Uncertainties about the time pattern of emissions after repair resulted in a range of estimates. Using the roadside pullover data, the IMRC calculated an emissions reduction of 17% for HC and 9% for $NO_x$. The IMRC also concluded that 10% of all vehicles that failed the initial Smog Check test never received a passing mark in later tests. This estimate is lower than that observed in Phoenix, where an estimated 29% of vehicles that failed the initial IM240 test never received a passing test or waiver in the following 3-15 months (Wenzel 1999a), and in Denver, where 27% of the emissions failures are unresolved (Air Improvement Resource 1999). Another 5-10% of the vehicles observed on-road in California were eligible for Smog Check testing, but no records exist of these vehicles reporting for a test.

Earlier independent evaluations of California's original decentralized idle-test program showed no emissions-reduction benefit (Lawson 1993; Lawson et al. 1995, 1996a). That result was based on data collected from California's random roadside surveys from 1989, 1990, and 1991 and it is in contrast to the estimate that the program using the CARB I/M model (the CALIMFAC model) was producing emissions reductions of 18% HC, 15% CO, and 7% $NO_x$ (IMRC 1993) at that time, and to data from vehicles that were given emissions tests before and after repairs.

**Colorado AIR Program**

The 1999 audit of Colorado's AIR program used test data on the outcomes of failing vehicles as well as EPA's Serious CO Area Model[10] to estimate emissions reductions (Air Improvement Resource 1999). Directed at reducing CO emissions, the AIR program operates in metropolitan areas along the Front Range (Denver area, Colorado Springs, Fort Collins, and Greeley). As described earlier, the program consists of two types of tests: a centralized biennial IM240 test used in the Denver area for 1982 and newer vehicles, and an annual basic idle test used in other areas and for vehicles older than 1982 in the enhanced area. The emissions reductions were estimated one time by analyzing the changes in emissions for fail-pass vehicles (vehicles that initially failed an I/M program and then passed a retest) tested during 1998 and part of 1999.

---

[10]The Serious CO Area model is a forerunner of the MOBILE6 model made available by EPA to states completing CO planning activities. It utilizes the lower emissions deterioration rates that will be contained in MOBILE6 and reduces the credits for oxygenated fuels.

The reductions were then used to estimate the benefits for the whole vehicle fleet. A second estimate of emissions reduction was made with EPA's Serious CO Area Model. This model reflects the assumptions that will be contained in the new MOBILE6, which probably will result in substantially lower credits for I/M programs than were estimated by MOBILE5. Overall, the evaluation concluded that, depending on the method of analysis, the AIR program reduced 1999 CO emissions by 8-17%. The lower estimate of emissions reductions was produced by using the in-program emissions data on fail-pass vehicles and by analyzing remote-sensing data from the area. The higher estimate was produced with the Serious CO Area Model.

Earlier evaluations of the Colorado program estimated different benefits. Stedman et al. (1997) estimated a 4-7% CO emissions-reduction benefit based on remote-sensing measurements. This evaluation showed no HC and $NO_x$ emissions reductions and no CO emissions reductions for pre-1982 vehicles. In another study, Stedman et al. (1997) estimated an 8-11% benefit based on the same measurements. ENVIRON International Corporation (1998) also funded a study that reported that the program obtained a 20-34% CO benefit using EPA's MOBILE5 model.

## Independent Evaluations of State I/M Programs

In addition to the evaluations of I/M programs in Colorado and California described earlier in this report, numerous evaluations have been done by state agencies, EPA, and independent researchers. The following section describes a selection of these evaluations. Pierson (1996) also summarizes earlier I/M program evaluations.

## Evaluation of Phoenix's Program

Several studies in the past few years have examined the performance of the enhanced centralized IM240 program in Phoenix, Arizona. In addition to the thousands of records of program data gathered, extensive remote-sensing data were also collected. Several independent researchers such as Wenzel (1999a) and Harrington et al. (1998, 2000) performed studies using this information. EPA also assessed the performance of the Phoenix program using only I/M test records (EPA 1997a). Results from the studies are shown in Table 3-4.

**TABLE 3-4** Summary of Results of Evaluation of Arizona's Centralized I/M 240 Programs

| | Per Vehicle Reduction in HC (Fleet Average) | Per Vehicle Reduction in NOx (Fleet Average) | % Reduction in HC | % Reduction in NOx | Cutpoints | Comments |
|---|---|---|---|---|---|---|
| EPA (1997a) estimate measured from program data (cars only) | 0.08 g/mi | 0.08 g/mi | 14.3% | 7.6% | Arizona cutpoints (cars only)[a] | Cars only, no trucks |
| Predicted using modified TECH5 model | 0.09 g/mi | 0.20 g/mi | 16.9% | 16.7% | | TECH5 model adjusted for Arizona |
| EPA estimate for enhanced I/M (1992b) compared with non-I/M | 0.29 g/mi per vehicle | 0.06 g/mi per vehicle | 28% | 9% | All vehicles HC 0.8 g/mi NOx 2.0 g/mi | Modeled results; cars only |
| Harrington et al. (2000) | 0.11 g/mi per vehicle | 0.12 g/mi per vehicle | 13% | 8% | Arizona cutpoints[a] | Data from I/M program used |
| Wenzel (1999a) I/M program data | | | 14.1% | 7.4% | Arizona cutpoints[a] | Close to half the emissions reductions appeared to be due to pretest repairs |
| Remote sensing data | | | 11.0% | | | |

[a]Arizona cutpoints: Cars: model years 1981-90, HC 2.0 g/mi; NOx 3.0 g/mi; model years 91+, HC 1.2 g/mi; NOx 2.5 g/mi; cutpoints for trucks are more lax.

The EPA analysis (1997a) compared predictions of the TECH5 component of the MOBILE model used in the Phoenix case with the emissions reduction calculated from the IM240 test data.[11] The results predicted by the model were only slightly greater for HC reductions, but they were substantially higher for $NO_x$ reductions (Table 3-4). Chapter 5 provides a detailed discussion of the emissions-reduction benefits estimated for I/M with MOBILE.

Also included in Table 3-4 are the original predictions for the IM240 program from EPA's regulatory impact analysis of enhanced I/M in 1992 (EPA 1992b). Even though these estimates are the results of comparisons between enhanced I/M and non-I/M programs, they are probably close to what Phoenix is actually being granted in SIP credits. This is due to the MOBILE model predictions of low emissions reductions (5% for HC) from basic I/M programs.

As shown in Table 3-4, the MOBILE model forecasted greater HC and CO emissions reductions than were actually found using in-program or remote-sensing data. The large reductions predicted by the model were originally based on the assumption that all failing vehicles would be repaired. In Phoenix, however, the program data showed that roughly 25% of them had still not passed 1 year after failing the test (Ando et al. 2000).

Harrington et al. (2000) examined the costs and emissions reductions of the Phoenix program by using all IM240 test results over a period of 17 months (January 1996 to May 1997). This study used emissions data of initial and final tests for failed vehicles and assumed that emissions repairs lasted 2 years. Given these assumptions, the study estimated that HC emissions were reduced by 13% and $NO_x$ emissions by 7% over the 2-year period. This finding was very similar to the EPA (1997a) results from program data.

Wenzel (1999a) compared emissions reductions based on IM240 test data with a large sample of remote-sensing readings. The results of this study for the Phoenix program data were similar to those of the Harrington et al. (2000) study, which was also based on test data from the program. Wenzel found, however, that the emissions reductions were lower when remote-sensing readings were used; HC reductions were 11% instead of 14%. Furthermore, the 11% remote-sensing readings included a relatively large share of pretest reductions, which would not be reflected in the program data. These preinspection repairs are observed in remote-sensing data, which show a reduction in emissions in vehicles 1-2 weeks before their inspection (Wenzel 1999a),

---

[11]The TECH5 component of MOBILE was modified in this work to reflect emissions reductions that occur in a single I/M cycle. These model modifications are described in EPA (1997a, pp. 12-13).

as well as survey data, which indicated that a significant fraction of motorists had their vehicles tuned up before inspection (IMRC 2000). The implication of these findings is that the remote-sensing results show substantially lower post-inspection emissions reductions than the in-program data.

## Evaluation of Minnesota's Program

Scherrer and Kittelson (1994) assessed the impact on air quality of an I/M program initiated in 1991 in Minneapolis. Direct measurements of ambient CO data at three monitoring sites were used. Assessing the effectiveness of I/M using CO air-quality data is appealing because a high fraction of CO is emitted by light-duty vehicles subject to such testing, and CO is relatively unreactive in the atmosphere. Minnesota's centralized I/M program consisted of an idle-test program for HC and CO that failed about 9.4% of vehicles during its first year (July 1991 to June 1992). This study used a multifactoral regression that corrected for vehicle activity and meteorological factors to discern I/M benefits from time series observations of CO concentrations. The study collected hourly ambient CO monitoring data in the city and meteorological data at the regional airport. The average ambient reduction of CO attributed to I/M was $1.3 \pm 1.4\%$, with individual sites showing a 5.8% decrease, a 1.5% decrease, and a 3.4% increase.

Using air-quality data to evaluate I/M emissions benefits raises many issues. The committee recognizes that observing the effects of I/M programs on air quality is difficult because the level of emissions reductions have been relatively modest and there are numerous confounding variables. One of the issues encountered in this study related to the methods used to correct for the effects of changes in vehicle activity patterns and the vehicle fleet itself. The wide range of changes in ambient CO levels, estimated at the three monitoring sites, also suggests that using a limited number of monitoring sites for the purpose of program evaluation might be unreliable. However, it is those monitors that define whether a locality is in nonattainment of the national ambient air-quality standards and trigger the need for an I/M program.

## Evaluation of Georgia's Program

The Air Quality Laboratory at Georgia Institute of Technology used remote sensing to determine the influence of city characteristics on motor vehicle emissions (Rodgers 2000). The reference method of evaluating I/M's benefits (discussed in Chapter 6) compares vehicle emissions in an I/M city with those of a reference fleet in a city with similar socioeconomic and meteorological characteristics but with a different I/M program. This reference fleet could be from a non-I/M city—in which case an evaluation would determine the reduction in emissions due to the I/M program—or from a city with a benchmark I/M program. In the latter case, the evaluation would compare how well the program performed relative to the benchmark. The Air Quality Laboratory studied whether the selection of the reference fleet could affect the evaluation. It looked at whether emissions in comparable cities were actually similar. Because of similar socioeconomic characteristics, fleet age distribution, and average model year emissions, the I/M cities of Nashville, Tennessee, and Atlanta, Georgia, had comparable fleets for application of the reference method. Other city comparisons (Boston, Massachusetts compared with Burlington, Vermont; Macon, Georgia compared with Augusta, Georgia), however, suggested that characteristics outside of I/M program status can result in dissimilar model-year emissions. That result points to the difficulty in finding a comparable fleet for use in the application of the reference method.

The Air Quality Laboratory also used remote-sensing data to evaluate the emissions-reduction benefits for Atlanta's I/M program. Until 1999, the I/M program included a decentralized idle test in the four counties in the central Atlanta metropolitan area. The Air Quality Laboratory study compared emissions in the I/M area with emissions in the surrounding nine counties, which were not subject to an I/M program at the time. From this study, a reduction in CO emissions of 7.5% was estimated. Note that no attempt was made to correct for socioeconomic differences between the I/M and non-I/M areas. Atlanta's I/M program expanded to include these nine surrounding counties in 1996. Using more recent data, the Air Quality Laboratory also estimated the benefit of the program by comparing emissions of vehicles that had been tested with those that had not been tested when the program expanded to include the surrounding nine counties. This method (the step method described in Chapter 6) yielded an 11% reduction in CO emissions.

## EPA's National Tampering Surveys

For a number of years, from the latter 1970s to the early 1990s, the EPA conducted motor vehicle tampering surveys at various locations throughout the country. EPA used data from these surveys to document the occurrence of tampering-related defects[12] in the motor vehicle fleet and to compare different I/M program types for effectiveness. Random roadside surveys allow for inspection of vehicles as they are driven on the road, but many EPA surveys of centralized programs were done in the test lane, rather than on the road, which introduces bias into the results. Motorists were given no advance notice that they will be stopped for an inspection. The data collected in those surveys also give a representative sampling of actual vehicle miles traveled, because the more a vehicle is driven, the more likely it is to be stopped. Participation in the surveys was voluntary, so the survey results probably are biased toward vehicle data from compliant motorists who are generally willing to participate in such surveys.

In each year's survey, EPA selected up to 15 cities as sampling sites. To obtain statistically meaningful data, 300-500 vehicles were inspected at each location. The mix of inspected vehicles was assumed by EPA to be a self-weighting sample, and no attempt was made to approximate the national vehicle mix. The sampling location and the method of stopping individual vehicles varied for each location in accordance with the type of I/M program in place. Sampling also occurred in non-I/M areas. The roadside inspection included the following:

- Basic vehicle identification data
- Check of all emissions-control system components
- Measurement of no-load, low-idle (~1000 rpm) HC and CO emissions
- Collection of fuel sample from unleaded-only fueled vehicles for lead analysis
- Inspection of fuel inlet restrictor (designed to prohibit fueling with leaded gasoline)
- Test of tailpipe for lead deposits

Lawson et al. (1995) performed a series of analyses using EPA's national tampering survey data, obtained through roadside surveys, to compare the effectiveness of centralized and decentralized I/M programs with no I/M program. One study used pass-fail rates for the 44,000 vehicles reported, according to tampering inspection and emissions-test results from the EPA

---

[12]"Tampering" is the malfunctioning of one or more emissions-control devices due to either deliberate disablement or mechanical failure.

survey data taken from 1985 to 1990. The data were adjusted for model year and mileage. The model-year categories are 1985-1990, 1980-1984, and pre-1980, corresponding roughly to fairly homogeneous emissions-control technologies, although some differences for catalyst technologies and trucks and light-duty vehicles span these model-year groupings. Mileage was divided into five categories, the highest including 100,000 or more miles, as recorded on the vehicle's odometer. Finally, within each model-year group and mileage interval, vehicles were categorized according to the type of I/M program where they were sampled.

As shown in Figure 3-4, each combination of mileage and year of manufacture was compared for mean values of overall failure rates from different types of I/M programs: none, decentralized, and centralized. This plot displays the following features: failure rates tend to increase with odometer reading and vehicle age and to be highest for the oldest technology vehicles. Neither centralized nor decentralized programs showed a much lower failure rate than vehicles from non-I/M program areas.

In a second study, data obtained in these surveys over an 8-year period (1985-1992) were adjusted for differences in vehicle age and odometer readings (Lawson et al. 1996a). The analyses also accounted for the type of I/M program in place in each of the areas where the surveys were made. Tampering and emissions failure rates for different I/M configurations during the 1985-1992 period are presented in Table 3-5, which shows that there were only small differences between different I/M program configurations. There was also only a 4% difference in tampering or emissions failure rates between non-I/M and centralized areas, a small difference compared with the overall emissions and tampering failure rates. Because EPA discontinued its motor vehicle tampering surveys after 1992, more recent analyses with nationwide data have not been possible.

## SUMMARY

Numerous variations of vehicle emissions I/M programs are in use today, each with its own attributes. One program type is the centralized program using transient emissions tests such as the IM240. Such programs enable the estimation of mass emissions of $NO_x$, CO, and HC under simulated driving conditions. Possible drawbacks from this type of program are higher testing equipment costs and greater inconvenience to the public because of fewer testing locations. Additionally, motorists requiring repairs must visit a separate

Model Years 1985-1990

Model Years 1980-1984

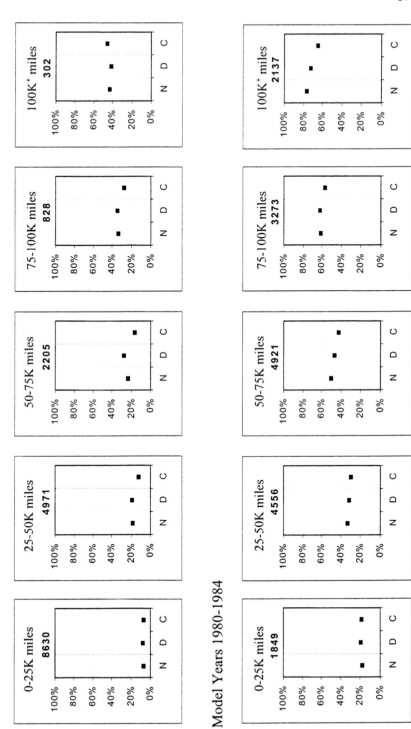

88

Model Years 1975-1979

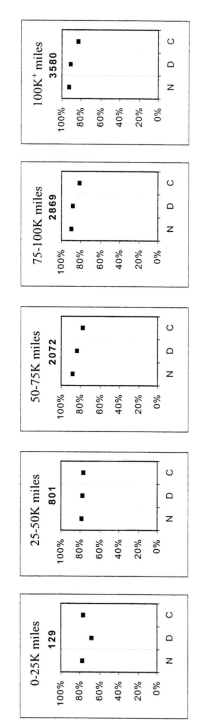

**FIGURE 3-4** Cross-classification diagram using EPA motor vehicle tampering survey data from the 1985-1990 surveys. Failure rates for 44,000 vehicles are shown by I/M program type as a function of year of manufacture and odometer readings (N = non-I/M region; D = decentralized I/M program; C = centralized I/M program). The number of vehicles in each model year and mileage group is shown at the top of each pane.

**TABLE 3-5** Normalized Tampering and Emissions Failure Rates by Program Type from EPA's 1985-92 Motor Vehicle Tampering Surveys

| Program Type | Tampering Rate (%) | HC >100 ppm (%) | HC > 400 ppm (%) | CO > 1 (%) | CO > 4 (%) |
|---|---|---|---|---|---|
| Non-I/M | 19.5 | 28.0 | 8.8 | 20.8 | 10.4 |
| Decentralized | 16.6 | 25.7 | 7.9 | 18.5 | 8.7 |
| Centralized (on-road) | 15.4 | 24.3 | 5.8 | 16.3 | 6.2 |
| Centralized (I/M lane) | 15.0 | 26.6 | 5.7 | 14.7 | 5.6 |

repair facility before they return to be retested. Another type of I/M program uses a decentralized idle test in which exhaust concentrations of HC and CO are measured. Such programs provide greater convenience to motorists because of the larger number of testing facilities, and because testing and repairs can occur at the same place. These programs, however, do not simulate $NO_x$ emissions and are more difficult to oversee. Many variations on these two program types exist. For example, the current California Smog Check program is a hybrid network that uses an ASM test to estimate CO, HC, and $NO_x$ concentrations.

Previous evaluations of I/M's emissions benefits have been based on MOBILE as well as direct estimates of vehicle emissions. The committee believes those evaluations based on direct estimates of vehicle emissions are far superior to those taken from models. Estimates of I/M benefits from direct measurements of vehicle exhaust using test data, remote sensing, and roadside pullovers have shown reductions to be significantly smaller than model-predicted reductions. This conclusion is based on a review of state-sponsored evaluations of the Colorado and California programs and independent evaluations of these programs and programs in Arizona, Minnesota, and Georgia. Although an exhaustive review of all previous evaluations is beyond the scope of this study, the committee believes those described represent some of the best examples of I/M evaluation. The committee recognizes that the number of evaluations will expand greatly in the future. As discussed in Chapter 1, this is the first phase of a two-part study. The second phase is expected to continue to review evaluations and to rely on them as critical sources of information.

# 4

# Emerging Emissions Testing
# Technologies

New technologies continue to be developed to provide faster, more convenient, and more accurate emissions testing. Since inspection and maintenance (I/M) programs have been in operation for approximately 30 years, the accumulated data can be used for motor vehicle profiling. In addition, on-board diagnostics (OBD) systems and remote-sensing technologies may eliminate traditional I/M testing for some vehicles. These emerging emissions technologies are described below.

### MOTOR VEHICLE PROFILING

Motor vehicle profiling can be used to help determine whether a vehicle is likely to be a high emitter. By examining past emissions performance of a vehicle (through existing I/M records), as well as performance for similar makes and models, the likelihood of whether a vehicle will pass or fail an I/M inspection may be determined. There are two types of profile:

• Low-emitter profile (LEP)—The LEP attempts to assign a probability that a vehicle or group of vehicles will pass an I/M test. It relies on I/M records indicating which vehicle makes, models, and model years have low incidences of I/M failure.

• High-emitter profile (HEP)—The high-emitter profile similarly attempts to predict the probability that a vehicle or group of vehicles will fail an I/M test. Examples of this type of profiling are provided by Wenzel and Ross (1996), who used California remote-sensing data, and Wenzel (1999a), who used Arizona IM240 data to identify vehicle makes and models with high malfunction rates. However, data from random roadside surveys in California have shown significant differences between the HEP and on-road data.

These profiles might be used to make I/M programs more cost-effective by targeting more frequent inspection to those vehicles most likely to need repair and exempting from testing vehicles with a small likelihood of high emissions. For example, depending on the state, many programs exempt vehicles 2-5 model years old (MECA 1999). The developers of one LEP estimated that such a "clean screening" model could screen out at least 50% of the vehicles from testing with little impact on emissions benefits (Klausmeier and Kishan 1998).

The California Bureau of Automotive Repair uses a HEP in their enhanced I/M program to help determine whether to send vehicles to test-only facilities, which are thought to perform more accurate tests. Eastern Research Group developed and maintains the computer program for performing this analysis (Eastern Research Group 1997). This HEP uses the prior inspection history of a vehicle; historical failure rates of vehicles of the same year, make, and model; and remote-sensing measurements of the vehicle. The California I/M Review Committee (IMRC 2000) reported the failure rates and initial emissions test results for HEP versus non-HEP vehicles. As shown in Table 4-1, the HEP made only a small improvement in identifying vehicles likely to fail, and the improvement was only for post-1986 model-year vehicles. The benefits of the HEP model are much smaller than those estimated by Klausmeier and Kishan (1998) from a small sample of data from California. However, updating the profile for recent test data might improve its performance.

If a HEP is used in I/M program design, it is important to consider the regressive impacts that will occur to low-income motorists who may be more frequently targeted for testing. To the extent such a policy is regressive, it could be combined with the most cost-effective supporting policies, such as repair assistance or scrappage programs, in an attempt to mitigate its negative effects.

**TABLE 4-1** Results of the HEP Used in the California Smog Check Program

|  | HEP Directed | Random Directed | Not Directed |
|---|---|---|---|
| Failure Rate | 26% | 22% | 23% |
| Initial emissions |  |  |  |
| HC (ppm) | 71 | 63 | 68 |
| CO (%) | 0.45 | 0.41 | 0.46 |
| NO$_x$ (ppm) | 520 | 485 | 494 |

Note: Vehicles could be directed using the HEP, randomly directed, or not directed to a test-only facility, but directed to a test and repair facility.
Source: IMRC 2000.

## ON-BOARD DIAGNOSTICS

The use of OBD technologies in I/M programs represents a major shift from current practice. As described in Chapter 2, the OBDII system on 1996 and newer vehicles uses sensors to monitor and modify the performance of the engine and emissions control components. It is possible to identify problems with OBD sensors or emissions control components by interfacing a diagnostic analyzer ("scan tool") with the vehicle's electronic processor to download any diagnostic trouble codes. These codes identify emissions-control systems and components that are malfunctioning. If the OBD I/M program is operating properly, OBDII inspections will fail vehicles if either the vehicle's emissions-control components are, or have been, malfunctioning or if the sensors monitoring emissions-control components are malfunctioning. This program is in contrast to a traditional I/M emissions-testing program where a vehicle is inspected to determine if it is emitting, at the time of its appearance at the testing station, more pollutants than a standard set by individual states. The U.S. Environmental Protection Agency (EPA 2001) has recently finalized an OBD rule that requires states to begin implementing OBD testing in I/M programs for 1996 and newer OBD-equipped vehicles.

The OBDII system does not actually measure emissions. Because this system does not measure emissions but rather alerts drivers that there is a problem that might result in excess emissions, evaluating the benefits from such a system is not straightforward. Direct emissions reductions from the repairs resulting from an OBDII alert cannot be estimated without subjecting the vehicle to at least two tests that measure emissions, one before and one after the repair. In addition, the objective of OBD is to prevent vehicles from becoming high emitters. It is difficult to quantify the emissions benefits of preventing vehicles from becoming high emitters.

An important aspect of the OBD system is that it is required to maintain a memory of past events, and store a history of previous problems, even though the problem no longer exists. Thus, a vehicle in an OBD I/M program might fail due to an intermittent problem. Another aspect of the OBD I/M system is that it might fail a vehicle due to a failed sensor. Though the information collected by the sensor might be used to minimize emissions, the onboard computer on OBDII-equipped vehicles can use an alternate strategy to control vehicle emissions until the failed sensor is repaired or replaced. The emissions using the alternate "fail-safe" strategy can be almost as low as if the control system was using the primary sensor. Thus, some repairs, particularly repairs to sensors, will result in little, if any, immediate emissions reductions. This can make OBD-directed repairs look ineffective in the short term.

As described in several studies below, the design of the OBDII system means that the malfunction indicator light (MIL or "check engine" light) will illuminate and diagnostic trouble codes issued for a potentially significant number of vehicles despite vehicle emissions being below the state's I/M emissions cutpoints and even the vehicle's certification standards. Furthermore, OBDII's strict malfunction criterion (the MIL illuminates if a problem is detected that could cause emissions to exceed 1.5 times the vehicle's emissions certification standards) were not set by individual states to meet their air-quality needs, but were set nationally according to the needs of areas with the most stringent requirements for vehicle emissions control.

If people respond to the MIL and the OBD system operates properly, there is little need for a periodic inspection. Vehicles will remain at low emissions levels throughout their lifetimes. However, there is a question as to whether drivers will seek repairs as the vehicle ages, and runs out of warranty. As described in several studies below, there is also the concern over the large number of vehicles with high emissions and no MIL illuminated.

There are a number of issues related to the OBD I/M programs that will first be highlighted. They are

- Readiness codes before and after repairs.
- Failure criteria.
- Emissions or pollutants of concern.
- Fast pass using OBDII.
- Human response to the MIL.

We discuss each in more detail below.  In addition, we also discuss recent regulations and results of studies related to the use of OBD in I/M.


## Readiness Code

Through the use of various sensors, the OBDII system tests the components of the emissions-control and fuel-management systems to ensure that they are operating correctly.  There is a specific criterion for each emissions-control system component that must be met before an OBDII system sensor is considered ready, meaning the component in question has been monitored.  These criteria are defined and implemented by each manufacturer.  For example, certain components are monitored as soon as the engine is turned on, after as many as 40 engine restarts, or only after the vehicle is driven under a certain load and speed.  In the case of monitoring the evaporative emissions-control system, readiness codes are not set until the vehicle is exposed to certain ambient temperatures.

A significant part of the problem is that the detection limits are set to very sensitive levels.  If, for instance, the system was just to detect if the gas cap was in place, the test could be completed almost on every trip.  Because the intent of the evaporative control system monitoring is to reliably detect a very small leak (e.g., a 1-millimeter diameter hole), the conditions necessary to make such a determination might not occur very often and perhaps never in the normal use of a certain vehicle.  If the OBD detection limits were set at higher levels, the tests could be completed more often.

EPA's OBD rule (EPA 2001) requires that all but two of these readiness codes be set to indicate that a particular emissions control component has been monitored by the OBDII system.  If more than two readiness codes are found unset, then the vehicle would be tested by an emissions tailpipe test or rejected from OBD testing.  EPA (2000c, 2001) estimates that the frequency of finding more than two readiness codes unset will be small.  However, McClintock (2000a) found in Colorado a much higher level of readiness codes being unset than the EPA's estimates.

The readiness codes are turned off when the battery is disconnected, possibly occurring as the result of repairs.  If that occurs, they must be reset before the vehicle can be subjected to another OBD check.  Resetting might be an issue for motorists attempting to retest their vehicles immediately after repairs.  Additionally, if it is easier to pass an emissions tailpipe test than an

OBDII check and the tailpipe test is an option for vehicles with unset readiness codes, motorists that fear failing an OBDII check may attempt to avoid this test by simply disconnecting the battery. The current OBDII system has no "stay-alive" memory that can persist through a battery disconnection. Future OBD systems might have such memory components and carry records of vehicle identification number, odometer reading, and a record of the MILs and their source and date. This information might provide a solution to the issue of unset readiness codes.

## Failure Criteria

Most I/M programs fail vehicles for excess emissions that are much higher than vehicles certification standards. The OBDII system, by design, illuminates the MIL (and fails a vehicle) if a problem is detected that might cause emissions to exceed 1.5 times the certification standard. In addition, MIL illumination occurs if the system determines that a monitor or sensor is not responding properly, even without increased emissions.

## Emissions or Pollutants of Concern

Many state I/M programs are designed to address a particular air-quality problem. Colorado's program is designed to control carbon monoxide (CO). The nonattainment areas in Texas are concerned about controlling nitrogen oxides ($NO_x$). Several states are concerned about hydrocarbons (HC) or $NO_x$, while others are concerned about both HC and $NO_x$, but one to a greater degree than the other. I/M cutpoints and standards are designed to control the emissions or pollutants of concern for each state. However, an OBDII program will fail a vehicle if any of the emissions (HC, CO, and $NO_x$) exceed the failure criteria.

## Fast Pass Using OBDII

States may consider using the OBDII system as a fast-pass test. This means that vehicles that demonstrate a clean OBDII system will be passed and not subjected to an emissions test. If the MIL is illuminated or there are unset readiness codes, the vehicle will not fail, but the vehicle owner will be given information for suggested repairs, and the vehicle will be required to undergo an emissions test. Under the current regulation (EPA 2001) the fast-pass test may be used only in the start-up of an OBDII test and for one cycle of vehicle inspection requirement. The fast-pass test could also be used for areas that are not required to implement an I/M program but are considering an OBDII test as a preventive control measure.

## Human Response to OBDII

The intent of the MIL is to inform motorists that they need to check their emissions control systems because there is an indication of some malfunction. However, many motorists are unlikely to spend the time and money to bring vehicles in for repair voluntarily, especially if the vehicle's emissions systems are outside the warranty period and the vehicle's operation is not affected. This might become especially problematic as the vehicle ages. Warranty periods for most components are relatively short compared with current vehicle lifetimes. The federal emissions control warranty is 96 months/80,000 miles for major emissions control components (such as the catalyst), and 24 months/24,000 miles for other components (such as sensors, PCV valve, EGR valve). Auto manufacturers have extended these warranties to 3 years/36,000 miles and 10 years/100,000 miles.

If motorists are required to have the OBD system checked as part of an I/M test, as with any I/M testing system, there is the possibility of cheating to avoid test and repair. We discussed above the possibility that motorists will simply disconnect batteries, causing unset readiness codes, which would allow them to take a more lenient IM240 tailpipe test rather than an OBD test. Other avoidance methods might also arise, although it is too early to determine how serious or widespread this problem could be.

Perhaps the most serious problem with motorist response to the MIL is the confusion that is likely to occur about what an illuminated check-engine light represents and what its relationship is to emissions and the cost-effectiveness of emissions reductions. Current studies, discussed later in this section, indicate little consistency between a MIL illumination and the probability of an IM240 failure. In addition, repairs of many vehicles with illuminated MILs do not produce substantial emission reductions, at least in the short-run. In part, it could be that many of the problems caught by OBDII are early-stage problems. Repairing these vehicles might result in much lower emissions later in the vehicles' lifetimes. Failures could also be due to evaporative emissions problems. Even after repair of these problems, improvements are difficult to measure. The inconsistencies between results of IM240 and OBD tests might produce motorists' confusion and serious skepticism about OBD I/M programs.

## Recent OBD I/M Regulations

EPA recently finalized a rule concerning the use of OBD in I/M (EPA 2001). It mandates the introduction of OBD tests for cars equipped with OBDII (1996 model year and later) and provides states the flexibility to completely replace traditional I/M tests with OBD checks.[1] The rule also extends the deadline by 1 year (until January 1, 2002) for states to implement OBD checks, and loosens some criteria for performing OBD inspections without all readiness codes being set. It also allows the states to phase-in the OBD test.

## Technical Analyses Regarding OBD I/M Tests

Table 4-2 contains a summary description of several recent studies regarding OBDII's use in I/M programs. Three EPA studies were summarized in a draft technical support document (EPA 2000c) that accompanied the OBD rule. The objectives of the EPA studies were to assess the effectiveness of OBD I/M testing for exhaust and evaporative emissions and to investigate implementation issues through the information collected from the Wisconsin enhanced I/M test lanes.

The first study evaluated the effectiveness of OBD I/M for tailpipe testing. EPA recruited 201 OBDII-equipped vehicles with either a malfunction indicator light (MIL) illuminated (194 vehicles) or no MIL illuminated but suspected of having high emissions (eight vehicles).[2] Once recruited, each vehicle was

---

[1]The Clean Air Act Amendments of 1990 and later regulations mandated that OBD checks be incorporated into I/M programs by January 1, 2001. However, until this proposed rule, states would have had to implement OBD checks in addition to traditional I/M programs. EPA concluded that there is no reason to subject vehicles to both IM240 and OBD checks (EPA 2000c).

[2]The discrepancy between the stated number of vehicles recruited (201) and the total number of vehicles in these two categories (202) exists because one vehicle was recruited twice for separate problems.

**TABLE 4-2**  Studies of OBD Issues Related to I/M Programs

| Study | Vehicle Recruitment | Vehicles Tested | Comments |
|---|---|---|---|
| EPA study of MIL illuminated vehicles | Solicitation, mainly from rental car agencies | 193 vehicles | Tailpipe comparison of IM240 with OBDII for vehicles with MIL on (EPA 2000c) |
| EPA study of high emissions, no MIL vehicles | I/M lanes | 8 vehicles | Vehicles suspected of high emissions with MIL off (EPA 2000c) |
| EPA evaporative emissions study | Same, with in-duced evaporative emission failures | 30 vehicles | Evaporative emissions effectiveness of OBDII (EPA 2000c) |
| CE-CERT (University of California, Riverside) | Rental car fleet and newspaper ads | 75 vehicles | Tailpipe comparison of IM240 with OBDII MIL on (Durbin et al. 2001) |
| Wisconsin | I/M lanes | 116,667 1996-1998 vehicles | Tailpipe comparison of IM240 with OBDII MIL on (EPA 2000c) |
| Colorado CDPHE study | I/M lanes (fails back to back IM240 fails and/or MIL on) | 3,162 vehicles in 2000; 1,466 vehicles in 1999 | Tailpipe comparison of IM240 with MIL on, including retest data (Barrett 2001) |
| Colorado CDPHE study | I/M lanes (fails back to back IM240 fails and/or MIL on) | 21 vehicles (out of a study design of 100) up to April 2001 | Tailpipe comparison of IM240 with OBDII MIL on, including repairs (Barrett 2001) |

given a Federal Test Procedure (FTP) emissions test as well as a laboratory IM240 emissions test.[3] Table 4-3 shows that of the 194 vehicles with the MIL

---

[3]The difference between a lane IM240 test, those conducted as part of an I/M program, and a laboratory IM240 test is that the latter can control better for factors such as the quality and calibration of the test equipment, ambient conditions, and tire pressure.

**TABLE 4-3** Results of EPA Study of Tailpipe Emissions for Vehicles with MIL Illuminated and Vehicles Suspected to Have High Emissions

| | No. of Vehicles | MIL Self-Cleared | FTP > 1× Certification Standards | FTP > 1.5× Certification Standards |
|---|---|---|---|---|
| Vehicles with MIL illuminated | 194 | 11 | 58 | 31 |
| Vehicles with no MIL illuminated but suspected to have high emissions | 8 | — | 5 | 4 |

Source: EPA 2000c.

illuminated, 11 had the MIL self-clear[4] before any emissions tests were completed, and 58 had emissions greater than the certification standards. Of the 58 vehicles with emissions greater than the certification standards, only 31 had emissions greater than 1.5 times the certification standards.

Table 4-3 indicates that 70% of the vehicles (136) had the MIL illuminated but emissions below certification standards. Of these 136 vehicles, 97 vehicles were identified to have a broken part (EPA 2000c). The remaining vehicles might have had an intermittent problem, but it no longer existed when the vehicle was tested. The problem might have been the result of a loose gas cap, a fuel-injector problem, or an intermittent electrical problem, or the vehicle could have been driven under an extreme driving condition. The OBDII system still stores much of this information in its memory and allows technicians to review the past history of the original problem. The large number of failing vehicles with relatively low emissions was also noted by

Durbin et al. (2001) in a study of 75 vehicles with MILs illuminated. That study found that 63% of vehicles with MILs illuminated had emissions below their certification standards, and 79% had emissions below 1.5 times their certification standards.

The eight vehicles in Table 4-3 with no MIL illuminated were recruited because of either high IM240 test lane results or other characteristics such as high mileage or driveability problems that suggest high emissions. Of those eight, four had emissions greater than 1.5 times their certification standards for

---

[4]The MIL self-clearing occurs when an intermittent problem is not detected on later system scans by the OBD system and the MIL turns off.

CO and/or $NO_x$ on the FTP test but no MIL illuminated. The OBDII catalyst monitoring system verifies the efficiency for HC. Thus, if the vehicle had high CO or $NO_x$, and low HC, it would not trigger the MIL.

This study also identified 21 vehicles with FTP emissions greater than two times their certification standards, and compared whether the OBD or laboratory IM240 test was better able to identify them. Of the 21, 19 were correctly identified by the OBD system, whereas only 13 were correctly identified by the laboratory IM240 test.

A second EPA study induced failures in the evaporative system on 30 vehicles to determine whether the OBD system could detect a range of such failures. These included missing, loose, or leaking gas caps and disconnected purge lines used to overload the carbon canister. Of these 30 vehicles, MIL illumination occurred in over 80% (25 vehicles). It should be noted that traditional I/M tests for evaporative emissions (the purge and pressure tests described in Chapter 3) are difficult to perform. Thus, the results of this study are encouraging in terms of the ability of OBD to identify problems in the evaporative system.

The third EPA study used data gathered in Wisconsin to assess failure rates and other issues associated with implementing an OBD I/M program. This study examined the relative failure rates for OBD I/M versus lane IM240 testing. For 1996 model-year vehicles, the OBD failure rate from the Wisconsin lane data was 2.4%, and the IM240 failure rate was 2.1%. However, the percentage of vehicles that failed both was only 0.2%, which indicates that only a small fraction (about 10%) of vehicles failing one also failed the other. Figure 4-1 shows data for the number of vehicles failing IM240 and OBD tests for model-year 1996-1998 vehicles. The large discrepancies between IM240 and OBD test failures are obviously of major concern.

The Wisconsin study also estimated the average time to perform an OBD I/M inspection (31 seconds) and identified atypical data link connector locations. The issue here is that the connector is placed out of sight and is difficult to locate as one moves from model to model. The study also looked at OBD readiness code data. Current regulations for OBD I/M testing require I/M programs to reject a vehicle with two or more readiness codes unset. Readiness codes were found unset in 5.8% of 1996 model-year vehicles, 2.3% of 1997 model-year vehicles, and 1.4% of 1998 model-year vehicles. The reason for these lower "not ready" rates on newer vehicles could be due to manufacturers; building better OBD systems or to lower mileage accumulation on these newer vehicles. Allowing states to proceed with OBD I/M testing with two

116,667 model year 1996-1998 vehicles
screened

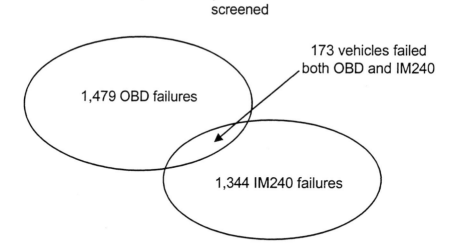

FIGURE 4-1 Number of OBD and IM240 failures from Wisconsin lane data for 1996 and newer vehicles.

or more readiness codes unset lowered the percentage of vehicles that would be rejected from 3.2% to 1.4%.

At the time of this report, the Colorado Department of Public Health and Environment (CDPHE) is investigating various aspects of OBDII. Under the Colorado's enhanced I/M program, new vehicles are exempt from testing for the first 4 years or until a change of ownership. If change of ownership occurs, the vehicles are inspected at that time and then are subject to the biennial inspection program from that time forward. A vehicle in the Colorado program can fail either if emissions are higher than the cutpoints or if the MIL is illuminated.

Two recent presentations examine I/M program data from testing of 1996 and newer vehicles in Colorado's I/M program (McClintock 2000b; Barrett 2001). Table 4-4 summarizes the results. The data show that, for 1996 and newer vehicles, about nine times more vehicles fail the MIL illumination test than the IM240 emissions test. Only a small fraction (about 2%) of the total vehicles tested failed both tests.

Barrett (2001) further reported that repair data for vehicles that fail either the MIL illumination or the IM240 tests showed similar repair cost per vehicle.

**TABLE 4-4** Number of 1996 and Newer Model-Year Vehicles Failing the IM240 and MIL Illumination Tests in Colorado's Enhanced IM240 Program

| Calendar Year | Number of 1996 Model Year and Newer Vehicles | | |
| --- | --- | --- | --- |
| | Failed IM240 Test | Failed IM240 + MIL | Failed MIL |
| 1999 | 182 | 36 | 1,320 |
| 2000 | 393 | 66 | 2,835 |

Sources: McClintock 2000b; Barrett 2001.

Both reported average repair costs at about $220 per vehicle (about 13% of vehicles that failed these tests reported repair costs). As shown in Table 4-2, the number of OBDII-induced repairs likely exceeded the IM240-induced repairs by almost an order of magnitude for these relatively new vehicles. However, the emissions reductions associated with OBDII repairs are much less than those resulting from IM240 repairs. For example, Barrett (2001) reported that for the retested IM240 failures, CO emissions were reduced from 47.1 g/mi to 5.7 g/mi, whereas for the retested MIL illuminated vehicles, CO emissions were reduced from 4.7 g/mi to 3.3 g/mi. This result is not surprising since the OBDII system will cause MIL illumination for a number of problems that do not cause high emissions in the short term but could lead to higher emissions or the nondetection of an emissions problem in the future.

### Summary of Technical Issues Regarding OBD I/M Tests

The combination of much higher failure rate, lower emissions reductions, and comparable cost of repair for OBDII-failed vehicles is likely to lead to higher repair costs and lower cost efficiency associated with an OBD I/M program. It should be noted, however, that the failure rate and repair cost information currently available come from first-generation OBDII systems and young vehicles with low overall failure rates. Additionally, the cost-effectiveness of an OBDII-based inspection system is difficult to compare with that of a traditional IM240 program and might require comparing emissions of OBDII-equipped vehicles in an I/M program with OBDII-equipped vehicles operating in an area that does not have an inspection program. OBDII-based inspection programs can be expected to have much greater amounts of pre-inspection repair, as one can expect very few motorists with a MIL illuminated to go to an inspection testing station. If an OBD I/M program is operating as it is supposed to, very few OBDII-equipped vehicles eligible for testing would be operating with high emissions in the area. These studies raise many important issues that should be reviewed by an independent group. In particular, both the Colorado and Wisconsin studies with recruitment of large numbers of vehicles from I/M lanes found many vehicles that failed the IM240 test but did not have the MIL on. This finding is a serious problem that needs to be thoroughly analyzed, because the IM240 failures are from higher-emitting vehicles. The problem could arise in manufacturer's design of OBDII systems, in the reproducibility of the IM240 test, or some other factor. In any case, this problem needs to be understood and corrected before I/M programs operate using OBDII alone.

## REMOTE SENSING

Remote sensing is a technique used to measure emissions from individual vehicles as they drive by a roadside sensor. Light of suitable wavelengths is projected across the roadway at tailpipe height and is partially absorbed by pollutants present in vehicle exhaust. Passing vehicles block the light beam as they drive by. Ratios of individual pollutants to $CO_2$ present in vehicle exhaust are determined by analysis of a series of sensor scans of the exhaust plume made after a vehicle has driven by. Background corrections are made by using readings taken just before the sensor beam is blocked by each passing vehicle. These ratios are used to calculate and report exhaust concentrations similar to those measured by a probe inserted into the tailpipe.

Remote sensing of vehicle emissions was pioneered by Stedman and coworkers at the University of Denver (Bishop et al. 1989). Researchers at General Motors (GM) developed a similar instrument (Stephens and Cadle 1991). More recent approaches to remote sensing of vehicle emissions (Nelson et al. 1998; Baum et al. 2000) have made it possible to measure a wider range of exhaust constituents, including ammonia, $NO_2$, NO, and some individual organic compounds. Other advances that have facilitated the collection and interpretation of remote-sensing measurements include pattern recognition software to read vehicle license plates automatically (Jack et. al 1995) and sensors to measure speeds and accelerations of passing vehicles. A typical remote sensor measures between 3,000 and 10,000 vehicles per day and provides the only test type that can be operated unmanned.

Although remote-sensing readings are commonly reported as the concentrations of exhaust constituents (e.g., % CO, or the amount of CO as a fraction of total exhaust gas volume), the underlying measurement is actually the mole ratio of the pollutant of interest (CO, HC, or NO) to carbon dioxide ($CO_2$). Tailpipe concentrations are calculated from the ratios measured by the remote sensor (Stedman et al. 1991). Ratios are determined by measuring the exhaust plume repeatedly within an interval of 0.5 second after the vehicle drives by and plotting the amount of pollutant detected versus the amount of $CO_2$. An example of the correlation of NO and $CO_2$ signals measured by remote sensing in the plume of a passing vehicle is shown in Figure 4-2. The remote sensor measures the amount of pollutant emitted relative to the amount of $CO_2$ because dilution of the exhaust plume varies with time, wind speed, vehicle speed, and other factors.

From remote sensor measurements of exhaust emissions ratios ($CO/CO_2$, $HC/CO_2$, and $NO/CO_2$) and knowledge of fuel properties, it is possible to derive mass emissions rates per unit of fuel burned by carbon balance (Stedman et al. 1991; Singer and Harley 1996). Therefore, although remote sensing is described above as a concentration test, it may also be used to provide mass emissions results but only per unit of fuel burned. Fuel economy (not measured by remote sensors) must be estimated to obtain mass emissions rates per distance traveled.

## Remote-Sensor Accuracy

### Carbon Monoxide

CO is the pollutant for which remote-sensing capabilities are best developed and demonstrated. Typically, this is the most abundant pollutant in vehicle exhaust, facilitating its measurement. One of the first assessments of remote-sensor accuracy in measuring CO emissions involved double-blind comparisons of remote-sensor readings with a specially equipped vehicle that had on-board instruments to measure exhaust emissions (Lawson et al. 1990). An observer in the vehicle manually selected different air-to-fuel ratios and recorded the on-board CO measurement as the vehicle passed by the remote sensor. The remote sensor was highly correlated with simultaneous on-board CO measurements ($r^2 = 0.94$), with a regression slope of 1.03 and an intercept of 0.08% CO, over a series of 34 vehicle passes with speeds ranging from approximately 15 to 50 mph.

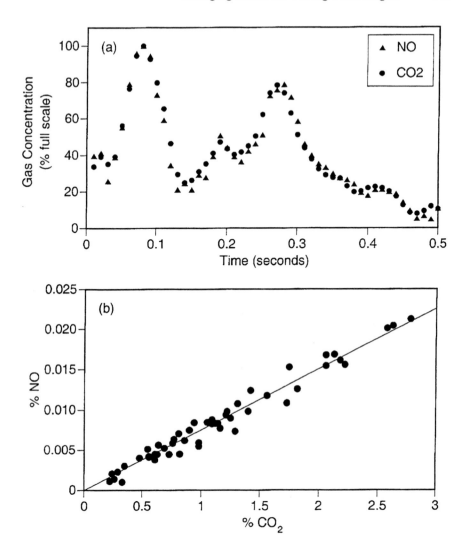

**FIGURE 4-2** Correlation of NO and $CO_2$ signals measured by remote sensing. Source: Popp 1999. Reprinted by permission of the author.

The comparisons between remote-sensor readings and on-board emissions measurements from an instrumented vehicle were repeated in 1991 (Ashbaugh et al. 1992, Stedman et al. 1994) in a study involving University of Denver (DU) remote sensors, a GM remote sensor, and an instrumented vehicle. Correlations between remote-sensor readings and the instrumented vehicle for

CO were high: $r^2 = 0.99$ for the DU remote sensor, and $r^2 = 0.96$ for the GM remote sensor. Corresponding slopes of linear regression lines for the DU and GM remote sensors relative to the instrumented vehicle were $0.98 \pm 0.02$ and $0.96 \pm 0.02$, respectively. These results confirm the accuracy of remote sensing in measuring CO emissions.

## Hydrocarbons

Measuring exhaust HC emissions by remote sensing is more challenging than measuring CO emissions for several reasons. HC emissions are typically much lower than CO emissions, and their infrared extinction coefficients are much less, making them more difficult to detect. Instead of dealing with a single well-defined molecule, HC encompasses hundreds of different organic compounds with different infrared spectra. Therefore, it is not surprising that in the intercomparison study (Ashbaugh et al. 1992) of remote sensing with an on-board infrared analyzers on an instrumented vehicle, remote-sensing measurements of HC emissions were found to be less accurate than those of CO. Correlations between remote-sensor HC measurements and instrumented vehicle readings were somewhat lower ($r^2 = 0.85$ for DU, $r^2 = 0.87$ for GM) than those for CO, and linear regression slopes were further away from 1.0 (slope was $1.08 \pm 0.06$ for DU, and $0.85 \pm 0.05$ for GM). The first DU remote sensor read systematically higher than the GM remote sensor by approximately 35% on average. The infrared filter used for HC measurements in the DU remote sensors was changed later (Guenther et al. 1995) and now matches more closely the filter used in the GM sensor. The earlier DU remote-sensor HC channel might have suffered from interference due to absorption by water vapor in vehicle exhaust. Further evaluation of remote-sensing capabilities for HC is needed.

Infrared analyzers that are used to measure HC emissions are optimized to measure absorption by the carbon-hydrogen bonds present in alkanes; typically, propane or hexane is used to calibrate the analyzers. Other compounds present in vehicle exhaust, such as alkenes and aromatics, have additional peaks in their infrared spectra at frequencies different from those of alkanes; however, no small set of remote-sensor channels is able to measure all the hydrocarbons present in vehicle exhaust. Therefore, remote sensors (as well as infrared analyzers typically used in idle and acceleration-simulation-mode (ASM) tests) detect only a fraction of total HC in vehicle exhaust (Stephens et al. 1996). To obtain a more accurate estimate of mass emissions rates,

Singer recommended that infrared analyzer results for HC should be multiplied by a factor of about 2 (Singer et al. 1998); the scaling factor may vary depending on the chemical composition of the HC emissions. Emissions tests, such as the FTP and IM240 described above, use a flame ionization detector (FID) to measure HC emissions. This detector is known to respond similarly to alkanes, alkenes, and aromatics and thus is better suited for measuring the HC mass present.


**Nitrogen Oxides**


$NO_x$ is defined as the sum of nitric oxide (NO) and nitrogen dioxide ($NO_2$), although the direct emissions from internal combustion engines are dominated by NO (Kirchstetter et al. 1996; Jiménez et al. 2000). Remote-sensing capabilities for NO have been developed more recently than those for CO and HC. Measurements of NO emissions are challenging because of overlapping absorption by other exhaust constituents: water vapor in the infrared and aromatic HC in the ultraviolet (UV). Various approaches have been used, including tunable infrared diode lasers (Nelson et al. 1998; Jiménez et al. 1999) and UV spectroscopy (Zhang et al. 1996a; Popp et al. 1999b). By modifying the UV absorption technique used in earlier DU remote sensors, Popp et al. were able to achieve a lower detection limit (i.e., increased sensitivity) and eliminate interference due to UV absorption by aromatic HC.

A limited comparison of $NO_x$ concentrations by remote sensing and on-board measurements in heavy-duty diesel truck exhaust has been reported (Jiménez et al. 2000). Remote-sensing measurements of the $NO_x/CO_2$ ratio agreed with similar measurements made on-board an instrumented diesel truck, although the authors note that remote-sensor accuracy was assessed over only a limited portion of the likely range of $NO_x/CO_2$ emissions ratios. An instrument comparison and further evaluation of remote-sensing methods for measuring $NO_x$ emissions is needed. Remote-sensing site selection is especially problematic for measuring $NO_x$ emissions accurately because of their dependence on operating conditions, but it might not be critical for identifying high $NO_x$ emitters.


**Particulate Matter**


Development of capabilities for remote sensing of particulate matter (PM) emissions is an area of active research. The Coordinating Research Council is currently sponsoring a study to evaluate the effectiveness of remote sensing to measure PM emissions from heavy-duty diesel vehicles (CRC Project E-56). Qualitative measurements of PM emissions using remote sensing will likely be available soon. Quantitative measurement of mass emissions rates for PM will be more difficult to achieve because the scattering and absorption of light by airborne particles are complex functions of particle size and chemical composition.

## Site Selection and Effects of Engine Load

An important consideration when measuring vehicle emissions by remote sensing is careful selection of roadside monitoring sites. Sites where vehicles might be sampled during cold-start operation should be avoided, because vehicle emissions are higher than normal until the engine and emissions-control systems have warmed up. Sites where driving conditions involve frequent heavy acceleration and high-load driving (e.g., accelerating on steep uphill grades) might yield unrepresentative emissions results associated with operation in commanded enrichment modes. (Enrichment modes have lower air/fuel ratios and increased CO and HC emissions.) To correct for effects of engine load on exhaust emissions, the roadway grade at remote-sensing sites should be noted, and the speed and acceleration of each vehicle passing by the remote sensor should be measured. This is now common practice, but information on vehicle speed and acceleration is rarely available in older remote-sensing studies.

Ashbaugh et al. (1992) and Zhang et al. (1993) noted that tailpipe HC concentrations measured by remote sensing were elevated at a site where vehicles were decelerating. The significance of this result is not that such driving modes are an important source of HC (fuel consumption is low under these conditions, hence mass emissions rates are also low), but rather that such sites should be avoided in remote-sensing studies.

Jiménez (1998) and McClintock (1998) developed more formal approaches to estimating engine load based on readily observed vehicle-operating parameters, such as speed and acceleration in addition to roadway grade. Vehicle-specific power (VSP) is estimated as the sum of loads due to aerodynamic drag (wind resistance), vehicle acceleration, rolling resistance (tire-roadway friction), and hill climbing, divided by the mass of the vehicle and commonly reported in kilowatts per metric ton. On a fleet-average basis, CO emissions appear to be less sensitive to engine load than other pollutants; they remain fairly constant over a VSP range of -5 to 20 kilowatts per metric ton (kW/t) (Bishop et al. 1999). HC emissions decrease with increasing engine load, over a VSP range of -15 to 15 kW/t (Bishop et al. 1999). $NO_x$ emissions often increase over the same VSP range, but further study of this relationship is needed.

## Coverage

If remote sensing is used to screen the vehicle fleet to help identify high-emitting vehicles, a significant issue is the need to measure by remote sensing the emissions from most of the vehicles operating in a given area. This need might require multiple remote sensors, which must be moved to different road-side sampling locations every few days. Current constraints, such as the need to measure across a single lane of traffic, make it difficult to achieve complete coverage of the fleet. A remote-sensing study conducted by the Bureau of Automotive Repair (Amlin 1995) using 10 remote-sensing vans in a 3-month period was able to obtain CO emissions measurements matched to readable license plates for 380,000 vehicles registered in Sacramento County, California. Emissions from 58% of these vehicles were measured more than once in this study. About 2 million remote-sensing measurements obtained at multiple roadside sampling sites were needed to achieve a 47% level of coverage for the 810,000 vehicles registered in Sacramento County. Improved coverage of the vehicle fleet could have been obtained by increasing the number of sites and days where remote sensors were operated; when the study ended, 30% of vehicles driving by the remote sensors were being observed for the first time. Note that remote sensors provided measurements for unregistered and out-of-county vehicles operating within Sacramento County; some of these vehicles would not be covered by traditional I/M programs.

## Need for Quality Assurance and Quality Control

As with any emissions testing program, a critical element is data quality. Success in using remote sensing in field studies has been mixed, with problems often apparent when multiple remote-sensing instruments and measurement teams are involved. Walsh and Gertler (1997) reviewed remote-sensing data collected in Texas during 1996 in Houston, Dallas/Ft. Worth, and El Paso. For the most recent 10-15 vehicle model years, HC emissions measured by one of the two remote sensors used in Houston were systematically lower by factors of 2-3 than those measured with the other. They concluded that the most probable cause was "related to calibration gases used by the individual instruments during the field study." There was also evidence of systematic differences in CO measurements from Houston relative to those measured in Dallas/Ft. Worth with different remote-sensing instruments. Walsh and Gertler (1997) noted that although the study sponsor was aware of the utility of a side-by-side comparison of the various remote-sensing units being used, it was not done because of budget and time constraints.

The experience described above with remote sensing in Texas is not unique: similar problems arose when multiple contractors and remote-sensing instruments were used in field studies in Phoenix and Sacramento. In such cases, there appears to have been too much emphasis on the number of vehicles and sites sampled and insufficient time and effort devoted to quality control.

## Use of Remote Sensing to Identify High Emitters

The question of whether remote sensing should be used to identify high emitters in I/M programs has been controversial. Proponents of remote sensing argue that current I/M programs waste time and money because about 20 vehicles have to be tested to identify one high emitter that is a candidate for repair; some vehicles might be adjusted by their owners or technicians to pass scheduled emissions tests, but they do not remain clean or are difficult to repair; and motorists might register their vehicles in ways that avoid I/M requirements. Opponents argue that remote sensing is not a reliable way to measure vehicle emissions, motorists might avoid known remote-sensor locations and/or take steps to frustrate remote-sensing device measurements, and use of remote sensing might lead to an unacceptably high rate of false failures, reducing public acceptance of I/M programs.

Several valuable studies have been conducted in which both remote sensing and standard I/M program tests have been used to measure emissions from the same vehicles. The most useful comparisons are made with I/M program tests administered at the roadside on vehicles pulled over immediately after their emissions were measured by remote sensing. Some analysts emphasize perceived inadequacies in the correlation between remote sensing and I/M test results for individual vehicles as a reason why remote sensing should not be used in I/M programs. More appropriate categorical analyses focus on the ability of remote sensing to identify high-emitting vehicles that will fail I/M program tests, as discussed below.

When comparing remote-sensing readings with roadside emissions inspection results, it is important to remember that the vehicle itself can be a significant source of variability, especially in the case of intermittent malfunctions in the emissions-control systems. Therefore, it is unrealistic to expect any emissions test to be 100% repeatable in making pass-fail determinations for individual vehicles, even for the same test administered repeatedly. For example, Knepper et al. (1993) measured emissions from 10 "normal" and 7 "high-emitting" vehicles, all 1986 or later model years. Emissions were measured in the laboratory using the FTP loaded-mode test described in Chapter 3. Knepper found that relative to normal emitters, the high-emitting vehicles showed greater emissions of CO and HC and greater variability of emission rates within each test vehicle. Variability in emission rates for the high-emitting vehicles was traced to changes in air/fuel ratio from test to test.

## Hawthorne (Los Angeles) 1989 Study

Lawson et al. (1990) describe a study in which vehicles were pulled over, and roadside inspections made immediately after vehicle emissions had been measured by remote sensing. Of 50 vehicles that were identified by remote sensing as having high emissions (more than 2% CO in their exhaust), 28 failed the CO portion of the roadside inspection and 15 failed for other reasons, for a total of 43 failing vehicles out of 50. The rate of false failures (error of commission) was 14%.

Of the 15 vehicles in the remote-sensing/pullover study that failed the roadside inspection for reasons other than high CO emissions, 8 were pre-1975 models that also would have failed for CO if a tailpipe concentration of less than 2% had been required to pass. (The actual CO concentration required to pass the roadside test ranged from 2.5% to 7% for pre-1975 vehicles, in contrast to levels of approximately 1% CO required for 1980 and newer cars.)

Of 10 additional vehicles that were measured by remote sensing to have low CO emissions, all passed the CO portion of the roadside inspection (2 of these 10 vehicles failed for reasons other than high CO emissions). The error of omission for this small sample of vehicles was 20%: remote sensing of CO emissions alone did not pick up other problems that led to failure of the roadside inspection.

## Rosemead Boulevard (Los Angeles) 1991 Study

A larger-scale combined remote-sensing/roadside inspection study was performed during summer 1991 in El Monte, California, as described by Stedman et al. (1994). Vehicles were identified as high emitters based on two remote sensors both reading greater than 4% CO. There was a preference for pulling over post-1980 model vehicles for roadside inspections because of the less stringent emissions requirements for older vehicles. Of 307 vehicles that had both remote-sensor and roadside inspection data available, 85% failed the exhaust emissions (idle test) portion of the roadside inspection, and the overall failure rate (including vehicles with tampered or noncomplying emissions-control systems identified during an underhood inspection) was 92%.

## Michigan 1992 Study

Stephens et al. (1995) assessed variability in vehicle emissions by examining correlations between multiple remote-sensor readings of CO and HC emissions and between remote-sensor and roadside IM240 emissions test results for 170 vehicles. In general, the correlations between remote-sensor and IM240 results improved as the number of remote-sensor measurements of a vehicle's emissions increased from 1 to 4. This finding indicates that the rate of false failures is likely to decrease when more than one high remote-sensing reading is required to identify a vehicle as a high emitter. It is unclear, however, whether simply raising the cutpoint would be a more effective method for identifying high emitters and reducing the number of false failures.

## Orange County (Los Angeles) 1995 Study

Lawson et al. (1996b) conducted a study in Orange County, California, in 1995, where high-emitting vehicles were identified by remote sensors and pulled over for repairs. In that study, measurements from two remote sensors separated by 100-150 feet were used to identify high emitters, whose criteria were average readings of 4% and 0.1% for CO and HC, respectively. During a 10-day period, remote-sensing readings were obtained for 19,000 vehicles at the two locations. Nearly 10% of the vehicles transiting the remote-sensing devices at the two sites exceeded the high-emitter cutpoint criteria, with a high emitter passing the remote-sensing devices every 2.1 minutes. More than 600 vehicles were pulled over for possible participation in the repair program, and 140 were selected for repairs and testing.

Once a car was chosen for participation in the program, it was given an IM240 test on EPA's transportable dynamometer; in nearly all cases, the IM240 test was given on the same day the vehicle was selected for program participation. Once the vehicle was given the IM240 test, it was transported to a repair garage where it was given the two-speed BAR90 idle tests and visual Smog Check inspection. In this unique data set, remote sensing, IM240, and BAR90 data were available for the same vehicles, with emissions readings taken on nearly the same day.

The average pre-repair IM240 emissions rates of the vehicles in this study were 70, 6.2, and 2.0 g/mi for CO, HC, and $NO_x$, respectively. Eighty-six percent of the vehicles in the program failed the IM240 test using EPA's 1997 standards for the IM240; 66%, 78%, and 27% failed for CO, HC, and $NO_x$ (even though the vehicles were not stopped for $NO_x$ emissions), respectively. Ninety-six percent of the vehicles that participated in the program failed the BAR90 inspection. This percentage includes those that failed a functional test, shown as an underhood failure in Figure 4-3. Of the five vehicles that passed the BAR90 test, four failed the IM240. Seventy-three percent of the vehicles in the program were classified as being "tampered" with or "arguably tampered." Additional data on pass/fail rates are shown in Figure 4-3. This study showed that remote-sensing identifications of high CO- and/or HC-emitting vehicles were confirmed in 86% to 96% of IM240 and BAR90 emissions tests administered on the same or the next day.

**Arizona High-Emitter Program**

The state of Arizona implemented a remote-sensing program to identify high-emitting vehicles in the Phoenix area, starting in 1995. The program was terminated 5 years later by state legislators, because of problems including costs in the final year of over $300 per high-emitting vehicle identified and

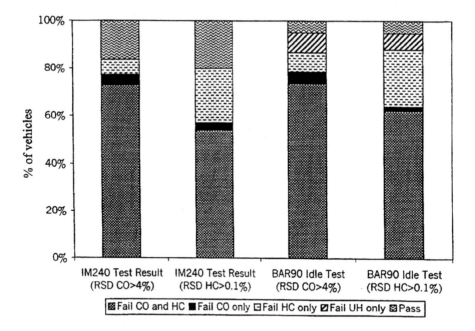

FIGURE 4-3 Results from Orange County study showing percentage of vehicles identified by remote-sensing device (RSD) that failed IM240 and BAR90 emissions tests. UH denotes under-hood inspection.

false failures attributed to cold-start operating conditions and mismeasured HC emissions. Appropriate remote-sensing sites were scarce, sites were lost as freeway ramps were widened, and the program was continually looking for new sites (J. Walls, Arizona Department of Environmental Quality, personal commun. February 16, 2001).

During a period from mid-May 1998 through early June 1999, over 2 million valid remote-sensing test records were collected, but only 2,987 vehicles were identified as high emitters (Wrona 1999). Owners of vehicles identified as high emitters were sent letters ordering them to submit their vehicles for IM240 testing within 30 days. About half (55%) of vehicle owners responded within this time period; an additional 15-20% of vehicle owners complied later, after their vehicle registration was suspended. Of vehicles that reported for testing, 42% passed the initial IM240 test, although a survey indicated that one-third of these vehicles underwent repairs prior to the test (Wrona 1999).

## Use of Remote Sensing to Screen for Clean Vehicles

Remote sensing is being used to identify clean vehicles so that they may avoid visiting an emissions test station for scheduled testing. For example, in the St. Louis area, a clean-screen program has been in operation since April 2000. If two or more successive low-emissions readings have been measured by remote sensing, the vehicle owner can opt to be excused from scheduled emissions testing. Daily locations and hours of operation of remote-sensing vans are advertised via a web site. This clean-screen approach may be preferable to issuing blanket exemptions to all vehicles of specified model years.

## ALTERNATIVE APPROACHES FOR CONTROLLING LIFETIME EMISSIONS

An I/M program attempts to ensure that a vehicle's emissions-control system is operating properly throughout the vehicle's lifetime. There are other approaches to controlling lifetime emissions. Shifting the burden of responsibility from vehicle owners to the manufacturers is one approach. Although requiring manufacturers to maintain vehicles throughout their lifetime might be unlikely, increasing warranties on emissions-control systems to 200,000 miles could accomplish at least part of this objective. Adopting national policies that force older vehicles from the fleet is another option. Vehicle scrappage programs have been used on only a limited scale in the United States. Other countries have taxation and inspection policies that help to maintain a young vehicle fleet, but these policies tend to be in effect in places with a large domestic automobile production sector (European Commission 1997; JAMA 2000). Developing outreach and financial-support programs targeting owners of high-emitting vehicles could be used to reduce the negative incentives for those needing emissions repairs. These and the methods described earlier in this chapter could be used to control lifetime emissions from vehicles and reduce or eliminate the need for traditional I/M testing.

## SUMMARY

Traditionally, I/M programs have used tailpipe emissions tests, often accompanied by visual underhood inspections, to assess vehicles registered in the program area. This approach is inefficient and costly because of the skewed distribution of emissions across the vehicle fleet; 10-20 must be tested to identify one high-emitting vehicle that is a candidate for repairs.

A variety of technologies that matured during the 1990s will affect emissions testing regimes in the future. These approaches include developing profiles of vehicles likely to have high or low emissions, use of OBD systems to detect and help guide repairs of emissions-related malfunctions, and the use of remote sensing to identify vehicles most likely to fail traditional tailpipe emissions tests.

The most significant form of profiling to date has been the excusing of new vehicles (typically up to 4 years of age) from regular I/M program testing. Smaller effects, if any, on emissions benefits and program costs have resulted from profiles that rely on inspection history and results of testing for vehicles of the same make, model, and model year.

Although OBD systems are present on an increasing number of vehicles, unresolved questions remain concerning their usefulness as a replacement for traditional emissions tests. These systems detect malfunctions "likely" to lead to increases in emissions above certification levels, but no actual emissions measurements are made. Studies of emissions levels on vehicles with MILs illuminated have shown that most of these vehicles do not have emissions much above their certification standard. A separate EPA study done with data from Wisconsin's I/M program showed very little overlap between vehicles that failed the IM240 and the OBD tests. The CDPHE also found a similar result. Instituting an OBD I/M program that fails a large number of marginal emitters could undermine a commitment to find high emitters and ensure that they are the repaired. Instituting an OBD I/M program that failed to detect high emitters could do the same. Furthermore, a critical human factor for OBD systems is the motorist's response to the MIL. The results of these initial studies emphasize the inadequacy of the current data set for assessing the effectiveness of OBD for I/M testing. The results also emphasize that much additional information is required before OBDII's reliability and effectiveness can be quantified in MOBILE. The modeling of OBD I/M options in MOBILE6 is discussed in the following chapter.

Roadside remote sensing has been shown to measure CO emissions reliably, with less certain results now available for HC and $NO_x$. Development of remote measurement capabilities for PM remains an important research priority. A variety of issues require careful attention in remote-sensing study design: site selection, effects of engine load, attention to quality assurance and quality control, and achieving adequate coverage of the in-use vehicle fleet. Studies in which vehicles suspected to have high emissions based on remote-sensing measurements are pulled over for further roadside testing have confirmed that remote sensing can identify vehicles likely to fail emissions tests with a success rate of 80-96%.

# 5

# Estimating Inspection and Maintenance Emissions Reductions Using the MOBILE Model

The U.S. Environmental Protection Agency (EPA) mobile-source emissions factor (MOBILE) series of computer models historically have been used by state and local air-quality planning agencies to estimate emissions benefits of inspection and maintenance (I/M) programs. In this chapter, the regulatory context of EPA's MOBILE program is discussed. Comparisons of I/M program evaluation data with MOBILE predictions are then provided, followed by a detailed explanation of proposed procedures for estimating I/M program effects in MOBILE6, EPA's latest version of the model. The chapter also includes a brief discussion of California's model for estimating on-road mobile-source emissions and I/M program effects, the EMFAC model.

## USE OF MOBILE IN REGULATORY APPLICATIONS

The Clean Air Act and its amendments require that areas that have not met the National Ambient Air Quality Standards (NAAQS) develop state implementation plans (SIPs) that describe how they will attain compliance. The 1990 Clean Air Act Amendments (CAAA90) prescribe minimal control measures and attainment dates, depending on the severity of the NAAQS exceedance. Among other things, these SIPs must contain three main items:

(1) a detailed and comprehensive current-year emissions inventory; (2) a detailed and comprehensive future-year (for the prescribed attainment year) emissions inventory forecast using federal, state, and local emissions-control programs; and (3) an analysis of future-year air quality showing attainment of the NAAQS by photochemical modeling.[1] To ensure that emissions reductions are occurring, SIPs must also specify emissions targets for every third year toward the attainment year, and so-called rate-of-progress inventories must then be submitted to EPA.

A second legislative requirement in the CAAA90, known as conformity, prohibits transportation projects if they impede progress toward meeting emissions targets and attaining the NAAQS. For the projects to proceed, metropolitan planning organizations (MPOs) must evaluate the emissions effects of transportation plans, projects, and programs, and pass a conformity demonstration with the U.S. Department of Transportation. Conformity is demonstrated if mobile-source emissions that are forecasted to result from transportation plans, programs, and projects do not exceed mobile-source emissions budgets established in the SIP. Conformity lapses if it cannot be demonstrated that the SIP mobile-source emissions budget will not be exceeded, or if 3 years have passed since the last conformity demonstration. During a conformity lapse, projects that are already under construction can proceed, but new projects requiring federal funding or approval cannot be advanced until the conformity lapse has been remedied.

For both of these applications, states and regions outside California use EPA's MOBILE emissions factor model for estimating emissions and emissions reductions from mobile-source control programs such as I/M (California has its own emissions factor model, EMFAC).[2] EPA introduced the first version of the model, MOBILE1, in 1978. Since then, there have been a series of model revisions with changes to modeling assumptions, methods, and the ways changes in the vehicle fleet are accounted for (e.g., with adoption of new emissions standards and other federal control programs). Many of the model revisions have incorporated data from testing programs that were designed to

---

[1]Carbon monoxide SIPs can use rollback modeling, which assumes that reductions in emissions produce a directly proportional reduction in pollutant concentrations (above background levels), to demonstrate future-year attainment.

[2]Although states are not mandated by any law or regulation to use MOBILE, SIPs developed with some other mobile-source emissions model would not be accepted by EPA (except for California, which must use the EMFAC model for their SIPs).

assess characteristics of vehicle emissions that previously had been ill characterized or were underestimated. For the past several years, EPA has been working on the most significant model revision in its history. The new model, MOBILE6, is expected to be released in 2001 for use in regulatory applications. The recent National Research Council (2000) report and the Holmes and Russell (2001) review of MOBILE describe the history of the model's revisions and provide more details about the uses and implications of MOBILE as a regulatory emissions modeling tool.

In the SIP process, MOBILE is used to estimate what are referred to as SIP credits. States use the model to estimate the emissions reduction in a future year with implementation of an I/M program (or changes to an existing I/M program). These SIP credits based on MOBILE are only an estimate of the real emissions reductions. Actual emissions reductions from an I/M program can be measured only with real data from vehicles that have and have not been through the program. SIP credits are very important to states, because if they do not accumulate enough credits to demonstrate future-year attainment, they can be penalized economically by withdrawal of federal transportation funds and limitations on new construction requiring environmental permits. On the other hand, if states claim too much credit for I/M and the emissions reductions are not fully realized, then progress toward attaining clean air standards is hindered.

It should be noted that MOBILE estimates emissions factors in grams per mile by vehicle class (e.g., passenger cars, light-duty trucks, and heavy-duty diesels). To estimate on-road mobile-source emissions, these emission factors are then multiplied by estimates of vehicle miles traveled (VMT) by vehicle class. In most urban areas, VMT estimates are derived from transportation demand models. This chapter addresses issues in the MOBILE estimates of I/M program effects. There are just as many issues and problems in the estimation of VMT, but coverage of these issues is outside the scope of this report.[3]

## MODEL PREDICTIONS COMPARED WITH
## PROGRAM EVALUATION DATA

As discussed above, one of the more important uses of MOBILE is for states to generate SIP credits for an I/M program to be implemented in a

---

[3]See EPA (1992c) for guidance on development of VMT forecasts.

future year. In the 1992 enhanced I/M regulatory impact analysis, EPA estimated that enhanced I/M would reduce light-duty vehicle (LDV) exhaust hydrocarbon (HC) emissions by 28%, carbon monoxide (CO) emissions by 31%, and nitrogen oxide ($NO_x$) emissions by 9% by the year 2000 from a non-I/M fleet (EPA 1992b). This prediction was made with version 4.1 of the model. EPA's predicted emissions reductions for enhanced I/M using MOBILE5, released shortly afterward, were likewise overly generous. Table 5-1 shows MOBILE5b predicted reductions in emissions estimates from the non-I/M case for light-duty gasoline vehicles (LDGV, passenger cars) for calendar years 1995 and 2000 under various I/M scenarios. The table shows the expected increased emissions reductions with more advanced testing, with the largest reductions occurring for the biennial IM240 with technician training. Predicted emissions reductions for calendar year 2000 are larger than for calendar year 1995, primarily because the base emissions (in the non-I/M case) are smaller in future years with fleet turnover.

There have been only a few comparisons of emissions reductions estimated from program data or remote-sensing measurements to MOBILE5 predictions. These comparisons are shown in Table 5-2 for several I/M programs across the country; evaluations for most of the I/M programs listed in the table were discussed in Chapter 3. Of the studies referenced in Table 5-2, the analyses of the Arizona IM240 program are arguably the most detailed and rigorous; these analyses show slight overpredictions by MOBILE5 of CO and HC emissions reductions and significant overprediction (by a factor of 2) of $NO_x$ reductions. Analyses of Colorado IM240 data also show significant overprediction of IM240 effects. Such overpredictions of the effectiveness of I/M programs hinder progress toward achieving air-quality goals, as states are granted too much SIP credit for planned I/M programs and therefore do not enact additional needed controls.

MOBILE6 was not available to the committee during most of the committee's work. However, the draft MOBILE6 model, just released, shows deterioration rates significantly lower than those in MOBILE5. Figure 5-1 compares VOC and $NO_x$ emission rates in MOBILE5 and in draft MOBILE6 with and without the effects of the Tier 2 and 2007 heavy-duty rulemakings. The figure shows that emission rates in draft MOBILE6 are significantly higher in past and current years and significantly lower in future years (after about 2005). If the emissions deterioration rates are closer to reality in MOBILE6 than in MOBILE5, this could be a major contributing factor to the MOBILE5 overestimation of I/M effects. EPA has been criticized in the past for overly pessimistic assumptions on deterioration rates for 1981 and later vehicles (see, e.g.,

**TABLE 5-1** MOBILE5b Predicted Exhaust Emissions Reductions for LDGVs in 1995 and 2000 for Various I/M Programs[a]

| | Year 1995 | | | Year 2000 | | |
|---|---|---|---|---|---|---|
| | CO (%) | HC (%) | $NO_X$ (%) | CO (%) | HC (%) | $NO_X$ (%) |
| Idle, annual | 17.9 | 17.8 | 0.8 | 18.8 | 19.1 | 1.2 |
| Idle, biennial | 14.9 | 14.5 | 0.8 | 16.8 | 16.9 | 1.3 |
| Idle/2500, annual | 25.5 | 22.3 | 0.6 | 29.0 | 24.8 | 1.0 |
| Idle/2500, biennial | 21.7 | 18.6 | 0.6 | 26.0 | 22.1 | 1.1 |
| Loaded idle, annual | 23.7 | 22.2 | 0.6 | 26.0 | 24.6 | 1.0 |
| Loaded idle, biennial | 20.2 | 18.5 | 0.6 | 23.3 | 21.9 | 1.1 |
| IM240 (1.2/20/3), biennial, without technician training | 32.8 | 31.0 | 13.1 | 36.8 | 32.4 | 16.8 |
| IM240 (1.2/20/3), biennial, with technician training | 39.6 | 36.3 | 19.5 | 45.4 | 39.2 | 24.8 |
| Acceleration simulation mode 2525/5015 (25,50,1), biennial | 33.6 | 30.7 | 19.6 | 41.9 | 39.4 | 24.4 |

[a]Fleet average grams-per-mile emission factors with I/M relative to non-I/M.
Note: All MOBILE5b runs used default fleet mix and registration distributions, 19.6 mph average speed, 75°F temperature, 8.7 pounds per square inch RVP, no RFG or oxygenate, and default operating fractions. All I/M programs were assumed to start in 1992, 20% stringency, 0% waiver rates, 100% compliance, test only, centralized.

Sierra Research 1994a). With these lower emissions rates for future years in MOBILE6, as shown in Figure 5-1, the I/M credits are likely to be lower in MOBILE6 than in MOBILE5. Early indications are that MOBILE6 will indeed reduce the emissions-reduction benefits from I/M compared with MOBILE5 (Clean Air Report 1999). There are serious policy implications if MOBILE6 SIP credits for I/M programs are significantly lower than MOBILE5.

One indication of I/M effectiveness in MOBILE6 compared with evaluation of benefits using program data can be gleaned from the most recent audit of the Colorado I/M program. In this audit, EPA's Serious Area CO Model was used to estimate the benefits of the state's I/M program. The Serious Area CO Model is a version of MOBILE5 that has some of the key features of MOBILE6 for CO emissions, including lower deterioration rates. The 1999

**TABLE 5-2** Estimated Emissions Reductions Attributable to I/M As a Percent of MOBILE5 Predictions[a]

|  | HC (%) | NO$_x$ (%) | CO (%) |
|---|---|---|---|
| **Phoenix, AZ: Centralized IM240** | | | |
| Random sample of 1995 program data (EPA 1997a) | 85 | 46 | 100 |
| All 1996-1997 program data with fast-pass/fast-fail converted to estimated full IM240 (Wenzel 1999b) | 83 | 43 | 90 |
| Random sample of 1996-1997 vehicles given full IM240 (Wenzel 1999b) | 89 | 46 | 83 |
| **Colorado: Centralized biennial IM240** | | | |
| All 1997 program data (ENVIRON 1998) | | | |
|     Idle | 86-103 | | 76-93 |
|     IM240 | 76-84 | 3-6 | 105-121 |
| Remote sensing in 1989 in I/M and non-I/M areas (Zhang et al. 1996b) | | | 21 |
| **Atlanta, GA: Decentralized idle (BAR97)** | | | |
| Comparison of remote-sensing measurements in I/M vs. non-I/M areas (Corley and Rodgers 2000) | | | Cars, 209 Trucks, 72 |
| **Minneapolis, MN: Centralized annual idle** | | | |
| Comparison of ambient CO concentrations (Scherrer and Kittelson 1994) with MOBILE5b fleet reductions (O'Connor et al. 1997) | | | 14 |

[a]Both program and MOBILE5 estimates are fleet average grams per mile emissions.

Colorado audit estimated an 8% reduction in CO emissions for the IM240 program, compared with 17% for the Serious Area CO Model (Air Improvement Resource 1999).

## MOBILE I/M INPUTS

To obtain emissions factors from MOBILE6, including credits for an I/M program, the user provides three types of input (1) program descriptive inputs,

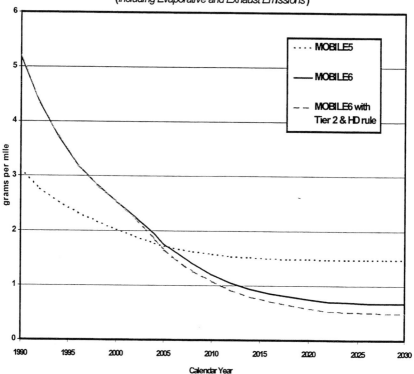

## All Highway Vehicles
### Volatile Organic Compounds (VOC) Emissions
#### (*Including Evaporative and Exhaust Emissions*)

**FIGURE 5-1** VOC and $NO_x$ emission factors in MOBILE5 and draft MOBILE6. The line rule-makings. Source: Beardsley 2001.

(2) program effectiveness input, and (3) fleet characterization inputs. The model estimates emissions credits for the effects of up to five I/M programs specified by the user. For example, if an area has two-speed idle testing for older vehicles and IM240 testing for newer vehicles, then the user provides program specifications for each of these two types of I/M programs.

The following I/M program descriptive inputs must be provided to MOBILE6:

- Program start year (calendar year when program begins).

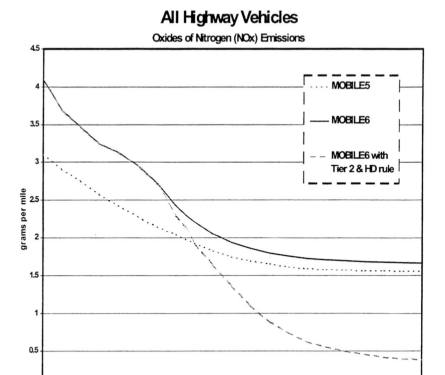

## All Highway Vehicles
### Oxides of Nitrogen (NOx) Emissions

marked "MOBILE6" is draft MOBILE6 without the effects of the Tier 2 and 2007 heavy-duty

- First (earliest) and last (latest) model years of vehicles subject to the requirements of the program.
- Model years exempted from the program.
- Test type (idle, 2500/idle, acceleration simulation mode (ASM), IM240, and on-board diagnostics (OBD)).
- Program type (inspection only, inspection and repair (computerized or manual)).
- Frequency of inspection (annual, biennial, change of ownership).
- Vehicle classes covered (LDGV, light-duty gasoline truck (LDGT) weight classes, heavy-duty gasoline vehicle (HDGV) weight classes).

- Cutpoints for HC, CO, and $NO_x$ for IM240 testing.
- Remote-sensing parameters.

The user is required to provide three MOBILE inputs related to program effectiveness: compliance rate, waiver rate, and stringency level. This section provides brief discussions of these parameters, including what they are and the common methods used by state agencies to determine their appropriate values.

## Compliance Rates

Compliance rate, typically the most important of these parameters in terms of emissions reductions, is defined as the level of compliance with the inspection program. However, compliance is a difficult concept, and it is not clear that EPA and the states have used a consistent definition or measurement of it in the past. Figure 5-2 shows a conceptual classification of vehicles in an area that has an I/M program. There are four types of noncompliant vehicles: (1) those that are not registered, (2) those that avoid the program by registering outside the area,[4] (3) those that are registered but never take the test, and (4) those that take the test and fail but never complete the test cycle with a passing test.[5] EPA guidance for MOBILE 5b (EPA 1997b) stated that the compliance rate specified should include all registered vehicles that successfully complete an I/M cycle, including both passing and waived vehicles. This definition includes only one of the four types of noncomplying vehicles shown in Figure 5-2, and in the past, states have tended to estimate the compliance rate as the proportion of registered vehicles that actually take an I/M test and thus underestimate the true noncompliance rate and overstate the I/M benefits. In MOBILE5, there is no default value for the compliance rate; it must be specified in the input file. However, EPA asks states to provide documentation if the compliance rate is over 96%. As a result, this 96% value has be-

---

[4]An analysis of Dayton, Ohio, area registration statistics showed that when the enhanced I/M program was implemented, registrations decreased by 10% in the counties in the I/M program and increased by a similar amount in the surrounding non-I/M counties (McClintock 1999b).

[5]Two other categories of vehicles could be considered in noncompliance: those that receive inadequate or ineffective repairs; and those that pass the inspection because of emissions variability, so they are never repaired. However, because both of these end up passing the test, they are not included in Figure 5-2.

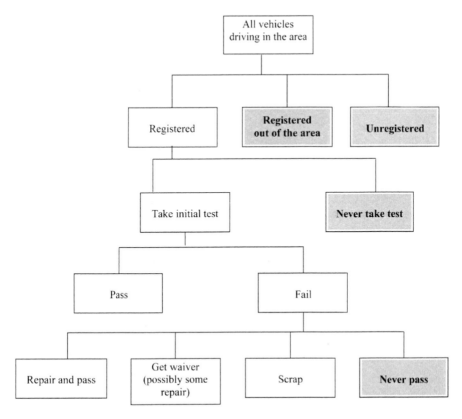

**FIGURE 5-2**  Classification of vehicles in an area subject to I/M. Shaded boxes indicate noncomplying vehicles. Source: Adapted from Harrington et al. 1998.

come a de facto default, because states could claim up to 96% compliance without any documentation.

Similarly, MOBILE6 defines noncomplying vehicles as "vehicles which show up for the initial test, but drop out of the process prior to a successful passing result or a waiver" (EPA 1999e). However, EPA now recognizes a second type of noncomplying vehicle—one that does not show up for its initial test—and says that the input compliance rate should take these vehicles into account (EPA 1999e). For MOBILE6, there is no default noncompliance rate; the rate must be specified in the input file. However, it is unclear what sort of documentation will be required by states in their SIPs to justify the rate that is used.

Although improved over MOBILE5, the MOBILE6 definition of compliance rate remains an underestimate of the true noncompliance rate, as it does not include unregistered vehicles and vehicles that avoid the program by registering out of the area. States will likely continue to estimate the compliance rate based on the number of registered vehicles, as there is no incentive to measure the proportion of vehicles that are unregistered or that are registered outside the region. Additionally, the registered fleet might not always accurately account for scrapped, moved, or change of ownership vehicles that are no longer in operation in the region. License-plate reading as part of remote-sensing measurement programs will help allow estimates of both of these components of the fleet being driven in the region. Once the total vehicle fleet is known, it is relatively easy to determine the complying vehicles from program data—the number of vehicles that get tested and are either repaired or waived are complying. Some of these might have been incorrectly or fraudulently passed, and remote sensing could also help identify them.

## Waiver Rate

Waiver rate refers to the fraction of vehicles that fail their initial tests but were never fully repaired because the repair cost limit (or some other criterion) has been met; these vehicles have complied with the program requirements but are still failing vehicles. This parameter is discussed in Chapter 3. In the model, separate waiver rates are used for pre-1981 and post-1980 LDVs. These rates must necessarily come from I/M program records. EPA recommends that, for historical inventory development, program-specific data be used to derive the waiver rates. For future inventories, the historical rates may be used.

## Stringency Rate

Stringency rate (or failure rate) is the expected failure rate for pre-1981 model-year vehicles.[6] Stringency rate is defined as the test failure rate ex-

---

[6]Stringency rate is input only because the older model years use a methodology (from the late 1970s) that calculates benefits based on failure rates rather than test procedures and cutpoints. For newer vehicles, MOBILE6 uses identification rates based on the proportion of total emissions from failing vehicles (not number of failing vehicles) identified.

pected in pre-1981 LDVs expressed as a percentage of tests administered (EPA 2000d). MOBILE6 restricts this percentage to between 10% and 50%. According to current EPA MOBILE5b guidance (EPA 1997b), this value can be estimated by one of two methods—testing a representative sampling of vehicles or determining actual program failure rates. Testing a representative sample is a relatively low-cost and quick way to obtain in-use failure rates. However, the major disadvantage of these sampling programs is the representation of the captured vehicles; typically, when volunteer vehicles are recruited for testing, high emitters are likely to be underrepresented. Actual program failure rates can be used "but only when there is no possibility of significant testing or data reporting errors and a determination can be made as to which tests were initial (first time) tests." The primary benefit of this approach is that the database is large, and because of their mandatory nature, I/M programs tend to capture a more complete fleet. However, because of the large number of reporting testing facilities involved and the possibilities for fraud, the quality of the data must be carefully checked.

For future-year inventories, compliance, waiver, and stringency rates used to determine the types and level of future-year control programs are commonly the values determined from the existing I/M program. For example, failure rates measured today are used to forecast emissions reductions in the future. This approach might not be reasonable. For example, MOBILE has emissions rates rising over time as vehicles age and the emissions-control system deteriorates, but some of the fixed parameters (e.g., failure rates on these older vehicles and age distribution of the fleet) stay constant. However, there is no obvious alternative to using the current-year failure rates for future-year inventories.

Fleet characterization inputs to MOBILE, although not directly descriptive of the I/M program, do affect calculated emissions reductions. The fleet characterization inputs are vehicle registration distributions and VMT mix. The vehicle registration distributions specify, by vehicle class, the percentage of vehicles by age (in years). Although there are default values in MOBILE5 (determined from national vehicle registration databases), it is common for states to input their own registration distributions obtained from state vehicle registration databases. However, as is the case for I/M program failure rates, the registration distributions from current data files are typically used for future-year emissions modeling. VMT mix specifies the proportion of total area VMT allocated to each vehicle class. The VMT mix is used to estimate average fleet emissions factors (grams per mile) as a weighted average of the vehicle class emissions factors. For SIPs in nonattainment areas, a standard VMT mix typically is not used because there are separate estimates of VMT by vehicle class from transportation models or other studies that can be used.

## REVIEW OF MOBILE6 I/M MODELING APPROACH

The MOBILE6 modeling approach and assessment of I/M credits were available to the committee from EPA only in draft form (EPA 1999e,f,g,h). In this section, we provide an overview of the draft MOBILE6 modeling approach for LDVs for estimating emissions reductions associated with identification and repair of malfunctioning vehicles. The I/M credit in MOBILE6 is estimated as the difference between emissions estimates with and without an I/M program. Below we provide a description of draft MOBILE6 emissions estimates without an I/M program and then a description of how the draft version of MOBILE6 estimates emissions with an I/M program.

### Non-I/M Basic Emissions Rate

The estimation of I/M effects begins with the basic emissions rates (BER) for each pollutant under a non-I/M scenario. These BERs are determined by vehicle type, model-year group, and technology type. The emissions factors were initially estimated from EPA and manufacturer test programs using the Federal Test Procedure (FTP). These were then adjusted by using high-emitter correction factors (additive adjustments) derived from first-year IM240 data from the Dayton, Ohio, I/M program. Full details of the source databases, the EPA analysis procedures, and the results are in EPA MOBILE6 draft documents (EPA 1999f,h,i,j,k,l).

The same FTP databases that were used to determine fleet average emissions were also used to determine emissions rates for normal and high emitters (by vehicle class, model-year group, and technology type). The vehicles were first classified as normal or high emitters. High emitters are defined as those vehicles that emit HC or $NO_x$ at levels more than two times their 50,000-mile certification level or CO at more than three times the certification standard. The current MOBILE5 model defines three classes of high emitters—high, very high, and super emitters. The draft MOBILE6 proposal is therefore a simplification of the modeling approach by combining all high emitters into one category. Depending on the I/M program and its cutpoints, a more discrete definition of high emitters would have allowed for various identification rates among different types of high emitters. However, the data on which EPA based its estimates did not argue for further delineation.

Emissions rates for normal emitters (by vehicle class, model-year group, and technology) were determined by simple linear regression. The emissions for normal-emitting 1988-1993 port fuel-injected (PFI) LDGVs as a function of mileage are shown in Figure 5-3 for all three regulated pollutants. For HC, the regression $r^2$ value for the data shown in the first plot in Figure 5-3 is only 0.20. The $r^2$ values for HC for the six technology groups for passenger cars range from only 0.04 to 0.30 at best (Appendix G in EPA 1999e). It is important to note the large amount of variability in the vehicle emissions data as a function of mileage; this factor is one of many contributing to uncertainty in the estimated I/M effects.

Average emissions rates for high emitters, however, were estimated from the FTP data as a simple average (by vehicle class, model-year group, and technology type) because the emissions were not seen to be strongly related to mileage. That could be either because the number of normal emitters was too small or because there is in fact no relationship between emissions and mileage for higher emitters. There is also very large variability in these high-emitter averages. For example, for 1988-1993 fuel-injected cars, the mean hot-running LDGV HC emissions for high emitters are 1.74 g/mi, but the emissions rates for the 58 cars in this group range from 0.14 to 31.18 g/mi.

Using the fleet average emissions rates and the emissions rates for normal and high emitters, the fraction of high emitters was simply calculated as

$$\text{Fraction of high emitters} = \frac{\text{Average emissions rate - Normal - emitter rate}}{\text{High - emitter rate - Normal - emitter rate}}.$$

$$(5\text{-}1)$$

It is important to note that the estimated emissions rates for normal and high emitters were not adjusted the same way the fleet average exhaust emissions rates were adjusted (using the Dayton IM240 data), although the same additive effects could be applied. However, because the fleet average emissions rates are adjusted using the Dayton IM240 data, the Dayton data are thus used to determine the fraction (but not the absolute levels) of high and normal emitters. Not adjusting the normal and high emissions rates introduces potentially serious underestimation of the high-emitter rates and the normal-

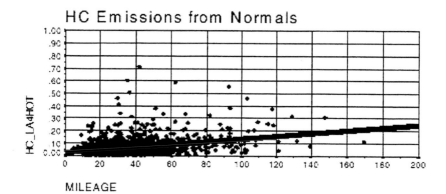

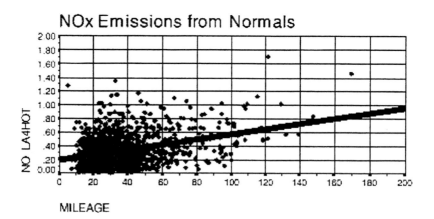

**FIGURE 5-3** Hot-running emissions (grams per mile) versus mileage (000 miles) for normal-emitting 1988-1993 model-year passenger cars with PFI. LA4 denotes the driving cycle. Source: EPA 1999e.

emitter rates and consequent bias in the estimated fraction of high emitters and the I/M credits calculated from these quantities (described below). In the draft MOBILE6 I/M documentation, EPA states that "additional fully preconditioned IM240 data (back to back IM240 tests) from Wisconsin and Colorado will soon be available in which to compare these results and modeling. These data may cause EPA to substantially revise the basic emission rates and I/M effects for MOBILE6" (EPA 1999e).

Figure 5-4 shows an example of the basic emissions rates of HC that have not been adjusted for I/M in 1990-1993 model-year cars (LDGVs) with PFI. The figure shows the average emissions rate calculated from the FTP data and adjusted using the Dayton IM240 data (EPA 1999k), the estimated normal- and high-emitter rates calculated from the FTP data alone, and the estimated high-emitter fraction of the fleet (EPA 1999e). For this example, the high-emitter fraction ranges from 2% for new vehicles to 30% for vehicles with about 200,000 miles. At zero miles, there is a small fraction of high emitters in the EPA calculation because the average emissions rate from the FTP and Dayton data is higher than the normal-emitter rate. If the normal emitters had been adjusted in the same manner as the average emissions, this would not have occurred.

## I/M Credits

The I/M credits are applied to the fraction of the fleet that is identified and repaired from emissions levels considered to be of high-emitter status due to either malfunctioning of, or tampering with, the emissions-control systems. The credit for I/M programs depends on several factors, including the identification rate, waiver rate, and after-repair emissions rates. The user inputs the waiver rate; identification rates and after-repair emissions are estimated by equations built into the model. The model is set so that the emissions rate for repaired vehicles is no lower than that for normal-emitting vehicles for the same vehicle class, model-year group, and technology type.

### Repair Emissions Rate

Under MOBILE5b, it is assumed that all repaired vehicles were repaired to emissions levels below the test cutpoints. In MOBILE6, this assumption is

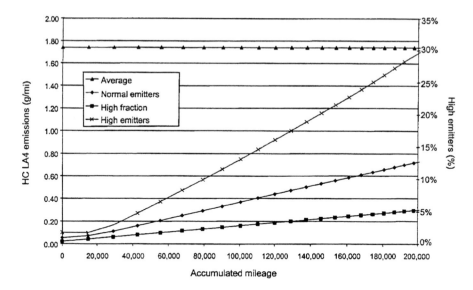

**FIGURE 5-4** Basic emissions rates of HC that have not been adjusted for I/M. Average emissions rates, normal- and high-emitter emissions rates, and the estimated fraction of high emitters in the fleet are shown. LA4 denotes the driving cycle.

modified. The after-repair emissions rates are a multiple of the normal emissions rates and are constrained to never fall beneath the normal emissions rates. They are a function of the test cutpoints and are calculated from several thousand before-and-after IM240 tests from the Arizona IM240 program (EPA 1999e).

The proposed after-repair emissions rates for MOBILE6 include the effects of technician training, because the technicians were trained in the Arizona IM240 program from which the rates are determined. The after-repair emissions rates are increased if there is no technician training. The amount of the increase was estimated from a small EPA study of 11 technicians who repaired three vehicles each; the emissions rates for the repaired vehicles were compared with emissions rates after the vehicles received any additional needed repairs by an expert technician (Glover et al. 1996).

A recent analysis of on-road emissions using remote sensing in the Denver area showed that on-road emissions reductions of "repaired" vehicles (i.e., those that failed, then returned and passed) in Denver's centralized IM240 program were only half as large as measured in the IM240 lanes (McClintock

1999a). Although only a small number of vehicles (22)[7] in the remote-sensing data set were matched to the IM240 program records—and there are issues that complicate the analysis (e.g., comparing emissions reductions from IM240 tests with remote-sensing measurements)—these results indicate that the MOBILE6 repair-effectiveness rates might be overstated. Chapter 7 contains a discussion of emissions-repair studies.

The waiver vehicles are those that still fail the emissions test after a set minimum amount was spent on only partially successful repairs. Although not fully repaired, they are assumed on average to have some repairs. The proposed default for MOBILE6 is that the waived vehicle emissions rate is 20% less than the failed vehicle emissions rate. This default is an assumption, as there was no available analysis of emissions from waived vehicles from operating IM240 programs at the time EPA prepared the draft MOBILE6 I/M credits (EPA 1999e). Figure 5-5 shows an example of the rates estimated for repaired and waived vehicles, for the same 1990-1993 PFI LDGV example as in Figure 5-4. Note that the change in emissions as a function of mileage for the repaired vehicles is not the deterioration rate for the repaired vehicles; rather, these emissions rates are used to determine the I/M credit at a given age. Note also for this example that the EPA methodology results in the repaired vehicle emissions multiple of the normal emissions rate increasing from 0 to about 100,000 miles and then decreasing until the repaired and normal-emitter rates are the same at about 170,000 miles. After 170,000 miles, the calculation actually results in repaired vehicle rates being less than normal-emitter rates, but they are set to the normal-emitter rates.

**Identification Rate**

The high-emitter identification rate (IDR) is the proportion of emissions from high emitters in the fleet that are correctly identified. If the cutpoints are set so that all high emitters are properly identified (i.e., fail the test), then the IDR is 100%. The IDR depends on the test method used (IM240, ASM, idle testing) and the test cutpoints (but not model-year group or vehicle technology). The lower the cutpoints, the higher the IDR; however, lower cutpoints also increase the chances that normal emitters will fail the test. To estimate

---

[7]In general, a large sample of vehicles should be measured repeatably using remote sensing to help establish emissions trends and repair effectiveness.

IDRs for MOBILE6, EPA used a database of 910 model-year 1981 and later cars and trucks that had both an IM240 test and an FTP test from EPA emissions factor testing in Ann Arbor, Michigan, and Hammond, Indiana, and also Arizona data on randomly recruited vehicles. These identification rates, used to calculate the average emissions of the fleet after a cycle of I/M testing and repair (described below), are estimated from a regression analysis of the logarithms of the test cutpoints (cut) as follows (EPA 1999e):

$$HC\ IDR = 1.1451 - 0.1365 \times \ln(HCcut) - 0.1069 \times \ln(COcut)$$

$$CO\ IDR = 1.1880 - 0.1073 \times \ln(HCcut) - 0.1298 \times \ln(COcut) \qquad (5\text{-}2)$$

$$NO_x\ IDR = 0.5453 + 0.7568 \times NOcut - 0.3687 \times NOcut^2 + 0.0406 \times NOcut^3$$

Another method that states commonly use to increase identification of failing vehicles is to require a passing inspection for change of vehicle ownership. This method can increase the fraction of the fleet that is inspected and increases the likelihood of failure identification and repair. In the draft MOBILE6 documentation, change of ownership is assumed to be a fixed fraction of the fleet based on an analysis of Wisconsin data, but there have been comments suggesting that this be a user input to reflect the actual change of ownership rates in an individual area.

**Noncomplying Vehicles**

As described above, the compliance rate input to MOBILE6 is assumed to represent vehicles that fail the initial test and do not complete the testing process, obtaining either a passing test or a waiver, and also those vehicles that do not show up for the required I/M testing. Although some of the no-show vehicles could be normal emitters, the draft MOBILE6 documentation indicates that EPA considers all noncomplying vehicles as high-emitting vehicles that are unaffected by the I/M program, and the input compliance rate should be set with this understanding. The high emitters, therefore, consist of three types of vehicles: (1) the identified high emitters that are repaired (but with emissions rates higher than normal emitters), (2) the identified high emitters that are partially repaired and receive waivers, and (3) noncomplying high emitters.

This treatment of noncomplying vehicles is different from the MOBILE5 assumptions in several ways. In MOBILE5, the noncompliance rate is defined as a share of the fleet as a whole; noncomplying vehicles are assumed to have higher emissions than normal vehicles. In MOBILE6, noncompliance is part of the high-emitter fraction only, and although MOBILE5 assumes that the failure rate of the noncomplying vehicles is higher than that of the complying vehicles, it did not assume that all of them are high emitters as is the case for MOBILE6.

**Average Emissions after I/M**

Average emissions after I/M are defined for each vehicle class, model-year group, and technology type from a combination of normal emitters, repaired vehicles, waived vehicles, and high emitters not repaired (either because I/M failed to identify them or because they are noncomplying). Table 5-3 shows the five subsets of vehicles that contribute to the average and the weighting factor for each subset. Once the average emissions rate after I/M has been calculated for each vehicle class/model-year group/technology-type combination, then sales weights are used to calculate the fleet average emissions after I/M across all LDVs in the fleet.

A significant problem with the draft EPA methodology is that the IDR has been defined as the fraction of *emissions* from the identified high emitters, yet this same IDR is used as $F_{ID}$ in Table 5-3, which is supposed to represent the fraction of high-emitting *vehicles* identified. Because the distribution of emissions from high-emitting vehicles is so skewed, the fraction of emissions from high emitters identified is substantially greater than the fraction of high-emitting vehicles identified. Using the estimated IDR for $F_{ID}$ in the estimation of average emissions after I/M results in an overestimate for the I/M credit (i.e., estimated average emissions after I/M are too low).

**Application of the I/M Credit**

The I/M credit in MOBILE6 is the difference in estimated emissions before and after I/M. Emissions before I/M are the basic emissions rates described previously, and average emissions after I/M are calculated as the weighted average across subsets of vehicles as shown in Table 5-3.

**TABLE 5-3** Calculation of Average Emissions after I/M

| Vehicle Subset | Weighting Factor | Emissions Rate |
|---|---|---|
| Normal emitters, no change in emissions after I/M | $1 - \underline{F}_H$ | $\underline{E}_N$ |
| High emitters not identified by I/M, no change in emissions | $\underline{F}_H * (1 - \underline{F}_{ID})$ | $\underline{E}_H$ |
| Noncomplying high emitters, no change in emissions | $\underline{F}_H \times \underline{F}_{ID} \times \underline{F}_{NC}$ | $\underline{E}_H$ |
| High emitters identified and given cost waivers, some repair below high-emitter level | $\underline{F}_H \times \underline{F}_{ID} \times \underline{F}_W$ | $\underline{E}_H * 0.80$ |
| High emitters identified and successfully repaired | $\underline{F}_H \times \underline{F}_{ID} \times \underline{F}_R$ | $\underline{E}_R$ |

Note:  The average for each vehicle-class, model-year, technology group is the weighted average emissions rate across five subsets of vehicles.

$\underline{F}_H$ = fraction of high emitters before I/M
$\underline{F}_{ID}$ = fraction of high emitters identified by I/M
$\underline{F}_{NC}$ = fraction of identified high emitters in noncompliance
$\underline{F}_W$ = fraction of identified high emitters given a waiver
$\underline{F}_R$ = fraction of identified high emitters fixed
$\underline{F}_{NC} + \underline{F}_W + \underline{F}_R = 1$

$\underline{E}_N$ = emissions rate for normal emitters
$\underline{E}_H$ = emissions rate for high emitters
$E_W$ = emissions rate for waiver vehicles
$\underline{E}_R$ = emissions rate for repaired vehicles
$\underline{E}_R \geq \underline{E}_N$ by constraint

MOBILE6 models the effect of I/M as a reduction in emissions at the time of inspection; this is referred to as the I/M credit. Emissions are modeled to increase between inspections at the same deterioration rate as vehicles not subject to an I/M program. This results in the so-called "sawtooth" pattern (also the basis for I/M credits in MOBILE5) shown schematically for a biennial program in Figure 5-6.

For an annual program, the I/M credit is calculated and applied once per year, and there is half the time for vehicle deterioration before the next test cycle. MOBILE5, the current regulatory model, has a very small increase in the emissions reduction in I/M benefits for an annual enhanced I/M program instead of a biennial program—only a 2-6% increase in emissions reductions,

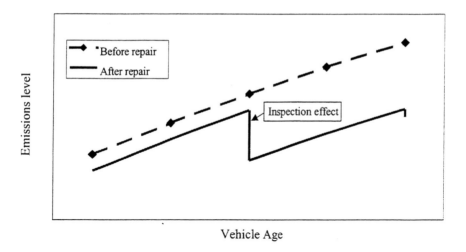

**FIGURE 5-6** Schematic of I/M credit algorithm (sawtooth) for a cohort of vehicles in a biennial program.

depending on the pollutant. If the I/M credit for an annual instead of biennial program in MOBILE6 is equally small, then states have no incentive to test vehicles more frequently and repair high emitters quickly. Although no analyses have been published that indicate significantly greater emissions reductions for annual programs, if repair durability is less than 2 years, annual programs are likely to reduce emissions more than only a few percent from biennial programs. When MOBILE6 is released, the additional credit modeled for annual programs should be compared with real-world data.

This sawtooth pattern for modeling I/M (the same approach used in MOBILE5) suffers from a number of problems and is inappropriate for a number of reasons, including the following:

- Vehicles with and without I/M are assumed to deteriorate at the same rate, but it is very likely that the repaired fleet will deteriorate at a rate different from that of the fleet that has not been repaired. Some repairs will be effective and lasting and others will be ineffective and cause emissions to increase back to the unrepaired level. A comparison of Arizona IM240 data with remote-sensing data shows that repair effectiveness diminishes over time (Wenzel 1999b).

- There is no explicit allowance in the model for repaired vehicles to revert back to high-emitter status. Analysis of Arizona IM240 data shows that 42% of cars that initially failed their IM240 and then returned and passed, failed again in their initial test in the next cycle 2 years later (Wenzel 1999b).
- The I/M credit algorithm does not allow for vehicles being scrapped or sold outside the area (and still used in the I/M area) rather than repaired. MOBILE6 includes vehicle scrappage, but it is not modeled as a function of high-emitter status.[8]
- There is no estimate of the effect of vehicles being repaired just before I/M testing so that they will pass the test the first time. Some of these repairs will not be done or not be long-lasting, and the vehicle will revert back to high-emitter status just after the test.

## OBD Effects

MOBILE6 includes emissions reductions for vehicles equipped with OBDII systems (1996 model years and later). OBDII is discussed further in Chapters 2 and 4. Estimates for these emissions reductions depend on three parameters, which have assumed levels because in-use data are not yet available (EPA 1999f):

- The ability of the OBD system to identify high emitters is assumed to be a fixed fraction of high emitters at 85%. The remaining 15% of vehicles that are high emitters but are not detected by the OBD system are assumed to remain as high emitters.
- The response rate is the fraction of owners who will respond to a malfunction indicator light (MIL) and have the vehicle repaired. MOBILE6 assumes that owners are much more likely to respond to a MIL in an OBD-based I/M area, where repairs are required. In OBD-based I/M areas, MOBILE6 assumes that the response rate is 90% over the lifetime of the vehicle. Without such an I/M program encouraging repair, the response rate is assumed to be 90% up to 36,000 miles (the standard full vehicle warranty period), 10% from 36,000 to 80,000 miles (the age limit for federally mandated emissions-control system warranty), and zero after 80,000 miles.

---

[8]MOBILE6 includes vehicle scrappage for vehicles destroyed in an accident or retired from the fleet. Emissions credits for scrappage programs are estimated outside the model.

- The emissions level after a repair in response to a MIL is assumed to be 1.5 times the appropriate 50,000-mile emissions standard; this is the threshold level for illuminating the MIL. Because of the low emissions for new vehicles and the low response rate at higher mileage, as currently modeled, the emissions reduction associated with OBD is low in the absence of an I/M program.

The MOBILE6 approach does not take into account the ability of the system to identify a failed component and take corrective action to minimize the effect of the emissions. For example, when an oxygen sensor fails, some OBD systems can revert to a known open-loop calibration that has good, but not optimal, emissions. Thus, some OBD identified failures might have little emissions increase, even if the owner ignores the MIL.

Figure 5-7 (EPA 1999f) shows MOBILE6 projected nonmethane HC basic emissions rates for light-duty Tier 1 vehicles with OBD systems from EPA's draft MOBILE6 documentation (EPA 1999f). The figure shows that MOBILE6 will generate a small emissions reduction for OBD systems in areas without OBD-based I/M and much larger emissions reductions in areas with OBD-based I/M. Such emissions reductions might be overly optimistic because they might be based on optimistic assumptions about owner response to the MIL in the I/M areas and pessimistic assumptions about response in non-I/M areas.

## Antitampering Programs

Antitampering benefits in MOBILE6 are intended to be as similar to MOBILE5 as possible with the same fractional reduction in high emitters associated with antitampering programs for vehicles before the 1996 model year. After 1996, OBD is assumed to catch all tampered vehicles. This description of the approach, obtained from conversations with EPA staff, was not available to the committee in written form.

## Evaporative Emissions and I/M

Evaporative emissions are modeled with three distinct groupings: normal (functioning), purge-failure, and pressure-failure vehicles. Purge failure refers to failure of the system that allows regeneration of the carbon canisters used

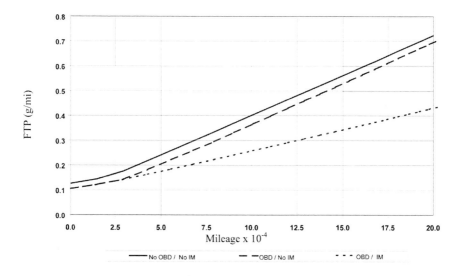

**FIGURE 5-7** MOBILE6 non-methane HC basic emissions rates for light-duty Tier 1 vehicles with OBD systems. Source: EPA 1999f.

to capture evaporative emissions through vapor purge into the combustion system. A purge failure can be a result of a failed valve or disconnected hose that leads to the intake manifold on the engine. A pressure failure refers to the loss of integrity of the system and can include a missing, split, or disconnected hose; a missing or failed gas cap; or a leak in the tank.

Purge and pressure failures have been measured in I/M programs through the use of flow rate and pressure tests on the vehicle during the exhaust emissions test. The test procedures can introduce their own problems, as not all vehicles have accessible components. Perhaps the greatest problem, however, is that the purge test is very invasive, with many hoses and components actually being damaged when these tests were first tried. Although MOBILE6 will model emissions reductions associated with pressure and purge tests, few areas are actually performing these tests. The future use of purge and pressure checks appears doubtful. A gas-cap check and a targeted physical inspection offer the most likely benefit of I/M programs on evaporative emissions.

## CALIFORNIA'S EMFAC MODEL FOR ESTIMATING I/M EMISSIONS REDUCTIONS

Historically, California has had more restrictive air-quality and automobile emissions standards than the rest of the United States. The Clean Air Act allows California to regulate automobiles in the state and use its own computer models to predict emissions inventories. The California Air Resources Board (CARB) has developed its own emissions inventory model, called EMFAC. Similar to MOBILE, EMFAC was developed well over a decade ago and has continually been improved over the years. The current version of EMFAC is EMFAC2000 (available at http://arbis.arb.ca.gov/msei/msei.htm).

EMFAC has a number of differences with MOBILE, as outlined in NRC (2000). For estimating emissions reductions from California's Smog Check I/M program, EMFAC uses a similar modeling methodology as MOBILE, with a sawtooth representation of inspection and repair over the life of a vehicle (section 4 in the online EMFAC2000 documentation at http://arbis.arb.ca.gov/msei/doctabletest/doctable_test.html). EMFAC has four categories for high emitters, compared with three in MOBILE5 and one in MOBILE6. The percentage of each technology group in these high-emitter groups (or regimes, in EMFAC terminology) is determined from vehicle surveillance program data and I/M recapture fleet data. These percentages are then multiplied by regime-specific identification rates (i.e., the percentage of vehicles that will fail a given I/M program), as described in section 8 in the online documentation (http://arbis.arb.ca.gov/msei/doctabletest/doctable_test.html). The identification rates in EMFAC2000 are based on failing fractions of vehicles in the various Smog Check programs.

For estimating the repair effectiveness, EMFAC uses a two-step process. During CARB's surveillance programs, high-emitting vehicles were extensively repaired to determine the maximum gain achievable through a "perfect" repair. These perfect repair values are then modified by "correction efficiencies," which are a function of the I/M program being simulated.[9] These efficiencies vary on the basis of such factors as I/M repair cost limits and estimates of technician training. After the identification and repair percentages have been determined, the percentages of vehicles in the different high-emitter

---

[9]Although it is questionable whether these "correction efficiencies" have been measured in a realistic repair setting.

regimes are modified. Last, the same standard deterioration rate is applied across all emissions regimes. Total reductions across entire fleets are then calculated by appropriately weighting the vehicle technology groups by VMT for a specific model year.

Like MOBILE, EMFAC has overpredicted emissions reductions from the state's I/M programs, thus generating SIP credits that were too large and contributing to problems in meeting air-quality standards. With EMFAC7G (the version prior to EMFAC2000), substantial emissions reductions were modeled for California's 1984 biennial two-speed idle I/M program—12% reduction in HC, 11% reduction in CO, and 5% reduction in $NO_x$. With a draft version of EMFAC2000 and additional analyses of I/M evaluation program data from tests of over 1,000 vehicles, CARB now suggests a 15% reduction for HC exhaust, 9% for CO, and 7% for $NO_x$ attributed to the 1984 program (CARB 2000b). Early independent evaluations of this program showed no emissions benefit (Lawson 1993; Lawson et al. 1995, 1996a).

As discussed in Chapter 3, CARB (2000c) recently evaluated the California enhanced I/M program. A draft version of EMFAC2000 predicts emissions reductions in 1999 from the program at 19% for HC, 6% for $NO_x$, and 18% for CO, but CARB's analyses of roadside tests showed emissions reductions of only 14% for HC, 6% for $NO_x$, and 13% for CO. However, these percentage reductions should be treated with caution due to a potential location bias in the roadside sampling that took place.

## SUMMARY

The MOBILE model will continue to be used to determine future emissions-reduction credits that states will receive from implementing I/M or from modifying their current I/M programs. MOBILE is a static, not a dynamic, model and is therefore a simplified representation of emissions changes from I/M. Historically, MOBILE has overestimated emissions reductions from I/M programs. It remains to be seen whether MOBILE6, which is a major revision from MOBILE5, will also overestimate I/M benefits or whether it will be a more accurate representation of I/M benefits. Indications are that MOBILE6 will estimate lower emissions reductions from I/M programs than are estimated by MOBILE5.

Estimates of model inputs, such as compliance rates, have a large effect on the I/M credits estimated by MOBILE. To date, states have been allowed to use optimistic estimates of these inputs, instead of justifying them with analysis of program data or other assessments. The model inputs should be set by default to pessimistic values, thus providing an incentive to states to document evidence for inputting more optimistic values. Such evidence should include program evaluations in the state or reliance on program evaluations from other states with similar I/M programs. Model-based forecasts should be closely linked to I/M program performance measurements.

There are also a large number of assumptions internal to the model that significantly affect MOBILE's emissions projections and I/M credits. These include the absolute number and average emissions of high emitters, average emissions of initially failing and passing vehicles, average repair effects, identification rates under different cutpoints, and OBD effects. Actual data from state programs and special studies could be used to improve model parameters and assumptions. In the long term, the overall I/M estimation methodology in MOBILE should be improved based on I/M evaluation data. For example, empirical data already show that the sawtooth modeling approach is not realistic. Human behavior, an important factor missing in the model, should be incorporated into future models. Further, embedded assumptions in the model should be given parameters as much as possible so that users can improve their I/M benefit forecasts with the latest available data.

In the short term, sensitivity analyses should be done to demonstrate the effects of changes in model inputs and in assumptions built into the model. The results should be incorporated into the MOBILE6 guidance documentation and related documents.

A model such as MOBILE will continue to be needed for forecasting future-year emissions and the effects of mobile-source control programs such as I/M. The model should not, however, be used to evaluate actual performance. Instead, program evaluation studies should be done to estimate current program effects, and results from actual I/M performance should be used to calibrate the MOBILE estimates. As stated elsewhere in this report, guidance from EPA is needed to accomplish these goals.

# 6

# Evaluating Inspection and Maintenance Programs: Methods for Estimating Emissions Reductions

Inspection and maintenance (I/M) program evaluation helps address whether the investment of human and capital resources required for I/M programs is beneficial. Although a judgment about whether I/M is beneficial is beyond the scope of this report, the committee charge does include a call for identifying evaluation criteria and methods. We will describe a set of criteria and discuss methods of evaluation using these criteria in this chapter and the next.

Ideally, the primary criterion should be the effect of an I/M program on air quality and the associated effects on human health and welfare. However, it is very difficult to separate the relatively modest emissions impacts of I/M programs from other policies designed to reduce emissions and from other anthropogenic and natural changes that influence air quality. Because of this difficulty, attempts to assess the impacts of I/M programs on ambient air emissions have been difficult—even for carbon monoxide (CO), a pollutant that is generated almost solely by light-duty vehicles (LDVs) (Scherrer and Kittelson 1994; ENVIRON 1998).

Thus, the criteria and methods of evaluation discussed in this chapter focus on the reduction in emissions brought about by I/M programs. Difficulties in estimating emissions reductions arise because vehicle emissions are variable over time and with driving method, emission tests themselves are variable and imperfect, and perhaps most important, the behavior of motorists, technicians, and even state enforcement authorities play a key role in the emissions reductions achieved. This chapter focuses on defining the emissions reductions to be measured, describes some of the obstacles to measuring them, and outlines possible methods for measuring them. Other discussions on emissions reductions are found in Chapter 3, which describes prior studies that have estimated emissions-reduction benefits from I/M programs, and in Chapter 5, which describes how emissions reductions are estimated in MOBILE.

A full evaluation of I/M requires that the criteria be defined more broadly than just the reduction in emissions. At a minimum, additional criteria include cost and cost-effectiveness of program designs, enforcement requirements, and such factors as public acceptance and political feasibility. These additional criteria are discussed in Chapter 7.


## METHODS FOR MEASURING EMISSIONS REDUCTIONS

There are several inherent difficulties in evaluating the emissions reductions from an I/M program. One is defining the baseline, the condition against which the I/M program is compared. Attempting to discern the benefits by comparing an area with an I/M program with a reference area (either an area with a reference I/M program or a non-I/M fleet) is confounded by differences between the area and its reference in climate, socioeconomic conditions, and other characteristics. Additionally, vehicle technologies are also continuing to improve, so the emissions benefits of a program depend on when they are being measured. Sorting out vehicle repairs or scrappage that occurs because of an I/M program versus what would occur even in its absence is also difficult. Finally, there are numerous statistical issues associated with evaluating I/M, some of which are summarized in Appendix C.

An I/M program has the potential to reduce emissions in a number of ways. Motorists might be persuaded to better maintain their vehicles as a result of the program. Emissions might be reduced as a result of repairs made in anticipation of an I/M inspection (referred to as pre-inspection repairs) or as a result of failing the inspection test. Finally, some vehicles may be scrapped or sold outside the I/M area because, given the age or condition of the vehicle, the owner did not think the repair was worth the cost. We summarize these sources of emissions reduction resulting from an I/M program in Table 6-1. It is important to contrast these sources of emissions reductions with the

**TABLE 6-1** Sources of Emissions Reduction from I/M

| Type of Emissions Reduction | Data Requirements |
| --- | --- |
| 1. Improved maintenance, which leads to lower emissions | |
| 2. Repairs to emissions equipment made before an emissions test in anticipation of the test | Roadside tests or remote sensing |
| 3. (a) Repair of a vehicle's emissions systems as a result of failing a test | In-program test data, comprehensive remote-sensing data, or roadside-pullover data |
| (b) Length of time repairs last for a vehicle repaired as a result of failing an I/M test | In-program test data, change-of-ownership test data, comprehensive remote-sensing data, or roadside-pullover data |
| 4. Early scrapping or transfer of high-emitting vehicles outside the I/M region (fleet effects) | In-program test data together with remote-sensing data or vehicle-registration data |

MOBILE modeling approach to I/M described in Chapter 5, which attributes most emissions benefits to the instantaneous repair of failed vehicles.

We emphasize at the outset that the components of emissions reductions arising from an I/M program, as described in Table 6-1, are very difficult to estimate. Human behavior and lack of complete evidence confound the estimation of emissions reductions at every turn. For example, emissions reductions as measured by in-program data on individual vehicles might not represent real emissions reductions on some vehicles but might result from partial repair or even retesting with no repair. Repair in anticipation of the I/M program might represent real and long-lasting emissions reduction from some vehicles but would not be accounted for if only I/M test observations were used for evaluation. Also important is the amount of emissions-reduction-related repairs that would be done without any I/M program.

Because of these issues, the approaches for evaluation described in this chapter include data needs and methods that attempt to account for all the factors that influence emissions reductions—technical, behavioral, and others. All the categories of emissions reductions listed in Table 6-1 must be evaluated to determine the effectiveness of a program. We first discuss sources of data for measuring emissions changes from I/M.

## Data to Estimate I/M Emissions Reductions

I/M programs have the potential to reduce tailpipe emissions of nitrogen oxides ($NO_x$) and CO and both tailpipe and evaporative (including liquid leaks) emissions of hydrocarbons (HC). Tailpipe emissions are easier to measure but depend on many factors related to the condition and operation of the vehicle; measurements can come from in-program (test results from centralized or decentralized I/M programs) or on-road (remote sensing, roadside pullovers) sources. Attributes of each are discussed below. Non-tailpipe HC emissions are very difficult and expensive to measure; they require special equipment, invasive test methods, and long test times. As a result, although many tailpipe emissions data are available, there are no evaporative emissions measurements that directly measure I/M effectiveness to reduce all sources of non-tailpipe emissions. As discussed in Chapter 1, evaporative emissions represent a significant but unquantified source of overall vehicle HC emissions.

## Data from I/M Programs

Tailpipe data from I/M programs (in-program data) can come from the program itself or from separate tests[1] run for the purpose of evaluating the program. Inspection lane data cover tailpipe, visual, and some functional tests, such as a test of the gas cap. Data can be from idle tests, steady-state loaded-mode tests (e.g., the acceleration simulation mode (ASM) test), or transient loaded-mode tests (e.g., the IM240). Chapter 3 contains descriptions of these tests. Idle tests measure concentrations of CO and HC; steady-state loaded-mode tests measure concentrations of CO, HC, and $NO_x$; and transient loaded-mode tests measure mass emissions of CO, HC, and $NO_x$. Data can also be gathered from visual and functional tests. Using in-program data is appealing because this information can be collected at little or no extra cost.

Because of the very large amount of data collected as part of ongoing I/M programs, detailed analysis can reveal information about the vehicle fleet and the I/M program. All tested vehicles are identified, and they can be followed

---

[1]Some examples of the separate in-program tests include running two consecutive tests on vehicles or, for a program that uses a fast-pass system, running full IM240 tests for the purpose of gathering unambiguous in-program data.

from cycle to cycle, giving estimates of emissions deterioration rates and repair effectiveness. These data also can be used to develop vehicle profiles (discussed in Chapter 4) and information about the performance of test stations.

Several factors might contribute to underestimating actual emissions reductions using in-program data. Several sources of emissions reduction listed in Table 6-1 cannot be measured with in-program data, such as the effect of an I/M program on improving vehicle maintenance before the I/M test or on emissions reduction gained by causing vehicles to leave the area or be scrapped early. Measuring the impact of I/M programs on these parameters is made difficult by the inherent turnover of the fleet and maintenance that would occur in the absence of a program.

Conversely, there are reasons why in-program data might overestimate actual emissions reductions. In-program data do not include emissions from vehicles that avoid testing. Avoidance can result in exaggerated emissions reductions in a number of ways. Owners might not bring their vehicles to be tested at all. That is a problem if it is assumed that all vehicles are tested and that failing vehicles receive repairs yielding some average emissions reduction. Owners might collude with technicians running the test program to falsify the emissions level of a failing vehicle so that it passes. Or owners might temporarily fix a vehicle to pass the test without fully repairing it. If vehicles are prepared for the test, they are not typical of vehicles on the road. In this case, again, in-program data overstates emissions reductions if it is assumed that all I/M repairs last some average length of time.

Finally, because of the statistical problem referred to as "regression to the mean," emissions of a failing vehicle likely will be lower on retesting, even in the absence of repairs.[2] Since only vehicles that fail are retested, this group has higher than average emissions. Thus, even in the absence of repairs, their emissions would tend to move closer to the mean of the fleet upon retesting. Not accounting for this phenomenon would tend to overstate actual emissions reductions from in-program data.

There are other more general problems with in-program data. The gold-standard tests to measure tailpipe emissions are the Federal Test Procedure

---

[2]Regression to the mean is a statistical phenomenon where the initial scores of a selected group within a normal distribution will tend to move toward the population mean in a follow-up test. Although the movement of an individual score cannot be predicted based on this phenomenon, the group average will likely move toward the population mean during follow-up tests.

(FTP) and the supplemental FTP (SFTP) dynamometer tests. These tests are used to certify that emissions from new vehicles do not exceed federal emissions standards. However, these tests are far too costly[3] and time-consuming to measure a large sample of vehicles. Most I/M tests suffer from a lack of consistent preconditioning and an inability to represent all the driving modes represented in the FTP and SFTP.[4] Environmental conditions also have been shown to affect emissions test results (Anderson and Wilkes 1998; EPA 2000b). Additionally, vehicle emissions vary from test to test, especially for many high-emitting vehicles (Knepper et al. 1993; Bishop and Stedman 1996; Coninx 2000). Many factors can contribute to variability in repeated emissions tests of the same vehicle. These factors, which are also summarized in Wenzel et al. (2000), include the presence of intermittent failures of emissions-control system components (such as a malfunctioning oxygen sensor) or fluctuations in back-to-back emissions test results because of differences in the measurement equipment, calibrations, or test personnel (e.g., different driving styles in tracking a target speed-time trace on a dynamometer).

Some test results, such as those for idle and ASM tests, also must be converted from concentration measurements to mass emission rates. The correlation of the idle test with the FTP is illustrated in Figure 6-1 for the same car tested in the same laboratory (Haskew et al. 1987). It includes 604 observations on model year 1981 and 1982 vehicles and is plotted on a logarithmic scale to reduce data scatter.

**Data from Roadside Testing**

Exhaust emissions test data can also be obtained from vehicles subject to roadside tests. Under such a program, vehicles are randomly pulled over and given an emissions test similar to the vehicle inspection test. Visual and functional tests can also be done to determine tampering rates (see the discussion

---

[3]A typical estimate for an FTP test is $800 to $1,000 per test for a vehicle delivered to the laboratory. The additional charge for an SFTP is $750.

[4]The FTP and SFTP have extensive protocols regarding fuel specifications and environmental conditions. Their driving cycles include driving modes not included in transient loaded-mode I/M tests, including cold-start and high accelerations. They are also done under laboratory conditions, with better-calibrated instruments and better-trained technicians.

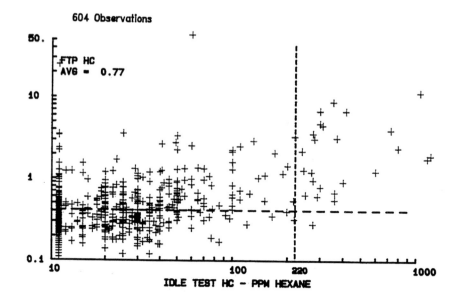

**FIGURE 6-1** EPA emissions-factor data from 1981-1982 industry closed-loop cars. The correlation of the idle concentration test with the FTP test is illustrated in the plot. The horizontal scale is the idle test concentration measurement in parts per million (ppm); the vertical scale gives the FTP mass test result for the same vehicle tested in the same laboratory. Logarithmic scales are used to keep the data on the plot. Source: Haskew et al. 1987. Reprinted by permission from SAE paper 871103; copyright 1987, Society of Automotive Engineers, Warrendale, PA.

of the results from the U.S. Environmental Protection Agency (EPA) national tampering survey in Chapter 3), and to check components of the evaporative emissions-control system. Roadside testing is fairly expensive because it requires portable testing equipment, technicians to do the testing, and officers to pull over vehicles. California's roadside test program measured emissions from about 10,000 vehicles per year from 1997 to the present. EPA's national tampering surveys, conducted from the late 1970s through 1992, measured about 7,500 vehicles per year between 1985 and 1992.

Because of the costs and time required to perform roadside testing and for political reasons, emissions on far fewer vehicles are measured in this manner than are measured in the inspection lanes. This implies that samples need to be carefully defined to avoid selection bias and to obtain a representative sample of the fleet. However, roadside testing represents an independent source of in-use evaluation data.  Many of the shortcomings of in-program data, such as motorists avoiding testing or making repairs solely to pass the test, are not present in roadside pullover data.  Roadside testing coupled with a vehicle's I/M history can demonstrate the effectiveness of an I/M program or changes to a program, the duration of repairs, the occurrence of pretest repairs, the level of compliance with the program, and whether there is a need to increase enforcement.

**Data from Remote Sensing**

Remote sensing is a third source of tailpipe emissions data (see Chapter 4 for a description of remote sensing).  Remote sensing allows a large number of in-use vehicles to be measured.  As with roadside testing, remote sensing can help assess the effectiveness of an I/M program or changes to the program, the duration of repairs, the occurrence of pretest repairs, the level of compliance with the program, and whether there is a need to increase enforcement.  Remote-sensing measures emissions for about one-half second of driving for each vehicle.  Care to select proper measurement sites is needed for remote-sensing evaluations of I/M programs so that cold-start and off-cycle emissions are avoided.  Other issues discussed in Chapter 4 relate to quality control and quality assurance, site selection, and coverage.  Measurements at a single site represent only one sample and one range of operating conditions.  The correlation of results from the vehicles measured by remote sensing to vehicles and operating conditions (such as the load on the vehicle) of the entire fleet or to results measured from a standard test procedure remains problematic.[5]  As with any measurement that estimates only concentration of pollutants, there is also the issue of converting measurements from concentration units to mass emissions.

Remote sensing provides the only way to estimate pretest repairs effec-

---

[5]The vehicle specific load (VSP) distribution (percentage of vehicles at different loads) can be calculated for a fleet of vehicles measured by remote sensing.  In an IM240 test, a single vehicle is subjected to different loads for different amounts of time.  The load distribution in the IM240 will be different in almost all cases than the load distribution of a fleet of vehicles measured in a remote-sensing campaign.  Jiménez et al. (1999) have recommended that the load distribution in the remote-sensing fleet be adjusted to that of the IM240 test by weighting the remote-sensing measurements by load so that the weighted load distribution is the same as that in the IM240 test.

tively. Extensive remote sensing can identify trends in emissions by model year before the I/M test to determine whether owners are taking actions to reduce emissions before their tests. As with roadside testing, remote sensing offers a way to determine the extent of noncompliance with an I/M program, including whether vehicles that fail I/M tests are still driven in the I/M area. Remote sensing can also determine the percentage of vehicles exempt from testing but driving in the I/M area, together with an estimate of their contribution to overall vehicle emissions.

## Data on Evaporative Emissions

The evaporative emissions reductions possible from periodic inspection and repair programs are difficult, if not impossible, to estimate. One needs to know the frequencies and impacts of evaporative system failures, the ability to detect failure, and the ability of the service industry to make effective and durable repairs. The only current data with which to estimate evaporative emissions from I/M tests on pre-on-board diagnostic (OBD) vehicles are limited to visual observations and gas-cap and fill-line pressure tests. There is no method for directly measuring evaporative emissions short of subjecting vehicles to a laboratory SHED (sealed housing for evaporative determination) test.[6]

## Duration of Vehicle Repairs Issues

The length of time that repairs remain effective is a central issue for evaluating I/M program benefits. If emissions reductions from vehicle repairs last on average 2 years, then emissions reductions from I/M are double what they would be if reductions lasted only 1 year. There has been some analysis of this issue, but it has certainly not been resolved, and further work must be done. The evidence to date is mixed. A number of studies find that at least some vehicles have reductions that last a very short time. Lawson (1993) observed that many high-emitting vehicles stopped in random roadside pullovers had either passed their emissions test in the previous 90 days or went on to pass their emissions test in the following 90 days. This finding suggested that some

---

[6]The SHED test involves placing the vehicle in a sealed enclosure and monitoring HC concentrations over time.

repairs were of short duration done simply to pass the test. The IMRC study (2000) found from change-of-ownership data that about 20% of vehicles that failed and later passed would have failed again immediately after the test, and McClintock (1999a) found in Colorado using remote-sensing data that a significant amount of the emission reduction estimated from lane data was lost within 1 month of the final IM240 test. Wenzel (in press) found in Arizona that half of on-road benefits disappear after 1 year and that 40% of the vehicles that fail in one I/M cycle, fail again in the next cycle. Rajan (1996) found in a California study that on average vehicle emissions of the repaired vehicles returned to their original level after 2 years. There is also evidence that some emission reductions last for much longer periods. Again, the IMRC study (2000) found that the 80% of vehicles that appeared to receive lasting repairs had emissions reductions for $NO_x$ that extended at least a year, and for HC, deterioration in those benefits began after 9 months. This study was not able to look beyond a year after repair.

In summary, there appears to be a distribution of repair duration of the vehicles that do have emissions reductions as a result of I/M. That distribution ranges from a matter of days to several years or beyond. There needs to be more study of the factors that influence how long repairs last, such as how different I/M program configurations might affect repair durability.

## Methods for Estimating I/M Tailpipe Emissions Reductions

The data sources described above can be used to estimate vehicle tailpipe emissions for model-year-specific emissions by a number of possible methods. We summarize three methods and describe the advantages and disadvantages of each. The reader is referred to Chapter 3, which discusses previous evaluations using some of the methods described below.

### Reference Method

This method compares the emissions by model year measured by the test program with those of a reference program. The reference program may be a null program (non-I/M) or a benchmark I/M program. The EPA has recommended comparison with a benchmark I/M program. Before comparing vehicle fleets in the test and reference program, they are adjusted for model year and, if possible, odometer reading. Other factors influence fleet emissions besides I/M. These parameters include vehicle types, vehicle models, socioeconomic characteristics of vehicle owners, altitude, climate, and fuel. Adjustments between the two fleets need to be made for these factors in order to estimate the effect of the I/M program. The effects of these other factors may be seen by comparing fleets from different areas having the same I/M program status. EPA released guidance on using the reference method for I/M evaluation where the Arizona I/M program is used as the benchmark (Sierra Research 1997; EPA 1998d). Critiques of this method are discussed in the following section.

An advantage of the reference method is that it can be applied at any point during the program's lifetime as opposed to only when there is an incremental change in the program (as with the step method of evaluation described below). It can account for the effects of multiple I/M cycles, pre-inspection maintenance and repairs, and deterioration of emissions repairs. If remote sensing is used to collect the data, deterioration of emissions for vehicles not inspected in the I/M program can also be estimated.

However, it is difficult to find two areas that are similar in all respects except for their I/M programs. To the extent that the test area and the baseline non-I/M area are different outside of I/M program status and those differences have an impact on vehicle emissions, the difference must be fully accounted for in the analysis. Unexplained differences would be incorrectly attributable to the I/M program.

## Critiques of the EPA-Approved Reference Method

The EPA guidance on the use of a benchmark program in Phoenix was critiqued by Wenzel and Sawyer (1998), and by Rothman (1998). The EPA guidance document, the Sierra Research report describing this method, and the critiques may be found at the EPA web site (http://www.epa.gov/oms/epg/progeval.htm). Comments in the critiques were not incorporated into the guidance document. Wenzel and Sawyer's concerns included possible sample bias in recruitment options; errors in the conversion of concentrations to mass emissions rates; and the fact that the method of model-year stratification, in which vehicles are grouped by model year, does not accurately group vehicles according to the technologies used in a vehicle's fuel delivery and computer control systems. Rothman's concerns included recruitment bias and use of the

MOBILE model to get the evaporative emissions from a pressure test. The author recommended complementary use of remote-sensing data from several independent sites.

This guidance for I/M evaluations of state programs also was discussed in the I/M Program Evaluation Panel at the 16th Annual Mobile Sources/Clean Air Conference, September 2000, sponsored by the National Center for Vehicle Emissions and Safety at Colorado State University. Richard Joy, of Sierra Research, stated that previous applications of the EPA Guidance on I/M program evaluation were not valid because vehicles in the benchmark program in Phoenix were not uniformly preconditioned. He said that Sierra Research had looked at the following alternative evaluation methods before coming up with this evaluation method and rejected them:

- Using the MOBILE model.
- Comparing I/M test results before and after repair.
- Comparing emissions test results from I/M to non-I/M areas.
- Comparing air quality before and after I/M implementation.

Comparison to a benchmark I/M program, with measurements based on adequately preconditioned (uniformly warmed up) vehicles, is recommended by Joy as the best way to evaluate other I/M programs. Potential problems to the benchmark evaluation method included the following:

- Accounting for seasonal, fuel, temporal, and geographical differences (to be corrected by applying MOBILE correction factors for these parameters).
- Loss of benefits due to program evasion and test fraud.
- Bias introduced in recruiting vehicles.

Application of this evaluation method requires emissions tests on a random sample of vehicles. According to Joy, the best method of recruiting vehicles would be by random roadside testing. However, some states do not allow roadside testing, and many others might not have the political will. Alternative recruitment methods all have shortcomings. Random selection after I/M testing does not capture vehicles avoiding testing. Recruiting vehicles by mail introduces selection bias, even when vehicle owners are threatened with registration denial for noncompliance.

During the panel discussion at the conference, David Amlin, of the California Bureau of Automotive Repair, noted that the California evaluation of emissions reductions using roadside pullover data (described in Chapter 3 and in CARB 2000b) showed different emissions reductions in Sacramento and Los Angeles. Depending on which city was used as the benchmark, the other city's I/M program could have been considered to be exemplary or insufficient. Socioeconomic differences, vehicle model differences, and other factors might be responsible for the differences in vehicle emissions reductions. Such factors are not accounted for or estimated in the current EPA guidance for evaluating I/M using the EPA-approved method.

## Step Method

When an I/M program is initiated or significantly modified, at some point about half the vehicles will fall under the new program and half will still be tested under the old program. In the step method, emissions of a random sample of vehicles tested under the new program are compared with those of vehicles yet to be tested to determine the effect of the change.[7] The method was applied to roadside pullover emissions data by Lawson (1993) and the California Air Resources Board (CARB 2000b) to evaluate different versions of the Smog Check program. The CARB evaluation is described in Chapter 3. Using emissions data collected with remote sensing, Stedman et al. (1997) also used the step method to estimate the incremental effect of the enhanced Colorado I/M program.

A critical advantage of the step method is that the tested and untested cohorts come from the same vehicle fleet.[8] Thus, there is no need to correct for differences in climate, fuels, or socioeconomic factors required in application of the reference method. Further, the method possibly can be able to detect an impact of the program on fleet composition. Motorists might re-

---

[7]It should be noted, however, that the application of the reference method to an ongoing benchmark I/M program, the step method, or the comprehensive methods is complicated by the possible residual effects of prior I/M cycles, which might affect the emissions reductions occurring during subsequent cycles.

[8]In the case of a step change in a biennial program where, for example, all even model-year vehicles have gone through the test and all odd model-year vehicles have not (or vice versa), corrections must be made for subfleet differences in vehicle age, mileage accumulation, or emissions-control technologies.

register their vehicles outside the I/M area to avoid being subject to the program, as was observed by Stedman et al. (1997, 1998) and McClintock (1999b). The step method would be able to observe that there are more such vehicles in the tested cohort than in the untested group. The step method can be applied to estimate the impact of a change to an I/M program or to estimate the deterioration in vehicle emissions from one test cycle to the next.

## Comprehensive Method

In this method, vehicles are split into groups according to their test results: initial pass, fail/pass, fail/waiver, and fail/no-pass (see Table 6-2). Average vehicle emissions by test group are followed over time using remote sensing (Wenzel 1999a; IMRC 2000) or using change of ownership I/M test data (IMRC 2000). Periodic test-cycle-to-test-cycle in-program data can also be used to estimate initial emissions reductions and repair deterioration for fail/pass cars. To get estimates of repair deterioration with better resolution (months rather than annual or biennial) from in-program data, initial test data from inspections made at intermediate times are necessary, such as emissions tests that can occur with change of ownership. The level and change of emissions over time give information about the emissions reduction seen as a result of the test and pretest repairs together with the emissions deterioration between one test and the next. The comprehensive method can be used over a number of cycles. As described in Chapter 3, this method was used by the California Inspection and Maintenance Review Committee (IMRC 2000) to help estimate the emissions reduction for the Smog Check II program.

A simplified version of this method involves calculating emissions reductions for vehicles that fail and are repaired. Initial inspection data for each failing vehicle are compared with observations of emissions at final retest (whether the vehicle passed or not). Ando et al. (2000) used this method to evaluate the emissions reductions from the Arizona program. It has the advantage of being relatively simple because it requires only data collected by the I/M program. It also follows individual vehicles instead of examining changes in average emissions by model years. However, it does not account for all sources of emissions reductions listed in Table 6-1. It is likely to overestimate emissions reductions due to I/M because of the regression to the mean problem and because it does not provide any estimate of the amount of cheating (fixing to pass the test). It will understate emissions reductions because it does

**TABLE 6-2** Vehicle Categories with Respect to I/M Status

| |
| --- |
| Pass |
|    • Passing emissions test, and low on-road emissions<br>   • Passing emissions test, but high on-road emissions |
| Fail |
|    • Passing within X months<br>   • Obtaining a waiver after repairs over some minimum expenditure<br>   • No final pass within X months<br>      Legal:   (1) Scrapped[a]<br>             (2) Sold outside the I/M region and no longer driven in it<br>      Illegal:  (1) Driven in the region, but without passing the I/M test<br>             (2) Sold outside the region but still driven in it<br>                (In some places this is against I/M rules.) |

[a]There is some natural scrappage rate, which is about 5% per year in California for vehicles 10 years old.

not provide an assessment of how much legitimate repair is occurring in antici-pation of the I/M test. Although the use in some states of fast-pass or fast-fail algorithms may make analyzing test data more difficult, Ando et al. (1999) suggested one method for estimating full IM240 emissions from partial test results.

## Methods for Estimating Emissions Reductions From Induced Fleet Change

In some cases, the methods described above will provide estimates of emissions changes resulting from both vehicle repair and changes in the make-up of the fleet. The step method can evaluate both of these effects. Other methods have provided only estimates of emissions reductions by model year. To aggregate these estimates to emissions reductions from the fleet, estimates of any changes in the fleet makeup resulting from the I/M program must be included. Because of the I/M program, some motorists might decide it is either too expensive or too onerous to get their vehicles through the inspection pro-cess. The latter group of vehicles can be of several types. If a vehicle fails and receives some repair, it might qualify for a waiver in the region. In other cases, motorists might decide to scrap a vehicle earlier than they otherwise would, instead of trying to get through the inspection process; or they might sell the vehicle in another market that is not subject to the same I/M requirements.[9] Table 6-2 summarizes all the possibilities for the fates of failing vehicles.

## Induced Scrapping

Motorists might fail the test, obtain an estimate of repair costs, and elect to scrap the vehicle instead of repairing it. Even if the potential repair bill exceeds the waiver amount, motorists might decide to scrap rather than face future repair cost uncertainty (most waivers are one time only). To evaluate this effect, we must compare the underlying "natural rate" of scrappage of vehicles with the scrappage rate with the I/M program.

If motorists do scrap their vehicles early because of I/M, the resulting emissions reductions depend on what the vehicles' remaining lifetimes would have been without I/M and the difference in emissions between the scrapped vehicles and the replacement vehicles or alternative transportation modes. If a scrapped vehicle is marginal rather than a high emitter, the emissions reduction induced is not large.

Although there is reasonably good statistical information about the expected remaining lifetimes of vehicles of different vintages, very little is known about the remaining lifetimes of vehicles having trouble passing the I/M test. These vehicles are more likely to be in worse overall condition and have lower economic value compared with vehicles of similar age that do not have trouble passing the I/M test. It is clear that their expected remaining lifetimes would be lower with an I/M program, but how much lower? Alberini et al. (1996) found that vehicles scrapped under the voluntary Delaware Vehicle Retirement Program were more polluting than the average older vehicle and had about half the expected remaining lifetime of the average older vehicle, or about 1.7 years. Dill (2000) reported that vehicles scrapped under a CARB buy-back program and under the Bay Area Air Quality Management District's vehicle buy-back program had a lifetime expectancy of about 3 years. These vehicles also had higher emissions than other vehicles of the same model year.

Finally, replacement transportation for scrapped vehicles is complicated by the fact that the purchase of another vehicle, whether new or used, starts a

---

[9]Many regions have no I/M requirements because air-quality measurements do not exceed state or federal standards.

series of transactions through the market that are virtually impossible to identify. The usual assumption is that scrapped vehicles are replaced by vehicles
that represent the average of all vehicles in the fleet.

Despite these difficulties, simplifying assumptions can be made to estimate
fleet effects from I/M. The induced scrappage rate can be determined jointly
with the induced relocation rate (see below) in the following way. From I/M
program data, the number of vehicles or share of the inspected fleet that fails
and never passes can be calculated. Some fraction of these vehicles will still
be driven in the region, either with lapsed registrations or through some other
illegal means. An estimate of this number can be determined by remote sensing or automatic license-plate readers together with I/M lane data (e.g., see
Colorado Air Quality Control Commission 1999 and IMRC 2000). Because
these vehicles have not been repaired and might still be driven in the area, they
should not be included in any estimate of emissions reductions. The remaining
vehicles can be considered either scrapped or relocated to another region; in
either case, emissions in the region fall. In a biennial I/M program, a reasonable assumption is that the vehicles scrapped because of the program are
scrapped 2 years earlier than they otherwise would (see discussion of the
Alberini et al. (1996) and Dill (2000) studies above) and that the emissions of
the replacement vehicles are the same as the fleet average. Further research
is needed to better understand how well such assumptions reflect reality.

**Induced Relocation**

Motorists or dealers might sell vehicles outside the region rather than pay
large repair bills. These vehicles can be treated just like the scrapped vehicles
described above for the purposes of this analysis, if it can be demonstrated that
they do indeed remain outside the program area.

## SUMMARY OF RECOMMENDATIONS FOR
## EVALUATION OF EMISSIONS REDUCTIONS

On the basis of our review of methods for evaluation here in Chapter 6
and results of previous evaluations of emissions reductions in Chapter 3, the
committee has a number of findings and recommendations. First, we summarize some key areas of uncertainty that future evaluations and studies need to
address.

- Little is known about the durability of repairs[10] in I/M programs. There is some evidence that a share of repaired vehicles go back to their failing emission levels within a few months, but other vehicles retain low emissions for longer periods (Rajan 1996; ENVIRON 1998; McClintock 1999a; Wenzel 1999a; IMRC 2000; Regional Air Quality Council 2000). Understanding how long repairs last is critical because the effectiveness of repairs has a large impact on the total emissions reductions achieved by an I/M program and the required frequency of retesting fail/pass vehicles.

- A related issue is that of vehicles with widely variable emissions (Knepper et al. 1993; Bishop and Stedman 1996; Coninx 2000). Are there vehicles with intermittent problems that produce emissions levels that vary between high and low for no apparent reason, so that they fail an initial test, pass the next without repair, and then appear again as high emitters on the road a short time later? How many vehicles pass a retest simply because their emissions were low that time rather than because they had received effective repairs? How many of these vehicles are there, and what are the implications for traditional I/M testing?

- There is evidence that there are significant numbers of vehicles whose emissions decrease in the weeks before their I/M test (IMRC 2000). These vehicles were earlier referred to as having had pretest repairs. The number of such vehicles and the extent and duration of their repairs need to be included in the evaluation of an I/M program. Additionally, it is necessary to consider how many of these vehicles would have received repairs without an I/M program.

- Many vehicles that fail in I/M tests never get repaired to a passing level. These vehicles need to be tracked to determine whether they are scrapped or still driven in the I/M region.

- The benefit of I/M programs in reducing non-tailpipe HC emissions is unknown. The potential for benefits from reducing evaporative emissions and liquid gasoline leaks should be evaluated.

In addition to shedding light on these questions, evaluations must quantify all emissions reductions attributable to I/M programs. Based on the issues discussed in Chapters 3 and 5 related to modeling, it is clear that the MOBILE

---

[10]Here we are referring to vehicles that obtain repairs after having initially failed the I/M test. We distinguished between these fail/pass cars and the fail/pass cars that do not get repairs but rely on improved preconditioning or the variable nature of vehicle emissions to pass an emissions test after initially failing.

and EMFAC models should not be used as evaluation tools. In the past, both have greatly overestimated the benefits of vehicle emissions-control programs, such as I/M programs. Evaluations of emissions benefits must be based on I/M-test and on-road vehicle measurements associated with the program being evaluated. Ideally, emissions benefits would be estimated with multiple sources of emissions data and multiple evaluation methods. Evaluations would be performed periodically at the same location and compared with results from other program evaluations. Such a comprehensive evaluation would quantify all sources of emissions reductions listed in Table 6-1.

The committee also recognizes that comprehensive evaluations can require a commitment of money and time not available to all state programs. The committee recommends that EPA ensure that at least some comprehensive evaluations are done that address the full array of emissions impacts incorporating multiple data sources and evaluation methods. The committee realizes that there must be incentives for some states to do such comprehensive evaluations on a long-term basis, possibly by spreading the costs across all states. Some states, such as California and Colorado, already have incentives in their state requirements for evaluating I/M programs. As described in Chapter 3, these states have already performed multiple evaluations by a variety of methods.

Any state undertaking such a comprehensive evaluation also needs to have a well-established procedure for collecting and analyzing vehicle emissions data from in-program and on-road sources. The guidance for data collection and evaluation should be peer reviewed, and comments gathered during the review should be addressed.

The committee believes that selecting three to five states with different program types and from different regions in the country would provide a sufficient range of full evaluations. Besides providing for an estimate of the emissions reductions, comprehensive evaluations could be used by all programs to improve forecasts of I/M benefits from the MOBILE and EMFAC models and to assess the potential emissions impacts from changes in program design. Full evaluations could also be used to help less comprehensive program evaluations estimate all potential sources of emissions impacts due to I/M. Some of the evaluations should be conducted independently of the agencies that manage the I/M program or have a role in setting I/M policy and all evaluations should be peer reviewed by independent scientists, economists, and statisticians. Results of evaluations should be made public so that all states can benefit from what is learned. EPA also should pursue publishing some aspects of these evaluations in professional journals so that they may be further reviewed and disseminated.

## States Conducting Comprehensive Evaluations

Comprehensive evaluations must account for all the emissions reductions in Table 6-1: emissions impacts from pretest repairs; the initial emissions reductions from repairs and the length of time repairs last; the amount of fraud in the program (including vehicles that fraudulently register outside an I/M area but still operate within the area); and the number of vehicles that are scrapped or sold because of the I/M program. One difficulty is the need to account for repairs that would have been done without an I/M program. There is no perfect method for evaluating all emissions impacts from I/M—the reference, step, and comprehensive methods all have their own inherent limitations. The ideal evaluation is a reference method comparing an I/M area with a non-I/M area, which would take into account normal repair (from the non-I/M area), pre-inspection repair, test fraud, and I/M benefit from repair (from the I/M area). However, there are a number of challenges to this approach, as discussed earlier in this chapter. The most appropriate evaluation method will vary with the type of I/M program in place and the availability of comparison sites; the best method must include a non-I/M fleet for baseline comparisons. The most appropriate method might also depend on the timing of changes in the I/M program. However, evaluation methods and data sources are complementary. Each adds information to reduce the uncertainty of the estimate and to better understand the effectiveness of the I/M program.

For a comprehensive evaluation, in-program data can be used to determine how many vehicles take the test. Program populations can be compared with actual vehicle registrations to evaluate how many vehicles are actually participating in the program. These data can also show the number of vehicles that pass the test after initially failing in each I/M cycle. However, a key issue for determining emissions reductions is to know how many of these vehicles were repaired and how long repairs last. Because repairs could be temporary or simply made for "passing the test," remote sensing and random roadside pullovers can be used to assess how well the repaired vehicles are staying repaired. Roadside testing and in-program testing are ways to discover tampering with emissions-control components. Remote-sensing or roadside-pullover data can be used to estimate the percentage of emissions reduction due to pre-inspection repairs. However, these must be distinguished from repairs that would have occurred without an I/M program. Program data can also identify how many vehicles fail the test and never pass. License-plate data collected as part of a remote-sensing database are necessary to determine how many of those vehicles are still driven in the region and to indicate whether changes to the makeup of the vehicle fleet are due to an I/M program.

## States Conducting Shortened Evaluations

For the states that cannot do a comprehensive evaluation, a shortened evaluation should be developed. The short evaluation should do the following:

- Not be based on the MOBILE model.
- Include all components of emissions reduction (from Table 6-1).
- Use the best evidence from data collected in full evaluations for the value of unknown emissions-reduction components.
- Use some on-road data from the local area if possible.

In a shortened evaluation, in-program data, registration data, and any local on-road data that can be collected will be used along with evidence from more thorough evaluations to estimate the emissions-reduction components in Table 6-1. To the extent data are not available to estimate some aspect of emissions reduction from a program's own data sources, data and assumptions based on the best comprehensive evaluations from other sources must be used. Information and assumptions should be updated over time as more evidence becomes available. The use of assumptions based on evaluations of other programs for certain key variables is a reasonable approach if there are not great differences among programs in these variables. For example, if the amount of pretest repair is reasonably consistent across states that have measured this parameter, then use of the average amount of such repair is a good proxy in areas that do not measure it directly. If large variations are found in aspects of I/M performance among states conducting thorough evaluations, then this shortened evaluation method would have to be reevaluated.

EPA will need to develop guidance for a shortened evaluation method. A review committee should be established to advise EPA in the selection of shortened evaluation methods and in selection of what information can be drawn from comprehensive evaluations to inform the shortened evaluation.

Assumptions used in the shortened evaluation can then be continually improved over time as more evidence becomes available. The shortened evaluation method must be linked with results from comprehensive evaluations. The shortened evaluation method should not go forward unless comprehensive evaluations are also being performed. Any shortened evaluation method needs to be validated. States conducting comprehensive evaluations of their I/M programs also should do a shortened evaluation. EPA will review the differences between the results of the comprehensive evaluation and the shortened evaluation and will modify the shortened evaluation method so that its results are more similar to the comprehensive evaluation. Validation of the shortened evaluation should be done at least once every 3 years.

One way of structuring the shortened method would involve the following steps:

- In-program data are collected over a test cycle and an estimate is made of emissions reductions for all failing vehicles: initial test results minus final test results (even for vehicles that still do not pass). In some cases, these results need to be adjusted to a standard emissions test (e.g., IM240 and FTP) to estimate the emissions benefit using correlation equations.[11]
- Adjustments are made to account for regression to the mean in test data. The magnitude of the adjustment can be made based on other more comprehensive evaluations.
- The adjusted in-program data are aggregated across all failing vehicles and an assumption is made about the expected average length of repair duration, not including fraud. (This assumption about repair duration would be taken from on-road evidence from comprehensive evaluations.)
- A further adjustment to the results would be made based on an estimate of fraudulent emissions reductions or emissions reductions that are made only for the period of the test. This estimate could be based on the audits of the testing stations run by the state, remote-sensing or roadside-survey data if any are available for the particular region, or some average estimate of fraud in other programs.

---

[11]There are inherent difficulties with correlating other test results with an IM240 test that evaluates emissions over only 30-240 seconds of a 2-year period and only when the vehicle is on its "best behavior" to "pass the test." However, such correlations must be done to estimate mass emissions reductions.

• Further adjustment should be made to reflect pretest repairs and repairs that would take place without an I/M program. This adjustment could be based on estimates from other more comprehensive evaluations.

• Retirement or relocation of vehicles as a result of I/M can be estimated based on the evidence from more comprehensive studies and from local vehicle-registration data and remote-sensing data.

## Performance Indicators

In addition, both types of program evaluations should compile performance indicators. Although they do not directly estimate emissions reductions, performance indicators are relatively easy to measure, supplement the evaluations described above, and provide relatively concise indicators of a program's success. EPA, and the states themselves, should use these performance indicators to rate states' I/M programs and to help direct improvements nationally. These performance indicators could include the following:

• An estimate of the total number of vehicles driven in the I/M region, the share of those vehicles that are eligible for inspection, and the share of those that actually are inspected.

• Failure rates by model year at the program cutpoints.

• Estimates of the average emissions of passing vehicles and average emissions of failing vehicles.

• Share of failing vehicles that actually get repaired to below program cutpoints and their average emission rates before and after repair.

• Share of failing vehicles that do not ever pass the I/M test, their average emissions, and an estimate of the number of those still driven in the area.

• The rate of repeat failures from one I/M cycle to the next.

• Estimates of the actual number of high emitters on the road.

These indicators could also be checked against assumptions used in modeling to make the models more realistic and improve the forecast of emissions reductions for the state implementation plan.

Over time, alternative programs to reduce in-use vehicle emissions might be developed by states. Systems that rely exclusively on remote sensing or OBD may be used as technology improves in the future. These programs would also need to be evaluated. Some of the issues associated with evaluating these emerging testing technologies are discussed in the following chapter.

# 7

# Evaluating Inspection and Maintenance For Costs and Other Criteria

Full evaluation of inspection and maintenance (I/M) programs requires a broader assessment than just an estimation of emissions reductions. Costs and cost-effectiveness are critically important criteria for determining whether social resources are being well spent and for making decisions about improving I/M program design. The distribution of costs among motorists can also affect public acceptance of I/M and can be a key factor affecting behavior and, ultimately, emissions reduction. Other factors that influence emissions reductions are compliance and enforcement levels and public acceptance. Finally, new technologies will profoundly affect the design and evaluation of I/M programs in the future. These issues are discussed in this chapter.

## EVALUATING COST AND COST-EFFECTIVENESS OF I/M

Evaluation of an I/M program must consider the costs of the program. Costs are important for a number of reasons. The level of program costs can change the behavior of those affected. We discussed in Chapter 6 the impact of high repair costs on motorists' decisions to scrap vehicles earlier than they otherwise would. High repair or compliance costs can also cause motorists or technicians to avoid an I/M program by driving their vehicles without legal registration or by tampering with the pollution-control equipment. In general, if an I/M program evaluation reveals that an existing program is expensive relative to alternative policies to reduce emissions, modifications might need to be made to make it more cost-effective, or it might be dropped and replaced by more cost-effective alternatives.

The first section discusses the concept of cost in the context of I/M and its measurement. Following is a review of the different components of I/M costs and how each is measured. Existing evidence about the magnitude of costs from earlier studies is also reviewed. We then move on to combining costs and emissions reductions in a discussion of the cost-effectiveness of I/M. A set of findings that includes discussion of costs and cost-effectiveness is contained at the close of this chapter.

## Measuring Costs

There are a number of different ways to measure the costs of I/M. Table 7-1 summarizes the cost components discussed in this and the following sections. On the one hand, there are motorists' costs, which are the relevant costs for determining behavioral responses to I/M and for determining which socioeconomic groups are most affected by I/M costs. However, for evaluating the overall costs or "social costs" of I/M, one must look at the full resource costs that are paid by all parties affected by the program. These two measures of cost can be different if, for example, some repairs to the emissions systems are done under warranty. Repairs done under warranty are not paid by motorists but still represent real costs, in this case, to vehicle manufacturers. However, many programs exempt newer vehicles from I/M programs until well past the emissions warranty period for many emissions-control components. Another difference can arise if I/M program costs, such as the cost of the emissions test, are partially subsidized by the state implementing them. Taxpayers in general might be paying for a portion of these programs. However, this cost to taxpayers represents a real cost of the program, even if those costs are not being paid directly by motorists in test fees. The full social cost of an I/M program is the measure of costs that should be used to examine cost-effective improvements in I/M and to compare I/M with alternative programs.

It is important to note that activities in primarily one cost category—vehicle repair—actively achieve emissions reductions.[1] The other categories, including

---

[1]Other costs that achieve emissions reductions include the additional cost of selling or scrapping one vehicle and buying another.

**TABLE 7-1** Evaluating I/M Costs

| Cost Category | Components of Cost | Comments |
|---|---|---|
| Cost of finding failing vehicles | Test or inspection cost (e.g., in I/M lane, by remote sensor, or on-board diagnostic readout) | Differs by test type (e.g., centralized vs. decentralized; remote sensing) |
| | Motorist costs including travel time and queuing time (for lane inspection) | Alternative possible assumptions about the value of time |
| Vehicle repair and associated fuel economy improvements | Resource cost of repair (if done at repair shop) Expenditures on parts and value of time (for self-repair) | Information about the costs and effectiveness of repair is incomplete |
| | Cost of reinspection | Some vehicles difficult to repair, requiring many trips to repair shops, increasing total cost of repair |
| | Fuel economy savings | Average fuel economy effects of emissions repair appear to be small |
| Program administration and oversight | Costs of administering program (aside from direct cost of testing) | These costs are a small share of the program; important to avoid double counting costs |
| | Enforcement costs | Enforcement efforts important to achieve emissions reductions; enforcement likely to affect compliance, but no research has been done on the magnitude of this link |
| | Evaluation costs | Thorough evaluation can be expensive; public-goods aspect of evaluation (evaluation in one state can provide evidence for other programs) |

the cost of the emissions test plus motorists' out-of-pocket and time costs, are simply transaction costs under the design of the current I/M program. Alternative program designs, such as the use of remote sensing or on-board diagnostics (OBD) for identifying high-emitting vehicles, have the potential to lower overall costs by reducing the costs of finding the high emitters.[2]

## Costs of Finding Failing Vehicles

### Testing Costs

The reported price of an emissions test under traditional lane tests can be used as an indicator of the cost of administering the test. However, this price might not always accurately capture the full resource costs of the testing process. Test price and true costs can diverge for several reasons. The states that have adopted centralized enhanced I/M have contracted out the emissions-testing services. The agreed-upon price of testing is an outcome of bargaining between the state and the contractor. Because the contractor has the status of a regulated monopoly, it is possible that the price could be higher than the approximate marginal cost of the service. However, evidence to date suggests that competitive bidding procedures in most states lead to prices that are at or even below cost.[3] Also, states might subsidize the costs of the test, and the price might underestimate the true cost. Another pitfall of counting test costs is that administrative costs to the state might be included in the test price. (Administrative costs typically are lumped with oversight and evaluation costs discussed later.)

Testing or inspection costs differ across I/M program types. Costs tend to be higher in decentralized programs than in centralized programs, primarily because of economies of scale in testing and because test fees for decentralized programs are in some instances market-driven (e.g., in the California and Pennsylvania I/M programs). High-volume testing spreads the fixed costs of the inspection across many vehicles.[4]

---

[2]Although remote sensing has the potential to lower the overall costs of finding high emitters, experience to date with using remote sensing within an I/M program for this purpose has not been entirely successful. Arizona recently abandoned a program to use remote sensing for this purpose.

[3]Contractors in some states are losing money with current contracts.

[4]For example, the price of a test in the enhanced decentralized program in California is over $40, whereas in Maryland's centralized program, it is $12.

Overall, the costs of finding a high-emitting vehicle have been relatively high in traditional lane programs in which all vehicles are tested on a regular basis. Alternative ways to identify high emitters that reduce the number of vehicles inspected or change the method of identification, such as through the use of vehicle emissions profiling or remote sensing, might result in lower costs. Harrington and McConnell (1993) found in a simulation analysis that an I/M program relying exclusively on remote sensing to identify high-emitting vehicles was more cost-effective than traditional I/M programs with universal inspection. Lawson et al. (1996b) reported high-emitter identification at costs as low as $9 per identified vehicle by remote sensing. It should be noted that Arizona recently halted a pilot program using remote sensing to identify high emitters (Arizona Department of Environmental Quality 2000), concluding that the emissions reductions achieved by the program did not justify the cost and inconvenience. There continues to be debate about the real effectiveness of this program, however. There was a period of time between the reading of the remote-sensing results and the contacting of the vehicle owner to come for a confirmatory test, and some of the vehicles might have been repaired during this time. Also, the cutpoints for the remote sensors and the IM240 confirmatory test appear to have been set at different stringency levels. It is important for programs to continue to search for cost-effective ways of identifying and reducing the emissions of high-emitting vehicles.

## Motorists' Costs

In a traditional I/M program, with vehicles inspected annually or biennially, a large share of the overall costs of I/M is paid by motorists for the inspection process. Studies of centralized enhanced I/M in Arizona (Harrington et al. 2000) and the decentralized program in California (IMRC 2000) found that over two-thirds of the total costs go toward the inspection process. These costs include test costs (described above) and motorist costs. Motorist costs include out-of-pocket expenses of bringing a vehicle in and the time costs associated with traveling to the test site, waiting for the vehicle during the test process, and waiting in line for the test. The out-of-pocket expenses, which include operating expenses of driving the vehicle to the station are likely to be fairly small, but the time costs can be large. For example, estimates of the average time spent to get to and from the inspection and the time at the inspection station in a centralized program range from 45 minutes to 1 hour (McConnell 1990; EPA 1992b; Harrington et al. 2000).[5]

## Repair Costs

### Laboratory Studies of Repair Costs

Several early studies on the cost of performing emissions repairs were done under controlled laboratory settings where a relatively small number of vehicles were repaired and tested by highly trained technicians. In early assessments of I/M, the U.S. Environmental Protection Agency (EPA 1981) forecasted that the repair of emissions equipment would be relatively easy and inexpensive. However, the difficulty and cost of repair for a relatively small number of vehicles is emerging as one of the biggest challenges facing current I/M programs. For example, some failing vehicles in the Arizona program were retested many times, and their emissions levels of hydrocarbons (HC) and nitrogen oxides ($NO_x$) bounced back and forth with sequential repairs (Harrington et al. 1998). As discussed below, both EPA (1992b) and California I/M pilot (CARB 1996) studies of repairs encountered significant numbers of vehicles that could not be brought into compliance with emissions standards.

EPA (1992b) forecasted the cost of repair in their assessment of the enhanced I/M program based on laboratory-based repairs and the cost of parts plus some markup.[6] The results of this study are presented in Table 7-2. However, many vehicles still did not meet the emissions standards after these repairs were made. Further, emissions reductions sufficient to meet the standards were assumed, but their costs were not estimated. Table 7-2 shows that the EPA cost estimates are lower than the other studies for the magnitude of emissions reductions assumed to have occurred. For example, the California I/M pilot study repaired 153 vehicles at an average cost of $420.

---

[5]The dollar value of the time spent depends on the value of the motorists' time, which is discussed by Deacon and Sonstelie (1985), Small (1992), and Calfee and Winston (1998). The most common estimate of the value of time used in similar studies is about half of the average wage rate. However, the value of time depends on what activity is being given up (leisure or work) to get a vehicle inspected, which is discussed by McConnell (1990).

[6]The sampling method used by EPA to recruit vehicles into this study was never made clear.

**TABLE 7-2** Comparison of Costs of Repair and Estimates of Repair Effectiveness Across Repair Studies

| | No. of Vehicles | Average Cost | HC Emissions | CO Emissions | NO$_x$ Emissions |
|---|---|---|---|---|---|
| | Change in Emissions (g/mi)[a] | | | | |
| EPA repair data set[b] | | | | | |
|   Tailpipe repair (IM240) | 266 | $120 | 1.89 | 32.1 | — |
|   Evaporative repair | | $38 | | | |
| Haskew et al. (1989) | 24 | $245 | 2.14 | 28.8 | |
| Sun Company (Cebula 1994) | 155 | $339 | 3.28 | 52.2 | 0.88 |
| Total Petroleum (Lodder and Livo 1994) | 103 | $390 | 1.18 | 12.26 | — |
| Orange County high-emitter repair study (Lawson et al. 1996b) | 91 | $630 | 4.96 | 42.7 | 0.40 |
| California I/M pilot study (CARB 1996) | 153 | $420 | 1.69 | 15.1 | 0.82 |
| Arizona enhanced I/M (Harrington et al. 2000) | | | | | |
|   Tailpipe repair (IM240) | 66,002 | $145 | 1.02 | 15.5 | 1.13 |
|   Evaporative repair | 15,917 | $29 | | | |
| California IMRC (2000) tailpipe repair (IM240) | | $128 | | | |

[a]All emissions measurements were made with the Federal Test Procedure, except for Arizona I/M and the Orange County studies, which used the IM240 test, and California IMRC, which used the Acceleration Simulation Mode test.
[b]Data set of vehicles repaired at EPA labs and used to estimate changes in HC/CO emissions resulting from repairs (EPA 1992b).

Several other laboratory repair studies have helped to shed light on repair and the cost of repair. Table 7-2 shows the costs and emissions benefits estimated for these studies. Haskew et al. (1989) reported the average cost of repairs for early-technology closed-loop-system General Motors vehicles that were repaired to pass Michigan's exhaust testing program. The Sun Company (Cebula 1994) and the Total Petroleum (Lodder and Livo 1994) studies were based on relatively small numbers of recruited vehicles, and the repairs were done by highly trained technicians who were told to repair vehicles up to a cost of $450. These studies were not connected with I/M. They were evaluations of scrap-or-repair programs initiated by major oil companies in search of emissions-reduction credits to offset emissions increases at their facilities. Remote sensing was used in both studies to identify high-emitting vehicles, whose owners were then offered an opportunity to sell the vehicle for a fixed price or to receive a free repair of the emissions system. The 1995 Orange County study (Lawson et al. 1996b) repaired 91 high-emitting vehicles (identified by remote sensing) using the BAR90 test, with an average repair cost of $630. The repair cost limit in that study was set at the blue book value of the vehicle being repaired. Sierra Research, under a contract with the American Petroleum Institute (API), also conducted a study of the causes of failures of high-emitting vehicles and examined the most effective repairs. However, no costs were included in that analysis (API 1996).

The California I/M pilot study, discussed in Chapter 1, also recruited vehicles to test the effectiveness of emissions repairs. In this study, automotive-service-excellence (ASE)-certified technicians with at least 15 years of experience in vehicle repairs were allotted up to $500 or more to repair failing vehicles.[7] There were 153 vehicles in the study that were either completely repaired to pass an emissions test or that exceeded the repair cost limit. Figure 7-1 depicts the cumulative frequency distribution of net emissions reductions. The net emissions reductions are defined as the sum of one-seventh the emissions reductions of carbon monoxide (CO) plus the emissions reductions of $NO_x$ and HC ($1/7(CO) + NO_x + HC$). This approach to aggregating emissions reductions is described in IMRC (1993). Because of the skewness of excess emissions among failing vehicles, 20% of the repaired vehicles produced 63% of the emissions reductions. Additionally, 19 of the 154 repaired vehicles had an increase in net emissions after repairs. Figure 7-1 shows that the increase in net emissions from these 19 vehicles was large enough to displace the small emissions reductions gained by a substantial number of vehicles. No net emissions benefits were achieved from the repair of the 50% of the vehicles with the lowest emissions reductions, in part because of the fraction that had a net increase in emissions ($1/7(CO) + NO_x + HC$). Figure 7-2 shows little relationship between repair costs and net emissions reductions in the California I/M pilot study.

---

[7]According to CARB (1996) when the repair costs exceeded $500 the technicians were asked to treat CARB as a client and request permissions for further repairs. This resulted in repair costs greater than the $500 limit for many vehicles.

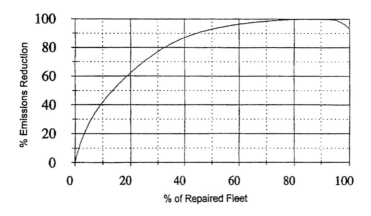

**FIGURE 7-1** Cumulative frequency distribution of net emissions reductions for vehicles repaired in the California I/M pilot study $(1/7(CO) + No_x + HC)$.

All these repair studies are not likely to represent repairs as they would be done in an operating I/M program. The training and experience level of the repair technicians is likely higher than it is for many small private repair facilities. Some repairs undertaken in these studies were more extensive than those that would be approved by a vehicle owner interested only in passing the I/M test. Even under these conditions, however, some vehicles could not be brought into compliance with the emissions standards. It should also be noted that the way in which vehicles were recruited, the cost limits placed on repairs, and the degree to which the vehicle owner participated in repair decisions varied across these studies.

In addition, diagnosis, repair, and the costs of repair can be different for vehicles equipped with new emissions control technologies and on-board diagnostic II (OBDII). Features of OBDII systems might make diagnosis and repair of vehicles easier, but the costs of repairing some vehicles whose emissions are close to the tight OBD standard could be high. Some of these repairs, such as those to sensors, will only affect the monitoring capability of the system and will not directly reduce emissions.

**In-Program Studies of Repair Costs**

Recently, data have been collected from ongoing I/M programs on the actual costs of repair for each round of I/M testing. Arizona and California

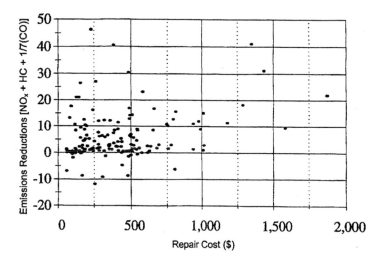

**FIGURE 7-2** Net emissions reductions versus repair costs for vehicles repaired in the California I/M pilot study.

currently require owners of all repaired vehicles to report the repairs and the cost of repair. These data have been analyzed by Ando et al. (2000) for the Arizona program and by the IMRC (2000) in California. These data are beginning to provide better estimates of repair costs (and the associated emissions reductions) because they are based on reported data for a large number of vehicles in ongoing I/M programs as opposed to laboratory studies where costs might be less a factor. However, the committee recognizes that the collection of repair cost data from motorists might be problematic due to some of the issues discussed later in this section.

Table 7-2 also includes the average per vehicle cost of repair and the average per vehicle change in HC, CO, and $NO_x$ emissions from in-program repair studies. It is important that repair costs be considered in the context of the associated change in emissions. For the in-program repair studies, Table 7-2 identifies whether the repair is to the tailpipe only or to the evaporative system (e.g., gas-cap repair). Evaporative systems repairs, at least the type done in I/M programs, tend to be much less expensive than tailpipe repairs, but the emissions reductions are difficult if not impossible to estimate. Examination of Table 7-2 shows that the costs of tailpipe repair in both the California and Arizona programs are somewhat higher than the EPA estimate of tailpipe repair and that emissions reductions are much lower than assumed by EPA.

However, the cost estimates for the California and Arizona programs are a good deal lower than the estimates in the Sun Company, Total Petroleum, and California I/M pilot studies, possibly because vehicles were being repaired to stricter cutpoints in these studies. Repairs done by experienced technicians in these laboratory studies might also be more complete and lasting than repairs done by the average technician, and costs were not as much of a factor as they are for vehicle owners. The average repair costs from the Orange County study are the highest of those shown in this table, in part because the vehicles repaired had a repair cost limit equal to the vehicles' blue book values. Owners are likely to want to pay the minimal amount necessary to do what it takes to allow their vehicle to pass the test, which is reflected in average costs of repairs for in-program studies.

Some difficult data issues have emerged with attempts to measure repair costs in ongoing I/M programs. Data problems in assessing costs of repair are hardly surprising under the current regulatory climate. Until recently, few states collected data on emissions repairs and their costs, and fewer still provided incentives to collect accurate data. In both the Arizona and California programs, there are a good deal of missing data in both the repair and cost information. In Colorado, only 13% of the failing vehicles actually report repair costs as required (Colorado Air Quality Control Commission 1999). In other cases, costs are reported as zero. Costs reported as zero are problematic when accounting for the full social costs of I/M because they can occur for several reasons: They can reflect repairs done under manufacturer warranty, they can reflect repairs done at home by do-it-yourself technicians, or they can simply reflect missing data. Even when repair costs have been reported, program administrators are often skeptical about the accuracy of the reported costs.

Despite these potential problems, studies of repairs of ongoing I/M programs in Arizona and California show very similar estimates of average repair costs: average repair costs in California are $128 per vehicle and in Arizona they are $120. Colorado's repair costs in 1999 ranged from $118 to $250, depending on program type and testing configuration (Colorado Air Quality Control Commission 1999).

Table 7-2 shows only estimates of the average costs of repair. It does not tell us anything about the variation in costs across vehicles. The underlying distribution of repair costs turns out to be very skewed, with the great majority of vehicles being repaired at relatively low costs and a small number of vehicles incurring very high costs for repairs. Figure 7-3 shows the distribution of repair costs by model year in the Arizona program. The average repair costs

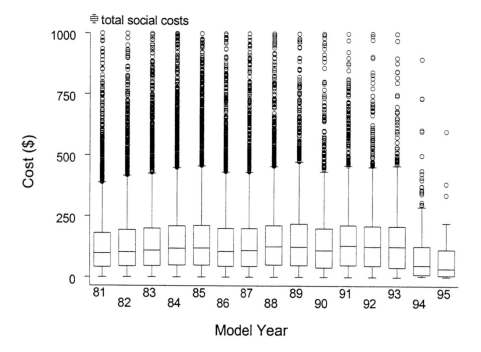

**FIGURE 7-3** Costs of repair by model year. This figure includes all costs of repair. Repair costs were estimated according to Harrington et al. (2000) when zero costs were reported. A circle represents one vehicle. Repair costs greater than $1,000 are not included.

are very similar by model year, as the midbar of each model-year box shows. However, the tails show that a relatively small number of vehicles have very high costs for all except the most recent model years. A part of the high costs are a result of the costs of numerous retests. Harrington et al. (1998) reported that 22% of failing vehicles in the Arizona program had more than one retest, and some had over 10 retests.

In addition to the variation in costs of repair across vehicles, there is also a great deal of variation in emissions reductions as discussed above. There is little, if any, correlation between costs and emissions reduced per vehicle (Figure 7-2). This suggests that some repairs are much more cost-effective than others (see the discussion of the California I/M pilot study as well as Slott 1994; Lawson and Koracin 1996; Ando et al. 2000). For example, Ando et al. (2000) found in the Arizona program that if the most cost-effective repairs could be identified, 87% of the emissions could be achieved at just 65% of the cost. This finding creates an opportunity for programs to target cost-effective repair and might be accomplished by more intensive efforts at technician training that could include training in specific diagnosis and repair procedures.

## Fuel-Economy Savings

As a result of repair, there is at least the potential for fuel-economy benefits, although currently there is no reporting of such benefits by I/M programs. A standard equation can be used to estimate fuel economy before and after repair.[8] In the Arizona program, Harrington et al. (2000) found that it was about 0.75 mile per gallon.[9] In contrast, EPA forecast that fuel economy benefits from enhanced I/M would be more than four times larger (EPA 1992b) because of the large emissions reduction benefits EPA forecasted for enhanced I/M. Some of the differences also might be due to assumptions in the EPA study associated with the nature of failures and repairs when the fleet changed from carbureted to fuel-injected vehicles.

## Program Administration and Oversight

Program administration and oversight costs include operation, enforcement, and evaluation costs. Operation costs include administration costs, direct costs for operation, cost incurred for outreach to the public, and running of special programs, such as repair assistance. In California's decentralized program, operation costs are over half of the Smog Check budget (IMRC 2000). Enforcement costs include the costs of monitoring the performance of testing facilities through overt and covert audits as well as costs associated with enforcing program requirements on noncompliance motorists. Enforcement efforts are a key component of administrative costs because a program with greater enforcement effort is likely to have higher levels of compliance from

---

[8]A standard equation is miles per gallon = $2,421/[(0.866 \times$ grams of HC per mile) + $(0.429 \times$ grams of CO per mile) + $(0.273 \times$ grams of $CO_2$ per mile)].

[9]However, use of this method can produce estimates of fuel-economy improvements for some vehicles that are clearly too high; using data from Arizona resulted in miles-per-gallon estimates that were as high as 100 miles per gallon for a few vehicles.

motorists, testers, and technicians. However, there is little empirical evidence about enforcement expenditures and almost none about how they affect emissions reduction from programs.

Evaluation costs include resources spent to estimate the level of emissions reductions and other assessments of a program. Evaluations can be a key method for directing improvements of I/M programs as their results can be used to enhance the emissions performance, cost-effectiveness, and public acceptability of a program. Evaluation costs vary a great deal, depending on the evaluation being done. For a full evaluation, as described in Chapter 6, that includes analysis of on-road data for the purpose of estimating pretest repairs, repair deterioration over time, and the extent of fraud in a program, a good deal of data will be collected. A full evaluation could cost as much as $4-5 million.[10] Less extensive evaluations that focus on collection of only certain types of information could also be done and would obviously be less costly. Even the shortened evaluation described in Chapter 6 would involve resources to evaluate the in-program data, to do any smaller sample of on-road data collection and analysis, and to evaluate the overall program results.

## Distribution of Costs Among Motorists

The distribution of I/M costs across socioeconomic groups is likely to influence the performance and acceptance of I/M programs. Under current I/M programs, the distribution of compliance costs among motorists varies a great deal. For example, in the Arizona program, repair costs for a single vehicle can vary from a few dollars for a gas-cap replacement to several thousand dollars for a variety of control-system problems from the catalyst to the air-injection system. The Arizona results also show that the anticipated repair costs differ substantially by age of vehicle, primarily because the probability of failure increases as vehicles age. The first two columns of Table 7-3 show the probability of failure and the average cost of repair by model year. Combining these two, column 3 shows that the expected costs by model year

---

[10]For example, if 20,000 vehicles are inspected over 4 years at roadside (5,000 vehicles each year) and 1 million remote-sensing readings are taken (250,000 each year), the costs would be close to $4 million (each roadside test is $50 and each remote-sensing measurement is about $1-2). Analysis of the data in a full evaluation would also require resources of at least $100,000-300,000.

**TABLE 7-3** Expected Costs of Repair in Arizona I/M for an I/M Cycle

| Model Year | (1) Probability Vehicle Will Fail Initial Test (%) | (2) Average Costs of Repair for Failing Vehicles ($/vehicle)[a] | (3) Expected Costs of Repair, All Vehicles ($/ vehicle) (1) × (2) | (4) Probability a Failed Vehicle Will Never Pass (%) | (5) Average Income of Owner in National Sample ($) |
|---|---|---|---|---|---|
| 1982 | 41.2 | 140 | 58 | 38.1 | 35,500 |
| 1983 | 38.5 | 148 | 57 | 38.9 | 39,000 |
| 1984 | 35.9 | 153 | 55 | 37.2 | 40,800 |
| 1985 | 28.8 | 155 | 45 | 32.8 | 41,700 |
| 1986 | 19.8 | 145 | 29 | 27.6 | 44,100 |
| 1987 | 14.2 | 142 | 20 | 25.1 | 46,000 |
| 1988 | 12.2 | 150 | 18 | 22.9 | 47,300 |
| 1989 | 8.1 | 144 | 12 | 18.5 | 48,000 |
| 1990 | 5.6 | 134 | 7 | 15.8 | 51,200 |
| 1991 | 6.8 | 152 | 10 | 18.6 | 52,000 |
| 1992 | 4.4 | 138 | 6 | 13.1 | 53,600 |
| 1993 | 2.6 | 130 | 3 | 8.1 | 54,900 |
| 1994 | 1.2 | 80 | 1 | 1.8 | 57,400 |
| 1995 | 1.0 | 62 | 0.59 | 1.1 | 61,000 |

[a]Includes expenditures reported by motorists and our imputations of costs when repairs are made but costs are not reported. For late-model vehicles these imputations include warranty repairs and therefore overstate the burden on the motorist.
Source: Adapted from Harrington and McConnell (2000). Data from Arizona enhanced I/M database, 1995-1996 (columns 1-4); 1995 Nationwide Personal Transportation Survey (column 5) (U.S. Department of Transportation 1997).

are 10 times higher for a 15-year-old vehicle than for a 4- or 5-year-old vehicle. In addition, Table 7-3 provides further evidence that older vehicles are much less likely than newer vehicles to eventually pass the emissions test.

How do the costs of repair fall on different income groups in society? We can shed some light on this issue by looking at car ownership by vintage. The last column of Table 7-3 links model-year holdings to average income of vehicle owners.[11] It is clear that older vehicles are more likely to be owned by households with lower average income; these vehicles also have the highest expected repair costs. Singer and Harley (2000) found that households in low-income neighborhoods in Los Angles tended to have older vehicles and higher-emitting vehicles for their age. Assigning motorists the liability for repairs means that those least able to pay are likely to be paying the highest costs. Politically, it has been difficult to enforce a regulation that appears to have such a regressive incidence. States have responded by allowing waivers for vehicle owners who have paid up to some repair cost minimum. That response is clearly not the best solution for achieving improved air quality; such alternatives as repair subsidies and repair insurance might offer more cost-effective solutions.

Moreover, future changes to I/M might have different distributional income effects on motorists. For example, the addition of OBDII systems to vehicles could increase the future cost of vehicle repair. That increase could create a greater burden for low-income drivers, who will have the burden of maintaining OBDII systems at the end of a vehicle's lifetime. The incidence of these costs on drivers of different income levels needs to be assessed. If OBD and OBD-related repairs are found to be regressive as some evidence suggests, policies will need to be designed to mitigate the impact on low-income motorists.

In general, low-income assistance programs might need to be expanded to improve the effectiveness of I/M and enhance its public acceptance. If properly designed, a low-income assistance program for I/M would reduce the burden that I/M might place on low-income motorists and reduce the incentive to avoid compliance with repair requirements.

## Overall Cost-Effectiveness of I/M

For policy evaluation, the costs of an I/M program must be combined with some measure of its effectiveness. A full economic analysis would require that costs be compared with the value of the air-quality and human-health benefits. However, it is difficult enough to measure emissions reductions and virtually impossible to link emissions reductions from this single program to an accurate measure of air-quality and human-health impacts.

---

[11]The data used to estimate these averages are from the 1995 National Personal Transportation Survey (U.S. Department of Transportation 1997).

Cost-effectiveness estimates provide a measure of a program's average cost per unit of pollution reduction. Costs of the program or some aspect of the program are divided by estimates of the associated emissions reductions to produce a measure of average cost per ton of reduced emissions. These estimates can be used to compare the average costs of I/M programs with alternative programs or to compare the costs of different program elements. As with evaluating emissions reductions, the baseline to which a new program is being compared is critical for cost-effectiveness calculations. As discussed later in this chapter, marginal costs and benefits should be assessed for deciding various program features, such as whether to exempt certain model years from testing.

**Multiple Pollutants**

One difficulty in estimating cost-effectiveness is that multiple pollutants might be reduced with I/M programs. If a region is concerned with pollution from only one pollutant, as in an area with a CO problem such as Denver, then cost-effectiveness calculations are very straightforward. Costs are divided by CO emissions reduced to calculate average costs per ton of CO reduced.

However, if both HC and $NO_x$ reductions contribute to ozone improvements and the program is in place to reduce ozone, then both pollutants must be accounted for in the cost-effectiveness calculation. Additionally, some regions attempting to reduce ozone are also attempting to reduce CO, and all three pollutants must be accounted for in estimating cost-effectiveness. How the pollutants are counted or "weighted" in the cost-effectiveness calculations is equivalent to determining how costs should be allocated among the different pollutants. The literature suggests that costs should be allocated on the basis of their relative importance in contributing to air pollution (Young et al. 1982; Sierra Research 1994b). If affected parties actually had to pay for the pollution control program, the allocation would be perceived as reasonable if payments were made in proportion to the value of the damages prevented. In many studies, $NO_x$ and HC emissions are simply added because they are said to contribute equally to ozone pollution (EPA 1992b; IMRC 2000). However, CO also contributes to ozone formation and is a pollutant of concern. The IMRC (1993) suggested that emissions could be aggregated according to the formula $1/7(CO) + NO_x + HC$. $NO_x$ and HC emissions also contribute to particulate pollution, but to different extents, implying that these emissions might be weighted differently. In California, one estimate is that the damages

186 Evaluating Vehicle Emissions I/M Programs

from a ton of $NO_x$ are over two times the damages from a ton of HC (Small and Kazimi 1995). In southern California's areas with the most severe ozone problems, $NO_x$ reductions actually would increase urban ozone levels (Blanchard and Tanenbaum 2000; Fujita et al. 2000), although $NO_x$ controls might be needed for controlling ambient ozone on a regional scale (NARSTO Synthesis Team 2000). Weighting is important for cost-effectiveness analysis, and weights are likely to vary across regions.

## Estimates of Program Cost-Effectiveness

Cost-effectiveness of an entire I/M program can be estimated by dividing the costs of the program by the weighted emissions reductions relative to some baseline. A number of studies have attempted to measure cost-effectiveness from empirical evidence from ongoing programs. Table 7-4 summarizes some of the studies but does not attempt to be an exhaustive listing. All the studies use weights that treat a ton of HC as equivalent to a ton of $NO_x$. The use of equal weights for HC and $NO_x$ is subject to many uncertainties, as discussed above.

## Cost-Effectiveness of Marginal Changes to I/M Programs

In addition to evaluating the cost-effectiveness of an entire program, it is also possible to look at improvements in an existing I/M program. How can I/M policies be made more cost-effective? Or can costs be spent in alternative ways that will produce larger emissions reductions? Here, we discuss a few of the existing studies and then look at other possible modifications that have been suggested but not yet analyzed in any ongoing program.

## Changes in Cutpoints

Should I/M programs have more strict or less strict cutpoints? I/M cutpoints were intended to indicate a vehicle in need of repair or adjustment. The EPA guidance on enhanced I/M suggests tightening cutpoints in the future, but there is evidence that tighter cutpoints might make programs less cost-effective. Closed-loop fuel-injection systems, which dominate the in-use fleet today,

**TABLE 7-4** Cost-Effectiveness Estimates of I/M Programs

| | $/ton (HC + NO$_x$) | Comments |
|---|---|---|
| EPA 1992b | $4,400 | Study of a generic enhanced I/M program, using MOBILE for emissions reductions; assumes very large fuel-economy benefits. |
| Harrington et al. 2000 | $5,508 | Based on in-program data for Arizona, for enhanced I/M program; 82,000 cars tested over a 17-month period 1996-97. |
| California I/M Review Committee 2000 | $4,400-9,000 | Emissions reductions based on a combination of in-program and remote sensing data, California enhanced I/M program. |

do not have adjustments or settings that one can adjust to get lower emissions. What does a technician do with a marginal failure vehicle if there is no apparent failed component? Replacing the catalytic converter will immediately lower emissions but at cost of over $200. Tightening cutpoints will result in the failure of additional vehicles that would have emissions only marginally higher than the new cutpoints. The effect on failure rates from tightening cutpoints is described in Chapter 3. Cutpoints are poorly chosen if they do not clearly indicate a vehicle with a failed component.

There is evidence that marginal emitters are difficult to repair successfully and that those vehicles might have higher net emissions after repair (see Figure 7-2 and discussion by Slott (1994) and Lawson (1995)). Looser cutpoints have been found by Harrington and McConnell (1993) and by Ando et al. (2000) to be considerably more cost-effective. There is evidence that trucks have looser cutpoints than cars and that repair on trucks is more cost-effective (Ando et al. 2000). As described in Chapter 3, the IMRC (2000) also examined the impact of tightening NO$_x$ cutpoints on the emissions reductions from the California Smog Check program. Additional study of cost-effectiveness of tightening cutpoints needs to be done before cutpoints are tightened beyond current levels.

**High-Emitter and Low-Emitter Profiling**

The concept of profiling is that the vehicles that are more likely to be high emitters are selected for more frequent testing and those vehicles that are more likely to be clean would be tested less frequently. Profiling appears to be cost-effective. A study by a workgroup of the Mobile Sources Technical Review Advisory Subcommittee (EPA 1999m) predicted that California's current high-emitter profiling program would be relatively cost-effective, but that study was done before the program began. As discussed in Chapter 4, the recent IMRC study (2000) finds that California's high-emitter profiling does not do much better than random selection at identifying high-emitting vehicles in any model year. Again, more analysis needs to be done to assess both the costs and the effectiveness of alternative methods for high- and low-emitter profiling.

## Model-Year Exemption

The IMRC (2000) looked carefully at the cost-effectiveness of I/M by model-year vehicle. That study found that I/M is much more cost-effective on pre-1991 model-year vehicles than on newer vehicles. The pre-1991 vehicles accounted for 95% of the emissions-reduction benefits and for only 60% of the costs. The cost-effectiveness of the older vehicles is about $3,500 per weighted ton of emissions (HC, CO, and $NO_x$) compared with $35,000 per ton from the newer model years.

## Remote Sensing

Remote-sensing measurements can be used either in addition to a testing program or in lieu of scheduled testing. Chapter 4 describes previous studies in which remote sensing was used to identify high-emitting vehicles. Harrington and McConnell (1993) examined both the cost-effectiveness of regularly scheduled I/M compared with a remote-sensing program and the effect of adding remote sensing to an ongoing periodic I/M program. The study found that as a tool for identifying high-emitting vehicles in need of repairs, remote sensing compared favorably with the conventional universal testing under current I/M programs. For a given level of emissions reductions, remote sensing resulted in lower inspection and driver costs and lower vehicle-repair costs than universal periodic testing. The study also found that if periodic I/M is in place, remote sensing between I/M tests improves overall cost-effectiveness of the program. However, as described previously, a program to use remote sensing to identify high emitters in Arizona was halted because of to implementation difficulties.

## Other Potential Program Modifications

A number of other improvements or modifications to I/M programs have been suggested but have not been carefully studied. Some states are implementing subsidies for repair or voluntary scrappage programs. Changes in waiver and exemption policies have been considered. Policies such as repair insurance have also been suggested. The cost and emissions reductions of different policies to improve enforcement also deserve more attention. Finally, as noted above, some repairs are much more cost-effective than others. Policies that induce cost-effective repairs, such as technician training and specification of repair procedures or even emissions-based fees,[12] should be further explored.

## COMPLIANCE AND ENFORCEMENT

Enforcement of program compliance ensures that vehicle owners bring vehicles to a test station to get tested and then get repairs and retests if they fail. It also ensures that stations perform proper inspections and repairs and that certifications of compliance are not fraudulently obtained. Those are some of the most critical elements of the program as well as the most difficult ones. If enforcement mechanisms are not effective, then motorists faced with the cost of repairs will simply not get tested or will fraudulently comply. That defeats the purpose of the program. Testing clean cars does not provide any benefit; only repairing or removing high-emitting vehicles reduces fleet-wide emissions.

Enforcement is important because there is evidence that motorists, testing personnel, and technicians have found many ways to avoid compliance with I/M. Decentralized programs have come under particular scrutiny because, it is argued, they present many opportunities for testing fraud. Hubbard (1998) found evidence of incentives for such behavior in California's decentralized

---

[12]For a simulation of the potential cost-effectiveness of an emissions-fee policy compared with the current I/M program in Arizona, see Ando et al. (2000).

I/M program. Hubbard found that consumers are able to provide incentives to station technicians who then allow them to pass. Motorists therefore shop around to find stations most likely to respond to incentives. Monitoring and enforcement costs are likely to be higher in a decentralized program with thousands of test stations, though testing fraud has been reported in all program types.

## Motorist Compliance

The level of motorist compliance with the program is typically referred to as the compliance rate. The compliance rate refers to the percentage or fraction of cars that are required to participate in an I/M program that actually do so. MOBILE5, which is discussed in Chapter 5, allows states to claim credits for a 96% compliance rate. This means that 96 of 100 eligible vehicles registered in an I/M program area are assumed to comply with vehicle-emissions-testing and to obtain repairs if they fail the test. Unfortunately, states are not required to verify their compliance rates to EPA. The new version of MOBILE, MOBILE6, requires states to input compliance rates. Studies have shown that some motorists illegally register their vehicles outside the I/M area but continue to drive in the area in states having an I/M program determined by county-line boundaries. Stedman et al. (1997) documented the migration of registration of high emitters outside Denver's centralized IM240 program area, but they continue to be driven in the area. Ohio experienced this illegal registration in non-I/M areas at the start of their IM240 program (McClintock 1999b).

Data collected in the Phoenix, Arizona, and in the Colorado I/M programs also suggest that a high number of high-emitting vehicles failing the I/M test never appear for reinspection (Wenzel 1999a; Wenzel et al. 2000; Ando et al. 2000). In Colorado, the percentage of unresolved failures in the enhanced IM240 program increased from 23% to 27% between 1998 and 1999 (Colorado Air Quality Control Commission 1999). However, many of the vehicles that never appear for reinspection can be observed operating in the I/M area by license-plate reading as part of a remote-sensing program (Wenzel 1999a; Wenzel et al. 2000). The negative effect caused by this poor compliance element has not been well documented.

There are two systems for enforcing compliance on vehicle owners: windshield stickers and registration denial. These two systems vary in effectiveness and cost. They are discussed in some detail in the following sections.

## Windshield-Sticker Enforcement

This enforcement mechanism consists of placing a plastic sticker in the windshield to show that a vehicle is in compliance. Enforcement occurs when a police officer identifies a vehicle that has either no sticker or an expired sticker. Although sticker enforcement has historically performed badly in the United States, it is still used in Mexico and certain local areas in the United States. The sticker system relies solely on police efforts to stop and ticket motorists only because they did not complete the testing process. Counterfeit and stolen stickers are another problem. Legitimate stickers must be produced and distributed and carefully handled to prevent unauthorized distribution. This adds another layer to the auditing and oversight requirements of the program. Another problem that reduces police incentives to enforce is that it is difficult to determine whether a car without a sticker is required to be tested.

## Registration Denial

Registration denial works by rejecting an application for initial registration or re-registration of a vehicle that does not have a certificate of compliance (or a waiver, if allowed). This system was mandated in the Clean Air Act Amendments of 1990 as the method for enforcing the enhanced I/M program. It works very well in the United States for several reasons. First, the police can tell by looking at the license plate on a car whether the registration is current. Second, the police are more willing to enforce vehicle-registration requirements because registration fees generate revenue for local government, the registration system provides a mechanism for dealing with stolen vehicles, and similar law-and-order functions are appealing to the police. Third, the police are no longer enforcing the air-pollution standards but rather the vehicle-registration requirement. Fourth, the vehicle-registration office, not the police, decides whether a vehicle is required to have a certificate of compliance. For registration-denial enforcement to work properly, a test schedule must be adopted that clearly determines when a vehicle is required to be tested. It also is important that the vehicle be properly identified when it arrives at the test station so that a clean vehicle is not used in place of the vehicle for which a certificate of compliance is needed. It is preferable under the registration-denial system to have the I/M program automatically update the motor vehicle department's computer system by indicating that a vehicle is in compliance.

## Testing Station Compliance

Another aspect of the enforcement of I/M programs focuses on the inspection procedure. Any fraudulent variation of the inspection procedure will negatively affect the I/M program. I/M inspection procedures can vary from testing a vehicle that is not fully warmed up to clean piping. Clean piping is the practice of inspecting a known clean vehicle but entering the vehicle identification of a dirty vehicle. States use various methods to prevent fraudulent testing. Most states have developed a process of covert or "undercover" vehicles that are sent to I/M testing stations to confirm correct testing operations. In Colorado's enhanced IM240 program, inspectors have been caught "clean piping" by entering data into the test system that belong to a vehicle not being tested. Video cameras are now used for surveillance at the centralized testing facilities. Software programs are also used to ensure proper testing. These programs verify testing frequencies, operator authorization, and other data. A variation from the norm triggers an overt or covert inspection by a state official. A fine or license suspension for test or repair stations may result from the state's enforcement operation. California publishes enforcement activities and associated penalties in its I/M newsletter. The federal government also requires annual reporting of compliance and enforcement data to EPA by states.

Audits provide an indication of the degree to which the testing aspect of an I/M program is being operated as it should. Two types of audits are done on testing stations:

- Overt audits (the station being audited is aware of the audit): This type of audit checks to see if the appropriate equipment is in place and is being operated properly. Also checks are made to see whether records are kept as required and whether technicians have the requisite training.

- Covert audits (the station being audited is unaware of the audit): Vehicles, set to fail tests in known ways, are taken to stations surreptitiously to see if the testing station properly fails the vehicle. Selection of stations for covert audits is based on information indicating abnormal operation or the time since the last audit.

## Quality Assurance

Additional safeguards are needed to ensure motorist compliance. Motorists will look for ways to avoid compliance that do not involve missing scheduled tests or fraudulently passing the test. It is essential, therefore, for the enforcement system to prevent avoidance to the extent possible. Several strategies need to be used. Vehicle owners must be prevented from avoiding testing through manipulation of the title or registration system. For example, if diesel vehicles are not tested, vehicle owners should not be allowed to declare that the vehicle is diesel powered without some proof or verification. Another way to avoid annual testing is to transfer the title of the vehicle or, in other words, to sell the vehicle. To avoid this manipulation, all vehicles should be required to be tested before they are sold. Additionally, any change in registration address from the I/M area to a non-I/M area should be verified through some other means. By changing the address on the registration—for example, to a relative's address in another city—the vehicle owner can avoid inspection even though the vehicle is still operated in an I/M area. Requiring proof of the move is necessary; however, city and county motor vehicle departments have very little incentive to police this requirement.

In addition, care needs to be taken to prevent the theft or improper issuance of certificates of compliance. Because registration clerks are in the position of deciding whether to issue a registration to a particular motorist, safeguards are needed to prevent and detect corruption of this function. Repair and retest stations also should be held liable for missing documents by paying monetary fines that exceed the "street value" of a certification.

## Evaluating Motorist and Station Compliance

Evaluating the adequacy of enforcement and the level of compliance in a program requires monitoring vehicles, testing stations, and repair facilities. The motorist compliance rate needs to be measured on an ongoing basis. A random roadside pullover of a statistically significant sample of vehicles to determine compliance is one mechanism for achieving such measures. Another mechanism is remote sensing or automatic license-plate readers. Both approaches can be used to help determine two critical measures of a program's performance: the fraction of vehicles required to participate in the I/M program but not showing up for their initial test; and the fraction of vehicles that have failed an I/M test and never return for a retest but that still operate in the area (unresolved failures). Using these performance indicators in program evaluation was discussed in Chapter 6. Other assessments are needed to understand whether vehicles are being registered outside the region, such as observing changes in vehicle registrations and emissions in areas adjoining I/M areas.

Instances of fraudulent testing, repairing, or issuing of compliance certifications also must be used to evaluate compliance with an I/M program. Tracking the number of overt and covert inspections and the number of enforcement actions taken against stations can provide evidence of the level of fraud occurring in a program and can target test stations for covert audits.


## PUBLIC ACCEPTANCE AND POLITICAL FEASIBILITY OF I/M AND PUBLIC AWARENESS OF AIR POLLUTION

Vehicle emissions I/M programs are a comparatively burdensome environmental mandate for the public. As one of the only mandates that requires individuals to demonstrate compliance, I/M has not proved to be a particularly popular policy with the public or politicians. I/M programs require owners to visit a testing facility periodically where about 7-15% of tested vehicles require some sort of repair, necessitating further investment of time and money. Additionally, the owners of vehicles most in need of repairs are sometimes those least able to afford them. This lack of public acceptance presents an ongoing challenge to the design and implementation of an effective I/M program.

Evaluations of human behavioral issues related to I/M programs are important, not only to determine how behavior might be affected but also to get a sense of the political acceptability of the program. If the public perceives costs as high relative to the emissions reduced or the effect on air quality, the program will be difficult to implement or enforce. Furthermore, because costs of I/M tend to fall disproportionately on low-income groups who are least able to pay, the will of regulators to enforce the program and therefore its effectiveness could be compromised. Given the import of public and political acceptance on the ultimate effectiveness of an I/M program, the committee believes that evaluation should include some critical behavior elements. Examples of social research that could help evaluate the public's reaction to I/M-related issues include Bishop et al. (2000b), who described the response of motorists to highway messaging of vehicle emissions, and Bohren (2000), who described human factors research on OBDII. There are other examples of studies on I/M and human behavior, but these issues have not been thoroughly studied. Clearly, there is a need for expanded research in the area of human behavior, regressive impacts, and public acceptance as they relate to I/M program design. Moreover, additional studies are needed to characterize fully the demographics and socioeconomics of high-emitter vehicle ownership.


## FUTURE TRENDS IN VEHICLE TECHNOLOGY
## THAT AFFECT I/M PROGRAM EVALUATION

Automobile manufacturers have made vast improvements in vehicle technology over the past 30 years. Laws imposed by federal and local governments to reduce emissions were often the motivating factor for many of these technological advances.


### Decreasing Failure Rate

One of the major benefits of new-vehicle technology is the reduction in the number of vehicles that fail I/M testing. The "New Vehicle Certification," required by EPA, is an example of legislation that has decreased the failure rate. Along with tightening the new-vehicle-emissions certification standard, vehicle manufacturers are also required to extend the time provided for emissions component warranties up to 80,000 miles.[13] This mandate, as well as the availability of more robust technology such as advanced catalytic converters, has helped to reduce significantly the in-use deterioration rate of emissions-control components.

Determining the actual benefit of reducing the in-use deterioration rate is extremely difficult. Data collection that addresses this issue includes collecting information on high-mileage new vehicles. Such information includes the following:

- High-mileage new-vehicle certification.
- In-use vehicle studies using vehicles voluntarily provided by the public.

---

[13]The federal emissions-control warranty is 96 months/80,000 miles for major emissions-control components (such as the catalyst), and 24 months/24,000 miles for other components (such as sensors, positive crankcase ventilation (PCV) valve and exhaust gas recirculation (EGR) valve). Auto manufacturers have tended to offer warranties for 3 years/36,000 miles and 10 years/100,000 miles.

- Roadside pullover studies
- I/M test lane data

As newer vehicles age and change ownership, the actual in-use deterioration rate might be different from that originally predicted. However, current data collected by McClintock (1999c) in Colorado suggest that newer vehicles are cleaner because of the tighter certification standards and are staying cleaner longer. EPA will reflect this in-use deterioration improvement in the development of their MOBILE6 model. As discussed in Chapter 5, this lower deterioration will reduce the forecasted benefits from I/M programs.


## OBDII Evaluation

OBD systems were developed to help technicians diagnose and service the computerized engine-management systems of modern vehicles. Early diagnosis followed by timely repair can often prevent more costly repairs to either electronic or mechanical powertrain components. For example, a poorly performing spark plug can cause the engine to misfire, a condition sometimes unnoticed by drivers. This engine misfire can, in turn, quickly degrade the performance of the catalytic converter. With OBD detection of the engine misfire, drivers would be faced with a relatively inexpensive spark-plug repair. However, without OBD detection, drivers could be faced with an expensive catalytic-converter repair in addition to the spark-plug repair.

The major difference between I/M programs incorporating OBDII compared with traditional vehicle testing is that OBD is a technology-based test that makes no measurement of emissions, whereas traditional vehicle testing is emissions based. In addition, the OBD technology is an early warning system, which is designed to create a warning before emissions increase. These characteristics OBDII raise some critical issues for evaluation. Before OBDII, evaluating the emissions-reduction benefits of vehicle testing was based on the principle of $A - B = C$, where $A$ is the average fleet emissions before vehicle inspection, $B$ is the average fleet emissions after failed vehicles are repaired and subsequently have reduced emissions, and $C$ is the net benefit of the repair and the overall reduced fleet emissions. The principle of OBDII is to prevent $A$ from including vehicles with emissions much higher than the rest of the fleet. That is a new approach to I/M, and therefore new program evaluation principles and methods need to be developed to assess the benefits of OBD technology.

# SUMMARY

Besides evaluating emissions-reduction benefits, evaluating costs, compliance, and public acceptability is critical for understanding the full impacts of I/M. Costs and emissions reductions are intricately linked, and both must be considered in evaluating I/M programs. Costs affect the performance of an I/M program because they can affect the behavior of vehicle owners and technicians in response to the program and therefore affect the emissions reductions achieved by the program. Considering costs is also important for determining how an I/M program can be designed or improved or, more broadly, for determining whether emissions-reduction efforts are best directed at I/M or alternative ways of reducing emissions. Compliance and enforcement issues are critical for evaluating whether vehicles required to be tested are properly tested and whether those that fail obtain proper repairs or are removed from the fleet. Finally, given the importance of public and political acceptance on the ultimate effectiveness of an I/M program, the committee believes that evaluation should include some critical behavior elements.

Some specific findings and recommendations related to these criteria are the following:

• Costs are easier to measure than emissions reductions, but there are still uncertainties about costs, especially about the costs of repair, the costs of enforcement, and the value of consumers' time. Increased efforts need to be directed toward obtaining complete, accurate, and reliable repair-cost data from I/M programs.

• Studies show that repairs done in I/M programs do not cost as much and do not result in emissions reductions as large as those done in laboratory studies of repairs. This finding suggests that repairs done in I/M programs might not be as complete and long-lasting as they could be. A desire to pass the test at the minimal possible cost affects the type of repairs motorists obtain. Additional studies linking costs of repair, type of repair (e.g., components), emissions benefits, and the duration of those repairs are needed to document whether effective repairs are being done in I/M programs and how those repairs compare with repairs provided under laboratory conditions where cost considerations are less and technician training is likely higher. The study of OBDII-related repairs should be a particular area of emphasis.

• The role of waivers in I/M programs should be assessed. Large sums of money are spent in I/M programs to find failing vehicles, so the impact of "excusing" vehicles from repairs might result in inefficient use of consumer resources and allow continued emissions from high-emitting vehicles. Potential approaches to replace repair cost waivers with other mechanisms aimed at providing relief to low-income motorists should be studied.

• Innovations in I/M that potentially could improve cost-effectiveness should be studied and possibly implemented into programs, such as more use of remote sensing, emissions profiling, different cutpoints (more lenient as well as more stringent), and scrappage and repair assistance policies.

• Not only do we know little about the cost and emissions impact of current programs, we know even less about alternative enforcement efforts. How much difference do enforcement efforts, such as auditing repair-facility performance or intermittent testing with remote sensors or roadside pullovers, have on emissions reductions from a program? There is no information about the link between high expenditures on enforcement efforts and the additional emissions reduction achieved.

• Little research has been done on how I/M affects motorists' behavior, including decisions about program avoidance and other noncompliance behavior as well as what types of vehicles to own or hold in the I/M region. Expanded research on these issues and other behavioral issues is needed.

• Introducing new-vehicle and testing technologies, including OBD and remote sensing, into I/M programs raises many issues. These include public concerns about the use of these new technologies and evaluation issues, such as how emissions benefits of OBD will be estimated.

# References

ADEQ (Arizona Department of Environmental Quality). 2000. ADEQ Response to the Reported Filing of a Citizen Suit Related to the Arizona Remote Sensing Program. ADEQ Communications: News Releases. September. [Online]. Available: http://www.adeq.state.az.us/comm/pr/2000/sept00.html. [June 21, 2001].

Air Improvement Resource, Inc. 1999. Office of the State Auditor Final Report: 1999 Audit of the Colorado AIR Program, November 22, 1999. Novi, MI: Air Improvement Resource, Inc.

Alberini, A., W. Harrington, and V. McConnell. 1996. Estimating an emissions supply function from accelerated vehicle retirement programs. Rev. Econ. Statist. 78(2):251-276.

Amlin, D. 1995. Remote sensing/high emitter profile pilot project results. Pp. 4.131-4.168 in Proceedings of the Fifth CRC On-Road Vehicle Emissions Workshop, San Diego, CA, April 3-5, 1995. Atlanta, GA: Coordinating Research Coucil.

Anderson, L.G., and E.B. Wilkes. 1998. Effects of Oxygenated Fuels Use on IM240 Emissions Test Results in Colorado. Presentation at the 91st Annual Air and Waste Management Associations Annual Meeting, San Diego, CA, June 14-18, 1998.

Ando, A..W., W. Harrington, and V. McConnell. 1999. Estimating full IM240 emissions from partial test results: Evidence from Arizona. J. Air Waste Manage. Assoc. 49(10):1153-1167.

Ando, A..W, V. McConnell , and W. Harrington. 2000. Costs, emissions reductions and vehicle repair: Evidence from Arizona. J. Air Waste Manage. Assoc. 50(4):509-521.

API (American Petroleum Institute). 1996. Analysis of Causes of Failure in High Emitting Cars. Pub. No. 4637. Prepared under contract by P. L. Heirigs, T. C. Austin, L. S. Caretto, T.R. Carlson, and R.L. Hughes, Sierra Research Inc., Sacramento, CA, for American Petroleum Institute, Washington, DC.

Ashbaugh, L.L., and D.R. Lawson. 1991. A Comparison of Emissions from Mobile Sources Using Random Roadside Surveys Conducted in 1985, 1987, and 1989. AWMA Reprint No. 91-180.58 presented at 84th annual meeting of the Air & Waste Management Association, Vancouver, BC. June.

Ashbaugh, L.L., D.R. Lawson, G.A. Bishop, P.L. Guenther, D.H. Stedman, R.D. Stephens, P.J. Groblicki, J.S. Parikh, B.J. Johnson, and S.C. Huang. 1992. On-road remote sensing of carbon monoxide and hydrocarbon emissions during several vehicle operating conditions. Pp. 885-898 in $PM_{10}$ Standards and Nontraditional Particulate Source Controls, Vol. II, J.C. Chow and D.M. Ono, eds. Pittsburgh, PA: Air & Waste Management Association.

Barrett, R. 2001. Colorado's I/M240 and OBDII Testing. Colorado Department of Public Health and Environment. Presentation at 20th North American Motor Vehicle Emissions Control Conference. April.

Baum, M.M., E.S. Kiyomiya, S. Kumar, A.M. Lappas, and H.C. Lord. 2000. Multicomponent remote sensing of vehicle exhaust by dispersive absorption spectroscopy. 1. Effect of fuel type and catalyst performance. Environ. Sci. Technol. 34(13):2851-2858.

Beardsley, M. 2001. MOBILE6: EPA's Highway Vehicle Emissions Model. Office of Transportation and Air Quality, U.S. Environmental Protection Agency. Presented at Coordinating Research Council On-Road Vehicle Emission Conference, San Diego, March 26, 2001. [Online]. Available: http://www.epa.gov/otaq/m6.htm [May 29, 2001].

Bishop, G.A., and D.H. Stedman. 1996. Motor vehicle emission variability. J. Air Waste Manage. Assoc. 46(7):667-675.

Bishop, G.A., S.S. Pokharel, and D.H. Stedman. 1999. On-Road Remote Sensing of Automobile Emissions in the Phoenix Area: Year 1. Department of Chemistry and Biochemistry, University of Denver, Denver, CO. Prepared for the Coordinating Research Council, Inc., Atlanta, GA. [Online]. Available: http://www.crcao.com. [May 22, 2001].

Bishop, G.A., S.S. Pokharel, and D.H. Stedman. 2000a. On-Road Remote Sensing of Automobile Emissions in the Los Angeles Area: Year 1. Department of Chemistry and Biochemistry, University of Denver, Denver, CO. Prepared for Coordinating Research Council, Inc., Alpharetta, GA. [Online]. Available: http://www.crcao.com. [May 22, 2001].

Bishop, G.A., J.R. Starkey, A. Ihlenfeldt, W.J. Williams, and D.H. Stedman. 1989. IP long-path photometry: A remote sensing tool for automobile emissions. Anal. Chem. 61:671A-674A.

Bishop, G.A., D.H. Stedman, R.B. Hutton, L. Bohren, and N. Lacey. 2000b. Drive-by motor vehicle emissions: Immediate feedback in reducing air pollution. Environ. Sci. Technol. 34(6):1110-1116.

Blanchard, C.L,. and S. Tanenbaum. 2000. Data Analysis Complementing Proximate Modeling of the Weekday/Weekend Ozone Differences in Southern California. NTIS PB 2001-1014. Final report. Envair, Albany, CA. Prepared for Coordinating

Research Council, Alpharetta, GA, and the National Renewable Energy Laboratory, Golden, CO.

Bohren, L. 2000. OBDII Human Factors Research. Presented at the 16th Annual Clean Air / Mobile Sources Conference, Snowmass, CO, September 21, 2000. National Center for Vehicle Emissions and Safety, Colorado State University. [Online]. Available: http://www.obdiicsu.com/ [May 30, 2001].

Cadle, S.H., P.A. Mulawa, E.C. Hunsanger, K. Nelson, R.A. Ragazzi, R. Barrett, G.L. Gallagher, D.R. Lawson, K.T. Knapp, and R. Snow. 1999a. Composition of light-duty motor vehicle exhaust particulate matter in the Denver, Colorado area. Environ. Sci. Technol. 33(14):2328-2339.

Cadle, S.H., P.A. Mulawa, E.C. Hunsanger, K. Nelson, R.A. Ragazzi, R. Barrett, G.L. Gallagher, D.R. Lawson, K.T. Knapp, and R. Snow. 1999b. Light-duty vehicle exhaust particulate matter measurements in the Denver, Colorado area. J. Air Waste Manage. Assoc. 49:PM164-PM174.

Calfee, J., and C. Winston. 1998. The value of automobile travel time: Implications for congestion policy. J. Public Econ.69(1):83-102.

Canale, R.P., S.R. Winegarden, C.R. Carlson, and D.L. Miles. 1978. General Motors Phase II Catalyst System. SAE Trans. 87:843-852.

CARB (California Air Resources Board). 1996. Comparison of the IM240 and ASM Tests in CARB's I&M Pilot Program. California Environmental Protection Agency Air Resources Board, Sacramento, CA. June 25, 1996.

CARB (California Air Resources Board). 1998. Proposed California Exhaust Emission Standards and Test Procedures for 2001 and Subsequent Model Passenger Cars, Light-Duty Trucks, and Medium-Duty Vehicles. California Environmental Protection Agency Air Resources Board, El Monte, CA. [Online]. Available: http://www. arb.ca.gov/regact/LEVii/ldvtp01.pdf [May 31, 2001].

CARB (California Air Resources Board). 2000a. The California Low Emission Vehicle Regulations (as of December 1, 1999). [Online]. Available: http://arbis.arb.ca.gov/ msprog/levprog/test_proc.htm [May 31, 2001].

CARB (California Air Resources Board). 2000b. Evaluation of California's Enhanced Vehicle Inspection and Maintenance Program (Smog Check II). Draft. California Air Resources Board, Sacramento, CA.

CARB (California Air Resources Board). 2000c. Public Meeting to Consider Approval of Revisions to the State's On-Road Motor Vehicle Emissions Inventory. California Environmental Protection Agency Air Resources Board. [Online]. Available: http://www.arb.ca.gov/msei/msei.htm. [May 30, 2001].

Cebula, F.J. 1994. Report on the Sunoco Emissions Systems Repair Program. Philadelphia, PA: Sun Oil Company.

Chatterjee, A., T. Miler, J. Philpot, T. Wholley, R. Guensler, D. Hartgen, R. Margiotta, and P. Stopher. 1997. Improving Transportation Data for Mobile-Source Emissions Estimates. NCHRP Report 394. Washington, DC: National Academy Press.

Chrysler Corporation. 1998. Emission and Fuel Economy Regulations. Environmental & Energy Planning. Chrysler Corporation, CIMS 482-00-71. Auburn Hills, MI.

Cicero-Fernàndez, P., J.R. Long, and A.M. Winer. 1997. Effects of grades and other loads on on-road emissions of hydrocarbons and carbon monoxide. J. Air Waste Manage. Assoc. 47(8):898-904.

Clean Air Report. 1999. States may lose half of current I/M emissions credit in new air model. April 15, p. 7.

Colorado Air Quality Control Commission. 1999. Report to the Colorado General Assembly on the Automobile Inspection and Readjustment Program. Final Report. [Online]. Available: http://www.cdphe.state.co.us/ap/studiesreports.asp

Coninx, P. 2000. Test Result Variability in Ontario's New Drive Clean Inspection and Maintenance Program and its Implications. Presented at the 10th CRC On-Road Vehicle Emissions Workshop, San Diego, CA, March 27-29, 2000.

Corley, E., and M.O. Rodgers. 2000. Evaluating Inspection/Maintenance Program Effectiveness: Reconciliation of the Denver Step and Atlanta Reference Methods. Presented at the 10th CRC On-Road Vehicle Emissions Workshop, San Diego, CA, March 27-29.

Davis, S.C. 1997. Transportation Energy Data Book, Edition 17. ORNL-6919. Center for Transportation Analysis, Oak Ridge National Laboratory, Oak Ridge, TN.

Davis, S.C. 1999. Transportation Energy Data Book, Edition 19. ORNL-6958. Center for Transportation Analysis, Oak Ridge National Laboratory, Oak Ridge, TN.

Davis, S.C. 2000. Transportation Energy Data Book, Edition 20. ORNL-6959. Center for Transportation Analysis, Oak Ridge National Laboratory, Oak Ridge, TN.

Deacon, R.T., and J. Sonstelie. 1985. Rationing by waiting and the value of time: Results from a natural experiment. J Pol. Econ. 93(4):627-647.

Dill, J. 2000. Vehicle scrappage programs. Paper presented at the Congestion Mitigation and Air Quality Improvement Program, Berkeley, CA, Oct. 13-14, 2000.

Dockery, D.W., C.A. Pope, X. Xu, J.D. Spengler, J.H. Ware, M.E. Fay, B.G. Ferris, Jr., and F.E. Speizer. 1993. An association between air pollution and mortality in six U.S. cities. N. Engl. J. Med. 329(24):1753-1759.

Durbin, T.D., J.M. Norbeck, R.D. Wilson, and M.R. Smith. 2001. Analysis of the Effectiveness of OBDII for Emissions Reductions. Presented at 11th Annual CRC Meeting, San Diego, CA, March 26, 2001.

Eastern Research Group. 1997. Profiling Vehicle Emissions with the High Emitter Profile Model. Prepared for California Bureau of Automotive Repair by de la Torre Kausmeier Consulting, Inc., and Radian International, LLC, Austin, TX.

Eastern Research Group and Radian International.1999. Models for Estimating California Fleet FTP Emissions from ASM Concentrations. Prepared for California Bureau of Automotive Repair by Eastern Research Group, Inc., and Radian International, LLC, Austin, TX.

ECOS/STAPPA/EPA ( Environmental Council of the States/ State and Territorial Air Pollution Program Administrators/ U.S. Environmental Protection Agency). 1998. Inspection and Maintenance Workgroup Resource Document. ECOS/STAPPA/ EPA Workgroup. Compiled by the Keystone Center, Keystone, CO.

ENVIRON International Corporation. 1998. Performance Audit of the Colorado AIR

Program. Final Report. Prepared for the State of Colorado, Office of State Auditor. Novato, CA: ENVIRON.

EPA (U.S. Environmental Protection Agency). 1976. Final Evaporative Emission Regulation for Light Duty Vehicles and Trucks. Fed. Regist. 41:35626.

EPA (U.S. Environmental Protection Agency). 1978. Evaporative Emission Regulations for Light-Duty Vehicles and Trucks. Fed. Regist. 43:36970.

EPA (U.S. Environmental Protection Agency). 1981. Update on the Cost-Effectiveness of Inspection and Maintenance. EPA-AA-INS-81-9. Office of Mobile Sources Air Pollution Control, U.S. Environmental Protection Agency, Ann Arbor, MI.

EPA (U.S. Environmental Protection Agency). 1991. Gaseous and Particulate Emissions Regulations for 1994 and Later Model Year Light-Duty Vehicles and Light-Duty Trucks; Final Rule. Fed. Regist. 56:25724.

EPA (U.S. Environmental Protection Agency). 1992a. Inspection/Maintenance Program Requirements. Final Rule. Fed. Regist. 57(215):52950-53014.

EPA (U.S. Environmental Protection Agency). 1992b. IM Costs, Benefits, and Impacts. Office of Mobile Sources, U.S. Environmental Protection Agency, Ann Arbor, MI [Online]. Available: http://www.epa.gov/OMS/regs/im/im-tsd.pdf [June 7, 2001].

EPA (U.S. Environmental Protection Agency). 1992c. Section 187 VMT Forecasting and Tracking Guidance. U.S. Environmental Protection Agency, Washington, DC.

EPA (U.S. Environmental Protection Agency). 1993a. Clean Cars for Clean Air: Inspection and Maintenance Programs. Fact Sheet OMS-14. EPA 400-F-92-016. Office of Mobile Sources, U.S. Environmental Protection Agency, Ann Arbor, MI. [Online]. Available: http://epa.gov/otaq/14-insp.htm. [Feb. 16, 2001].

EPA (U.S. Environmental Protection Agency). 1993b. Control of Air Pollution from New Motor Vehicles and New Motor Vehicle Engines: Evaporative Emission Regulations for Gasoline and Methanol-Fueled Light-Duty Vehicles, Light-Duty Trucks, and Heavy-Duty Vehicles. Fed. Regist. 58(March 24):16002.

EPA (U.S. Environmental Protection Agency). 1993c. Quantitative Assessments of Test-Only and Test-and-Repair I/M Programs. Office of Air and Radiation, U.S. Environmental Protection Agency, Washington, DC.

EPA (U.S. Environmental Protection Agency). 1994. Control of Air Pollution from New Motor Vehicles and New Motor Vehicle Engines: Refueling Emission Regulations for Light-Duty Vehicles and Light-Duty Trucks. Fed. Regist. 59(April 6):16262.

EPA (U.S. Environmental Protection Agency). 1996. Final Regulations for Revisions to the Federal Test Procedure for Emissions from Motor Vehicles. Final Rule. Fed. Regist. 61(205):54851-54906.

EPA (U.S. Environmental Protection Agency). 1997a. Analysis of the Arizona IM240 Test Program and Comparison with the TECH5 Model. EPA 420-R-97-001. Office of Mobile Sources, U.S. Environmental Protection Agency, Ann Arbor, MI. [Online]. Available: http://www.epa.gov/otaq/regs/im/az-rpt/az-rpt.htm [June 6, 2001].

EPA (U.S. Environmental Protection Agency). 1997b. MOBILE5 Vehicle Emission Modeling Software MOBILE5b Emission Factor. User Guide Modifications (Chapter 2). [Online]. Available: http://www.epa.gov/oms/m5.htm#m5b [June 7, 2001].

EPA (U.S. Environmental Protection Agency). 1998a. National Air Pollutant Emission Trends Update: 1970-1997. EPA 454/E-98-007. Office of Air Quality Planning and Standards, U.S. Environmental Protection Agency, Research Triangle Park, NC.

EPA (U.S. Environmental Protection Agency). 1998b. Exhaust Emissions Certification Standards for Light Duty Vehicles and Light Duty Trucks. EPA 420/B-98-001. Office of Mobile Sources, U.S. Environmental Protection Agency, Ann Arbor, MI.

EPA (U.S. Environmental Protection Agency). 1998c. Minor Amendments to Inspection and Maintenance Program Evaluation Requirements. Amendment to the Final Rule. Final Rule. Fed. Regist. 63(6):1362-1368.

EPA (U.S. Environmental Protection Agency). 1998d. Inspection and Maintenance (I/M) Program Effectiveness Methodologies. EPA 420-S-98-015. Office of Air and Radiation. U.S. Environmental Protection Agency, Washington, DC.

EPA (U.S. Environmental Protection Agency). 1999a. Control of Air Pollution from New Motor Vehicle Standards: Proposed Tier 2 Motor Vehicle Emissions Standards and Gasoline Sulfur Control Requirements. Final Rule. Fed. Regist. 64(92):26003.

EPA (U.S. Environmental Protection Agency). 1999b. Determination of Running Emissions as a Function of Mileage for 1981-1993 Model Year Light-Duty Cars and Trucks. Draft. EPA 420-P-99-010. M6.EXH.001. Office of Mobile Sources, U.S. Environmental Protection Agency, Ann Arbor, MI.

EPA (U.S. Environmental Protection Agency). 1999c. Additional Flexibility Amendments to Vehicle Inspection Maintenance Program Requirements; Proposed Amendment to the Final Rule. Final Rule. Fed. Regist. 64(161):45491-45500.

EPA (U.S. Environmental Protection Agency). 1999d. Listing of all Operating State I/M Programs Including the Main Program Elements for Each Program. EPA420-B-99-008. Office of Mobile Sources, U.S. Environmental Protection Agency, Ann Arbor, MI. [Online]. Available: http://www.epa.gov/oms/epg/state.htm [June 28, 2001].

EPA (U.S. Environmental Protection Agency). 1999e. MOBILE6 Inspection / Maintenance Benefits Methodology for 1981through 1993 Model Year Light Vehicles. Draft. EPA420-P-99-007. M6 IM 001. Office of Air and Radiation, U.S. Environmental Protection Agency, Washington, DC. March. [Online]. Available: http://www. epa.gov/otaq/m6.htm#docs [June 7, 2001].

EPA (U.S. Environmental Protection Agency). 1999f. Determination of NOx and HC Basic Emission Rates, OBD and I/M Effects for Tier 1 and Later LDVs and LDTs. Draft. EPA420-P-99-009. M6.EXH.007. Office of Air and Radiation, U.S. Environmental Protection Agency, Washington, DC. March. [Online]. Available: http://www.epa.gov/otaq/m6.htm#docs [June 7, 2001].

EPA (U.S. Environmental Protection Agency). 1999g. Inspection/Maintenance in MOBILE6: A Technical Overview. Presentation by Ed Glover, MOBILE6 Workshop, Ann Arbor, MI, June 29, 1999. [Online]. Available: http://www.epa.gov /OMS/models/mobile6/wksp3/m6-pres3.htm [June 21, 2001].

EPA (U.S. Environmental Protection Agency). 1999h. Determination of CO Basic Emission Rates, OBD and I/M Effects for Tier 1 and Later LDVs and LDTs. Draft. EPA420-P-99-017. M6 EXH.009. Office of Air and Radiation, U.S. Environmental

Protection Agency. May. [Online]. Available: http://www.epa.gov/otaq/m6. htm#docs [June 7, 2001].

EPA (U.S. Environmental Protection Agency). 1999i. The Determination of Hot Running Emissions from FTP Bag Emissions. Draft. EPA420-P-99-014. M6 STE 002. Office of Air and Radiation, U.S. Environmental Protection Agency, Washington, DC. [Online]. Available: http://www.epa.gov/otaq/m6.htm#docs [June 7, 2001].

EPA (U.S. Environmental Protection Agency). 1999j. Determination of Start Emissions as a Function of Mileage and Soak Time for 1981-1993 Model Year Light-Duty Vehicles Draft. EPA420-P-99-015. M6 STE 003. Office of Air and Radiation, U.S. Environmental Protection Agency, Washington, DC. [Online]. Available: http://www.epa.gov/otaq/m6.htm#docs [June 7, 2001].

EPA (U.S. Environmental Protection Agency). 1999k. Determination of Running Emissions as a Function of Mileage for 1981-1993 Model Year Light-Duty Cars and Trucks. Draft. EPA420-P-99-010. M6 EXH 001. Office of Air and Radiation, U.S. Environmental Protection Agency, Washington, DC. [Online]. Available: http://www.epa.gov/otaq/m6.htm#docs [June 7, 2001].

EPA (U.S. Environmental Protection Agency). 1999l. Analysis of Emissions Deterioration Using Ohio and Wisconsin IM240 Data. Draft. EPA420-P-99-013. M6 EXH 002. Office of Air and Radiation, U.S. Environmental Protection Agency, Washington, DC. [Online]. Available: http://www.epa.gov/otaq/m6.htm#docs [June 7, 2001].

EPA (U.S. Environmental Protection Agency). 1999m. Recommendations Report. Prepared by the Innovative and Incentive Based Policies Workgroup, Mobile Sources Technical Review Advisory Subcommittee, and presented at the subcommittee quarterly meeting, Alexandria, VA, April 14, 1999. Clean Air Act Advisory Committee, U.S. Environmental Protection Agency, Washington, D.C.

EPA (U.S. Environmental Protection Agency). 2000a. National Air Pollutant Emission Trends, 1900-1998. EPA-454/R-00-002. Office of Air Quality Planning and Standards, U.S. Environmental Protection Agency, Research Triangle Park, NC.

EPA (U.S. Environmental Protection Agency). 2000b. Guidance on Use of Remote Sensing for Evaluation of I/M Program Performance. Draft. EPA-AA-TRPD-IM-00-X. Office of Air and Radiation, U.S. Environmental Protection Agency, Washington, DC.

EPA (U.S. Environmental Protection Agency). 2000c. Amendments to Vehicle Inspection Maintenance Program Requirements Incorporating the On-board Diagnostic Check. Notice of Proposed Rulemaking, Fed. Regist. 65(183):56844-566856.

EPA (U.S. Environmental Protection Agency). 2000d. User Guide to MOBILE6. Mobile Sources Emission Factor Model. Draft. EPA-420-P-00-005. Office of Air and Radiation, U.S. Environmental Protection Agency, Washington, DC. [Online]. Available: http://www.epa.gov/otaq/m6.htm#m6draft [June 7, 2001].

EPA (U.S. Environmental Protection Agency). 2001. Amendments to Vehicle

Inspection Maintenance Program Requirements Incorporating the On-board Diagnostic Check. Final Rule. Fed. Regist. 65(183):56844-566856.

European Commission. 1997. Vehicle Taxation in the European Union 1997. Reference XXI/306/98-EN, Brussels, Belgium. Sept. 8, 1997.

Fujita, E.M., B.E. Croes, C.L. Bennett, D.R. Lawson, F.W. Lurmann, and H.H. Main. 1992. Comparison of emission inventory and ambient concentration ratios of CO, NMOG, and NO$_x$ in California's South Coast Air Basin. J. Air Waste Manage. Assoc. 42(3):264-276.

Fujita, E.M., J.G. Watson, J.C. Chow, N.F. Robinson, L.W. Richards, and N. Kumar. 1998. Northern Front Range Air Quality Study. Volume C: Source Apportionment and Simulation Methods and Evaluation. Final Report. Colorado State University, Fort Collins, CO.

Fujita, E.M., R.E. Keislar, W. Stockwell, D.E. Campbell, P.T. Roberts, T.H. Funk, C.P. McDonald, H.H. Main and L.R. Chinkin. 2000. Weekend/Weekday Ozone Observations in the South Coast Air Basin. Retrospective Analysis of Ambient and Emissions Data and Refinement of Hypotheses. Executive Summary, Final Report to the National Renewable Energy Laboratory [Online]. Available: http://www.arb.ca.gov/aqd/weekendeffect/Fujita_arbwkshp991116/index.htm [June 21, 2001].

Gertler, A.W., J.C. Sagebiel, D.N. Wittorff, W.R. Pierson, W.A. Dippel, D. Freeman, and L. Sheetz. 1997. Vehicle Emissions in Five Urban Tunnels. Desert Research Institute, Nevada University System, Reno.

Glover, E., B. Croy, and B. Hall. 1996. Can Auto Technicians be Trained to Repair IM240 Emission Failures? SAE 960091. Warrendale, PA: Society of Automotive Engineers.

Grimm, R.A., R.J. Bremer, and S.P. Stonestreet. 1980. GM Micro-Computer Engine Control System. SAE 800053. Warrendale, PA: Society of Automotive Engineers.

Guenther, P.L., D.H. Stedman, G.A. Bishop, S.P. Beaton, J.H. Bean and R.W. Quine. 1995. Hydrocarbon detector for the remote sensing of vehicle exhaust emissions. Rev. Sci. Instrum. 66(4):3024-3029.

Gumbleton, J.J., and L.L. Bowler. 1982. General Motors' Computer Command Control-System Development. SAE 820901. Warrendale, PA: Society of Automotive Engineers.

Harrington, W., and V.D. McConnell. 1993. Cost Effectiveness of Remote Sensing of Vehicle Emissions. Pp. 53-75 in Cost Effective Control of Urban Smog, R.F. Kosobud, W.A. Testa, and D.A. Hanson, eds. Federal Reserve Bank of Chicago.

Harrington, W., and V.D. McConnell. 2000. Coase and car repair: Who should be responsible for emissions of vehicles in use? Pp. 201-237 in Property Rights, Economics and the Environment, M. Kaplowitz, ed. Stamford, CT: JAI Press.

Harrington, W., V. McConnell, and M. Cannon. 1998. A Behavioral Analysis of EPA's Mobile Emission Factor Model. DP 98-7. Washington, DC: Resources for the Future.

Harrington, W., V.D. McConnell, and A. Ando. 2000. Are vehicle emission inspection programs living up to expectations? Transp. Res. Part D 5:153-172.

Harvey, G., and E. Deakin. 1993. A Manual of Regional Transportation Modeling Practice for Air Quality Analysis, Version 1.0. National Association of Regional Councils.

Haskew, H.M., and T.F. Liberty. 1999. Diurnal Emissions from In-Use Vehicles. SAE 1999-01-1463. Warrendale, PA: Society of Automotive Engineers.

Haskew H.M., J.J. Gumbleton, and D.P. Garrett. 1987. I/M Effectiveness with Today's Closed Loop Systems. SAE 871103. Warrendale, PA: Society of Automotive Engineers.

Haskew H.M., D.P. Garrett, and J.J. Gumbleton. 1989. GM's Results—The EPA/ Industry Cooperative Test Program. SAE 890185. Warrendale, PA: Society of Automotive Engineers.

Holmes, K.J., and A.G. Russell. 2001. Improving mobile-source emissions modeling. EM (February):20-28.

Hubbard, T.N. 1998. An empirical examination of moral hazard in the vehicle inspection market. RAND J. Econ. 29(2):406-426.

Ihara, K., K. Ohkubo and Y. Nuira. 1987. Thermal Effect on Three-Way Catalyst Deactivation and Improvement. SAE 871192. Warrendale, PA: Society of Automotive Engineers.

IMRC (California Inspection and Maintenance Review Committee). 1993. Evaluation of the Smog Check Program and Recommendations for Program Improvements, 4th Report to the Legislature. California Inspection and Maintenance Review Committee, Sacramento, CA.

IMRC (California Inspection and Maintenance Review Committee). 1995a. An Analysis of the USEPA's 50-Percent Discount for Decentralized I/M Programs. Prepared by J. Schwartz. California Inspection and Maintenance Review Committee, Sacramento, CA. February 24, 1995.

IMRC (California Inspection and Maintenance Review Committee). 1995b. Reply to EPA Summary Response to the California Review Committee Report on I/M Effectiveness. Prepared by J. Schwartz, California Inspection and Maintenance Review Committee, Sacramento, CA. March 20, 1995.

IMRC (California Inspection and Maintenance Review Committee). 2000. Smog Check II Evaluation. California Inspection and Maintenance Review Committee, Sacramento, CA. [Online]. Available: http://www.epa.gov/otaq/im.htm.

Ingalls, M.N., L.R. Smith and R.E. Kirksey. 1989. Measurements of On-Road Vehicle Emission Factors in the California South Coast Air Basin. Vol. 1. Regulated Emissions. PB898220925XSP. Southwest Research Inst., San Antonio, TX. Prepared for the Coordinating Research Council, Atlanta, GA. June.

Jack, M.D., T.P. Bahan, M.N. Gray, J.L. Hanson, T.L. Heidt, F.A. Huerta, D.R. Nelson, A.J. Paneral, J. Peterson, M. Sullivan, G.C. Polchin, R.H. Rubin, and C.B. Tacelli. 1995. Remote and on-Board Instrumentation for Automotive Emissions

Monitoring. SAE 951943. Warrendale, PA: Society of Automotive Engineers.

JAMA (Japan Automobile Manufacturers Association, Inc.). 2000. Motor Vehicle Statistics of Japan. Japan Automobile Manufacturers Association, Inc., Tokyo, Japan. [Online]. Available: http://www.japanauto.com/library/. [May 31, 2001].

Jiménez, J.L. 1998. Understanding and Quantifying Motor Vehicle Emissions with Vehicle Specific Power and TILDAS Remote-Sensing. Ph.D. dissertation. Department of Mechanical Engineering, Massachusetts Institute of Technology, Cambridge, MA.

Jiménez, J.L., M.D. Koplow, D.D. Nelson, M.S. Zahniser, and S.E. Schmidt. 1999. Characterization of on-road vehicle NO emissions by a TILDAS remote sensor. J. Air Waste Manage. Assoc. 49(4):463-470.

Jiménez, J.L., G.J. McRae, D.D. Nelson, M.S. Zahniser, and C.E. Kolb. 2000. Remote sensing of NO and $NO_2$ emissions from heavy-duty diesel trucks using tunable diode lasers. Environ. Sci. Technol. 34(12):2380-2387.

Kirchstetter, T.W., B.C. Singer, R.A. Harley, G.R. Kendall, and W. Chan. 1996. Impact of oxygenated gasoline use on California light-duty vehicle emissions. Environ. Sci. Technol. 30(2):661-670.

Klausmeier, R., and S. Kishan. 1998. Description of the high and low emitter profile models. Memorandum to J. Somers and P. Lorang, U.S. Environmental Protection Agency, from R. Klausmeier, de la Torre Klausmeier Consulting, Austin, TX, and S. Kishan, Radian International, Austin, TX. Feb. 19, 1998. [Online]. Available: http://www.epa.gov/otaq/rsd.htm.

Klausmeier, R., S. Kishan, A. Burnette, and M. Weatherby. 2000. Smog Check Station Performance Analysis Based on Roadside Test Results. Technical Note. Prepared by Eastern Research Group for California Bureau of Automotive Repair Engineering and Research Branch, California Department of Consumer Affairs. [Online]. Available: http://smogcheck.ca.gov/pdfdocs/station_performance.pdf

Kelly, N.A., and P.J. Groblicki. 1993. Real-world emissions from a modern production vehicle driven in Los-Angeles. J. Air Waste Manage. Assoc. 43(10):1351-1357.

Knepper, J. C., W.J. Koehl, J.D. Benson, V.R. Burns, R.A. Gorse Jr., A.M. Hochhauser, W.R. Leppard, L.A. Rapp, and R.M. Reuter. 1993. Fuel Effects in Auto/Oil High Emitting Vehicles. SAE 930137. Warrendale, PA: Society of Automotive Engineers.

Lawson, D.R. 1993. Passing the test—Human behavior and California's Smog Check Program. J. Air Waste Manage. Assoc. 43(12):1567-1575.

Lawson, D.R. 1995. The costs of "M" in I/M—Reflections on inspection/maintenance programs. J. Air Waste Manage. Assoc. 45(6):465-476.

Lawson, D.R., and D. Koracin. 1996. Analysis of the 1995 El Monte I/M Pilot Study Data Set. Pp. 6.9-6.20 in Proceedings of the Sixth CRC On-Road Vehicle Emissions Workshop, San Diego, CA., March 18-20, 1996. Atlanta, GA: Coordinating Research Council.

Lawson, D.R., and R.E. Smith. 1998. The Northern Front Range Air Quality Study, report to the Governor and General Assembly. Fort Collins, CO: Colorado State University, Office of the Vice President for Research and Information Technology,

Cooperative Institute for Research in the Atmosphere. [Online]. Available: http://www.nfraqs.colostate.edu [May 25, 2001].

Lawson, D.R., P.J. Groblicki, D.H. Stedman, G.A. Bishop, and P.L. Guenther. 1990. Emissions from in-use motor vehicles in Los Angeles: A pilot study of remote sensing and the inspection and maintenance program. J. Air Waste Manage. Assoc. 40(8):1096-1105.

Lawson, D.R., P.A. Walsh and P. Switzer. 1995. Effectiveness of U.S. Motor Vehicle Inspection/Maintenance Programs, 1985-1992. Final Report. Prepared for California I/M Review Committee.

Lawson, D.R., P.A. Walsh and P. Switzer. 1996a. Analysis of U.S. Roadside Vehicle Emissions and Tampering Survey Data and Evaluation of Inspection and Maintenance Programs. Final Report. Desert Research Institute, Nevada University System, Reno, NV; Stanford University, CA.

Lawson, D.R., S. Diaz, E.M. Fujita, S.L. Wardenburg, R.E. Keislar, Z. Lu, and D.E. Schorran. 1996b. Program for the Use of Remote Sensing Devices to Detect High-Emitting Vehicles. Final Report. Prepared for South Coast Air Quality Management District by Desert Research Institute, Reno, NV.

Lodder, T.S., and K.B. Livo. 1994. Review and Analysis of the Total Clean Cars Program. Colorado Department of Public Health and Environment, and the Regional Air Quality Council, Denver CO.

Marr, L.C., G.C. Morrison, W.W. Nazaroff and R.A. Harley. 1998. Reducing the risk of accidental death due to vehicle-related carbon monoxide poisoning. J. Air Waste Manage. Assoc. 48(10):899-906.

McClement, D., J.A. Dueck, and B. Hall. 1997. Measurement of Diurnal Evaporative Emissions from In-Use Vehicles. CRC Project E-9. CRC Rep. No. 609, PB99-107286INZ. Prepared by Automotive Testing Labs, Inc., Mesa, AZ, for the Coordinating Research Council, Atlanta, GA.

McClintock, P. 1998. The Colorado Enhanced I/M Program 0.5% Sample Annual Report. Prepared for the Colorado Department of Public Health and Environment, by Remote Sensing Technologies Inc., Tuscon, AR. [Online]. Available: http://www.epa.gov/OMS/models/rsd/denv-rsd.pdf

McClintock, P.M. 1999a. Remote Sensing Measurements of Real World High Exhaust Emitters. NTIS PB99-140378. Prepared by Applied Analysis, Tiburon, CA, and Remote Sensing Technologies, Inc., Tucson, AZ, for the Colorado Department of Public Health and Environment, Denver, CO.

McClintock, P. 1999b. I/M Impact on Dayton Registration Transactions. Memorandum to P. Lorang and L. Platte, EPA OMS, from P McClintock, Applied Analysis. July 5, 1999.

McClintock, P. 1999c. Identifying and Reducing Program Avoidance in Centralized I/M Programs. Presented in Human Dimensions in I/M Programs, National Center for Vehicle Emissions Control and Safety (NCVECS), 15th Annual Mobile Sources/Clean Air Conference, Snowmass Village, CO, Sept. 16, 1999.

McClintock, P. 2000a. OBD-II Testing in I/M Programs. Presentations on OBD II,

National Center for Vehicle Emissions Control and Safety (NCVECS), 16th Annual Mobile Sources/Clean Air Conference, Steamboat Springs, CO, Sept. 19-22, 2000. Online. Available: http://www.obdiicsu.com/ [June 25, 2001].

McClintock, P. 2000b. OBD-II Testing in I/M Programs. Presentation to NESCAUM, October 19th, 2000.

McConnell, V.D. 1990. Costs and benefits of vehicle inspection: A case study of the Maryland Region. J. Environ. Manage. 30(1):1-15.

MECA (Manufacturers of Emission Controls Association). 1999. I/M Implementation Status Report. Prepared by A. Santos. MECA, Washington, DC. [Online]. Available: http://www.meca.org/

NAPA Echlin. 2001a. Training Programs. Dana Engine Controls. http://www. napaechlin.com/cpc7c.htm.

NAPA Echlin. 2001b. Training Programs. Dana Engine Controls. http://www. napaechlin.com/cpc8c.htm.

NARSTO Synthesis Team. 2000. An Assessment of Tropospheric Ozone Pollution—A North American Perspective. [Online]. Available: http://www.cgenv.com/Narsto/ assess.doc.html [May 31, 2001].

Nelson, D.D., M.S. Zahniser, J.B. McManus, C.E. Kolb and J.L. Jiménez. 1998. A tunable diode laser system for the remote sensing of on-road vehicle emissions. Appl. Phys. B Lasers Opt. 67(4):433-441.

NRC (National Research Council). 1998. Research Priorities for Airborne Particulate Matter: I. Immediate Priorities and a Long-Range Research Portfolio. Washington, DC: National Academy Press.

NRC (National Research Council). 1999. Ozone-Forming Potential of Reformulated Gasoline. Washington, DC: National Academy Press.

NRC (National Research Council). 2000. Modeling Mobile Source Emissions. Washington, DC: National Academy Press.

O'Connor, K., E.L. Carr, P.S. Stiefer, S.D. Vu, J.L. Fieber, and B.E. Koenig. 1997. Redesignation Request for the Seven County Minneapolis-St. Paul Carbon Monoxide Nonattainment Area. Final Technical Support Document. SYSAPP-97/43. Prepared by Systems Applications International, Inc. San Rafael, CA, for Minnesota Pollution Control Agency, St Paul, MN.

Pierson, W.R. 1996. Motor vehicle inspection and maintenance programs—How effective are they? Atmos. Environ. 30(21):i-iii.

Pierson, W.R., A.W. Gertler and R.L. Bradow. 1990. Comparison of the SCAQS Tunnel Study with other on-road vehicle emission data. J. Air Waste Manage. Assoc. 40(11):1495-1504.

Pierson, W.R., D.E. Schorran, E.M. Fujita, J.C. Sagebiel, D.R. Lawson, and R.L. Tanner. 1999. Assessment of nontailpipe hydrocarbon emissions from motor vehicles. J. Air Waste Manage. Assoc. 49(5):498-519.

Pokharel, SS., G.A. Bishop, and D.H. Stedman. 2000. On-Road Remote Sensing of Automobile Emissions in the Chicago Area: Year 3. Department of Chemistry and Biochemistry, University of Denver, Denver, CO. Contract No, E-23-4. Prepared for

Coordinating Research Council, Inc., Alpharetta, GA. [Online]. Available: http://www.crcao.com. [May 22, 2001].

Pollack, A.K., P. Bhave, J. Heiken, K. Lee, S. Shepard, C.Tran, G. Yarwood, R.F. Sawyer, and B.A. Joy. 1999. Investigation of Emission Factors in the California EMFAC7G Model. Prepared by ENVIRON International Corp., Novato, CA, for Coordinating Research Council, Inc., Atlanta, GA. NTIS PB99-149718INZ.

Popp, P.J. 1999. Remote Sensing of Nitric Oxide Emissions from Planes, Trains and Automobiles. Ph.D. Dissertation. Department of Chemistry and Biochemistry. University of Denver.

Popp, P.J., S.S. Pokharel, G.A. Bishop, and D.H. Stedman. 1999a. On-Road Remote Sensing of Automobile Emissions in the Denver Area: Year 1. Department of Chemistry and Biochemistry, University of Denver, Denver, CO. CRC Project No. E-23-4-99 Prepared for Coordinating Research Council, Inc., Atlanta, GA. [Online]. Available: http://www.crcao.com. [May 22, 2001].

Popp, P.J., G.A. Bishop, and D.H. Stedman. 1999b. Development of a high-speed ultraviolet spectrometer for remote sensing of mobile source nitric oxide emissions. J. Air Waste Manage. Assoc. 49(12):1463-1468.

Pun, B.K., C. Seigneur, and W. White. 2000. Data Analysis for a Better Understanding of the Weekday/Weekend Ozone and PM Differences. Draft final report. Prepared for Coordinating Research Council, Alpharetta, GA, by Atmospheric and Environmental Research, Inc., San Ramon, CA and Washington University, St. Louis, MO.

Rajan, S.C. 1996. Diagnosis and repair of excessively emitting vehicles. J. Air Waste Manage. Assoc. 46(10):940-952.

Regional Air Quality Council. 2000. Options to Reform the Current I/M Program, Report to the Governor, General Assembly, and the Air Quality Control Commission, Denver, Colorado. August 30, 2000. [Online]. Available: http://www.raqc.org/reports.htm

Rodgers, M. 2000. I/M Analysis. Presented at the workshop of the Committee to Review the Effectiveness of Vehicle Emission Inspection and Maintenance Programs. Irvine, CA, Feb. 15, 2000.

Rothman, E.D. 1998. Assessment of the Report "Development of a Proposed Procedure for Determining the Equivalency of Alternative Inspection and Maintenance Programs." Center for Statistical Consultation and Research, University of Michigan, Ann Arbor, MI. [Online]. Available: http://www.epa.gov/OMS/regs/im/imreadme.htm. [May 29, 2001].

Sawyer, R.F., R.A. Harley, S.H. Cadle, J.M. Norbeck, R. Slott and H.A. Bravo. 2000. Mobile sources critical review: 1998 NARSTO assessment. Atmos. Environ. 34(12-14):2161-2181.

Scherrer, H.C. and D.B. Kittelson. 1994. I/M Effectiveness as Directly Measured by Ambient CO Data. SAE 940302. Warrendale, PA: Society of Automotive Engineers.

Sierra Research. 1994a. Investigation of MOBILE 5a Emission Factors. Evaluation of

IM240-to-FTP Correlation and Base Emission Rate Equations. Report No. SR94-06-04. Prepared for American Petroleum Institute by Sierra Research, Inc., Sacramento, CA.

Sierra Research. 1994b. The Cost-Effectiveness of Further Regulating Mobile Source Emissions. Report No. 94-02-04. Prepared for American Automobile Manufacturers Association by Sierra Research, Inc., Sacramento, CA, and Charles River Association.

Sierra Research. 1997. Development of a Proposed Procedure for Determining the Equivalency of Alternative Inspection and Maintenance Programs. Report No. SR97-11-02. Prepared for the U.S. Environmental Protection Agency, Regional and State Programs Division, by Sierra Research, Inc., Sacramento, CA. [Online]. Available: http://www.epa.gov/OMS/regs/im/imreadme.htm [May 30, 2001].

Singer, B.C., and R.A. Harley. 1996. A fuel-based motor vehicle emission inventory. J. Air Waste Manage. Assoc. 46(6):581-593.

Singer, B.C., and R.A. Harley. 2000. A fuel-based inventory of motor vehicle exhaust emissions in the Los Angeles area during summer 1997. Atmos. Environ. 34(11):1783-1795.

Singer, B.C., R.A. Harley, D. Littlejohn, J. Ho, and T. Vo. 1998. Scaling of infrared remote sensor hydrocarbon measurements for motor vehicle emission inventory calculations. Environ. Sci. Technol. 32(21):3241-3248.

Slott, R.S. 1994. Economic incentives and inspection and maintenance programs. Pp. 115-135 in New Partnerships: Economic Incentives for Environmental Management. Proceedings of an International Specialty Conference, Rochester, NY, Nov. 3-4, 1993. Air and Waste Management Association, Pittsburgh, PA.

Small, K.A. 1992. Urban Transportation Economics. Chur, Switzerland: Harwood Academic.

Small, K.A., and C. Kazami. 1995. On the costs of air pollution from motor vehicles. J. Transp. Econ. Policy 29(1):7-32.

South Coast Air Quality Management District. 2000. Multiple Air Toxics Exposure Study in the South Coast Air Basin. South Coast Air Quality Management District, Diamond Bar, CA. [Online]. Available: http://www.aqmd.gov/matesiidf/matestoc.htm [June 7, 2001].

St. Denis, M.J., P. Cicero-Fernandez, A.M. Winer, J,W, Butler and G. Jesion. 1994. Effects of in-use driving conditions and vehicle/engine operating parameters on "off-cycle" events: Comparison with federal test procedure conditions. J. Air Waste Manage. Assoc. 44(1):31-38.

Stedman, D.H. 1989. Automobile carbon monoxide emission. Environ. Sci. Technol. 23(2):147-148.

Stedman, D.H., G.A. Bishop, and M.L. Pitchford. 1991. Evaluation of a Remote Sensor for Mobile Source CO Emissions. EPA 600/4-90/032. Prepared by the Department of Chemistry, University of Denver, CO, for the Environmental Monitoring Systems Laboratory, Las Vegas, NV.

Stedman, D.H., G.A. Bishop, S.P. Beaton, J.E. Peterson, P.L. Guenther, I.F. McVey, and Y. Zhang. 1994. On-Road Remote Sensing of CO and HC Emissions in California. Final Report. Prepared by the Department of Chemistry, University of Denver, Denver, CO, for the California Air Resources Board, Sacramento, CA.

Stedman, D.H., G.A. Bishop, P. Aldrete, and R.S. Slott. 1997. On-road evaluation of an automobile emission test program. Environ. Sci. Technol. 31:927-931.

Stedman, D.H., G.A. Bishop, and R.S. Slott. 1998. The use of remote sensing measurements to evaluate control strategies: Measurements at the end of the first and second year of Colorado's biennial enhanced I/M program. Pp. 6.15-6.24 in Proceedings of the 8th CRC On-Road Vehicle Emissions Workshop, San Diego, CA, April 20-22, 1998, Vol.1. Coordinating Research Council, Inc., Atlanta, GA.

Stephens, R.D., and S.H. Cadle. 1991. Remote sensing measurements of carbon monoxide emissions from on-road vehicles. J. Air Waste Manage. Assoc. 41(1):39-46.

Stephens, R.D., M.T. Giles, P.J. Groblicki, R.A. Gorse, K.J. McAlinden, D.B. Hoffman, R. James, and S. Smith. 1995. Real-world emissions variability as measured by remote sensors. SAE 940582. Pp. 243-250 in Auto/Oil Air Quality Improvement Research Program, SAE SP-117. Warrendale, PA: Society of Automotive Engineers.

Stephens, R.D. P.A. Mulawa, M.T. Giles, K.G. Kennedy, P.J. Groblicki, S.H. Cadle, and K.T. Knapp. 1996. An experimental evaluation of remote sensing-based hydrocarbon measurements: A comparison to FID measurements. J. Air Waste Manage. Assoc. 46(2):148-158.

U.S. Congress. 1995. Hearings before the Subcommittee on Oversight and Investigations of the Committee on Commerce, House of Representatives: 104th Congress, First Session on Inspection and Maintenance Programs. Clean Air Act Amendments, Serial No. 104-16. March 23-24. Washington, DC: U.S. Government Printing Office.

U.S. Department of Transportation. 1997. NPTS User's Guide for the Public Data Files 1995 Nationwide Personal Transportation Survey. [Online]. Available: http://www-cta.ornl.gov/npts/1995/doc/index.shtml [June 29, 2001].

Walsh, P.A. and A.W. Gertler. 1997. Texas 1996 Remote Sensing Feasibility Study. Final Report. Prepared for Texas Natural Resource Conservation Commission, by Desert Research Institute, Energy and Environmental Engineering Center, Reno, NV.

Watson, J.G., E. Fujita, J.C. Chow, B. Zielinska, L. W. Richards, W. Neff, and D. Dietrich. 1998. Northern Front Range Air Quality Study. Final Report. DRI 6580-685-8750.1F2. Prepared for the Office of the Vice President for Research and Information Technology, Colorado State University, Fort Collins, CO. [Online]. Available: http://www.nfraqs.colostate.edu. [May 25, 2001].

Watson, J.G., J.C. Chow, and E.M Fujita. 2001. Review of volatile organic compound source apportionment by chemical mass balance. Atmos. Environ. 35(9):1567-1584.

Wayne, L.G., and Y. Horie. 1983. Evaluation of CARB's In-Use Vehicle Surveillance

Program. CARB Contract No. A2-043-32. Prepared by Pacific Environmental Services, Inc., for California Air Resources Board, Sacramento, CA.

Wenzel, T. 1997. I/M Failure Rates by Vehicle Model. Paper presented at the 7th CRC On-Road Vehicle Emissions Workshop, San Diego, CA. April 1999.

Wenzel, T. 1999a. Evaluation of Arizona's Enhanced I/M Program. Presentation at the Ninth Road Vehicle Emissions Workshop, San Diego, CA, April 21, 1999. [Online]. Available: http://enduse.lbl.gov/projects/vehicles/Evaluation.html [May 30, 2001].

Wenzel, T. 1999b. Evaluation of Arizona's Enhanced I/M Program. Presentation to the NRC Committee to Review the MOBILE Model, March 4, 1999. [Online]. Available: http://enduse.lbl.gov/projects/vehicles/Evaluation.html [May 30, 2001].

Wenzel, T. In press. Evaluating the long-term effectiveness of the Phoenix IM240 program. Environ. Sci. Policy (2001).

Wenzel, T.P., and M. Ross. 1996. Emissions from Modern Passenger Cars With Malfunctioning Emissions Controls. SAE 960067. Warrendale, PA: Society of Automotive Engineers.

Wenzel. T., and R. Sawyer. 1998. Review of Sierra Research Report "Development of a Proposed Procedure for Determining the Equivalency of Alternative Inspection and Maintenance Programs." Lawrence Berkeley National Laboratory, Berkeley, CA. [Online]. Available: http://www.epa.gov/OMS/regs/im/imreadme.htm [May 30, 2001].

Wenzel, T., B.C. Singer, and R.S. Slott. 2000. Some issues in the statistical analysis of vehicle emissions. J. Transp. Stat. 3(2):1-14.

Wrona, N. 1999. Questions Concerning the State's Remote Sensing Program. Draft. Memorandum to Herschella Horton, Assistant House Minority Leader, and John Loredo, House Minority Whip, from Nancy Wrona, Director, Air Quality Division, Arizona Department of Environmental Quality. Nov. 3, 1999.

Yanowitz, J., M.S. Graboski, L.B. Ryan, T.L. Alleman, and R.L. McCormick. 1999. Chassis dynamometer study of emissions from 21 in-use heavy-duty diesel vehicles. Environ. Sci. Technol. 33(2):209-216.

Young, H.P., N. Okada, and T. Hashimoto. 1982. Cost allocation in water resources development. Water Resour. Res. 18(3):463-475.

Zhang, Y., D.H. Stedman, G.A. Bishop, P.L. Guenther, S.P. Beaton, and J.E. Peterson. 1993. On-road hydrocarbon remote sensing in the Denver area. Environ. Sci. Technol. 27(9):1885-1891.

Zhang, Y., D.H. Stedman, G.A. Bishop, S.P Beaton, P.L. Guenther, and I.F. McVey. 1996a. Enhancement of remote sensing for mobile source nitric oxide. J. Air Waste Manage. Assoc. 46(1):25-29.

Zhang, Y., D.H. Stedman, G.A. Bishop, S.P. Beaton, and P.L. Guenther. 1996b. On-road evaluation of inspection/maintenance effectiveness. Environ. Sci. Technol. 30(5):1445-1450.

# Glossary[1]

**Air/fuel (A/F) ratio**—The ratio, by weight, of air to gasoline entering the intake in a gasoline engine. The ideal (stoichiometric) ratio for complete combustion is approximately 14.7 parts of gasoline to 1 part of fuel, depending on the composition of the specific fuel.

**Air-quality model**—A computer-based mathematical model used to predict air quality based upon emissions and the effects of the transport, dispersion, and transformation of compounds emitted into the air.

**Ambient air**—The air outside of structures. Often used interchangeably with "outdoor air."

**BAR97**—The name for the test and equipment used in the California Enhanced Smog Check program. The BAR97 test is a *steady state, loaded-mode* emissions test. "Loaded-mode" refers to the fact that the test is run on a treadmill-like device called a *dynamometer,* which simulates actual driving with the engine in gear. "Steady state" refers to the fact that the car drives under a constant load throughout the test.

---

[1]Sources: California Air Resources Board at www.arb.ca.gov/html/gloss.htm; Davis 1997; EPA at www.epa.gov /otaq/epg/keyterm.htm; EPA at www.epa.gov/oar/ oaqps/peg_caa/pegcaa10.html; EPA at www.epa.gov/oms/stds-ld.htm; Harvey and Deakin 1993; IMRC 2000.

**California Air Resources Board (CARB)**—A part of the California Environmental Protection Agency whose mission it is to promote and protect public health, welfare and ecological resources through the effective and efficient reduction of air pollutants while recognizing and considering the effects on the economy of the state.

**California Inspection and Maintenance Review Committee (IMRC)**—An advisory committee created to evaluate and recommend improvements for the California Smog Check I/M program.

**Carbon monoxide (CO)**—A colorless, odorless poisonous gas resulting from the incomplete combustion of hydrocarbon fuels.

**Clean Air Act (CAA)**—The original Clean Air Act was passed in 1963, but our national air pollution control program is actually based on the 1970 version of the law. The 1990 Clean Air Act Amendments (CAAA90) are the most recent and far-reaching revisions of the 1970 law.

**Clean screening**—The use of methods such as remote sensing measurements or vehicle profiling by states to excuse cars from a scheduled inspection and maintenance (I/M) emissions test.

**Closed-loop fuel control**—A fuel metering system that uses feedback for more effective emissions control. The air/fuel ratio of a contemporary vehicle is "closed-loop," using a sensor in the exhaust to evaluate the mixture exiting the engine, and adjusting the air/fuel ratio through the use of an on-board computer to optimize emissions performance.

**Cold-start emissions**—Tailpipe emissions that occur before a vehicle is fully warmed up. Vehicle emissions are higher during the first few minutes of operation, because the engine and the catalytic converter must come to operating temperature before they can become effective.

**Conformity (transportation conformity)**—A process to demonstrate whether a federally supported activity is consistent with the air quality goals in State Implementation Plans (SIPs). Transportation conformity demonstrates that plans, programs, and projects approved or funded by the Federal Highway Administration, or the Federal Transit Administration for regionally-significant projects do not create new violations, increase the frequency or severity of existing violations, or delay timely attainment of NAAQS. General conformity refers to projects approved or funded by other federal agencies.

**Criteria air pollutants**—A group of six common air pollutants (CO, lead, nitrogen dioxide, ozone, particulate matter, and sulfur dioxide) regulated by the Federal Government since the passage of the Clean Air Act in 1970 on the basis of information on health and/or environmental effects of each pollutant.

**Cutpoint**—For each pollutant, the emissions level above which a car is considered to have failed the emissions test for that pollutant.

**Data link connector**—The connector where the scan tool interfaces with a vehicle's OBD system. Also know as the diagnostic link connector.

**Diagnostic trouble codes**—Codes stored in the engine's computer that identify emission control systems and/or components that are malfunctioning and can be retrieved using a scan tool..

**Dynamometer**—A treadmill-like machine that allows cars to be tested under the loads typical of on-road driving.

**Emissions budget**—Allowable emissions levels identified as part of a state implementation plan for pollutants emitted from mobile, industrial, stationary, and area sources. These emissions levels are used for meeting emission reduction milestones, attainment, or maintenance demonstrations.

**Emissions factor**—The predicted ratio of the amount of pollution produced to the amount of raw material processed or burned, or of the amount of pollution produced to the activity level. By using the emission factor of a pollutant and data regarding quantities of materials used by a given source or the activity level of a given source, it is possible to compute emissions for the source. In the case of mobile source emissions, estimated emissions are the product of an emission factor in mass of pollutant per unit distance (e.g., grams per mile) and an activity estimate in distance (e.g., average miles traveled). In the case of stationary source emissions, estimated emissions are the product of an emission factor in mass of pollutant per unit energy (e.g., pounds per million Btu) and the amount of energy consumed.

**Emissions inventory**—Estimates of the amount of pollutants emitted into the atmosphere from major mobile, stationary, area-wide, and natural source categories over a specific period of time such as a day or a year.

**Environmental Protection Agency (EPA)**—The federal government agency that establishes regulations and oversees the enforcement of laws related to the environment.

**Exceedance**—An air pollution event in which the ambient concentration of a pollutant exceeds a National Ambient Air Quality Standard (NAAQS).

**Evaporative emissions**—Hydrocarbon emissions that do not come from the tailpipe of a car. Evaporative emissions can come from evaporation, permeation, seepage, and leaks in a car's fueling system. Often used interchangeably with *non-tailpipe emissions*.

**Fast pass**—Fast pass is a process that recognizes very clean cars early in the IM240 test cycle and passes them without the need to complete the full test.

**Federal Test Procedure (FTP)**—A certification test for measuring the tailpipe and evaporative emissions from new vehicles over the Urban Dynamometer Driving Schedule, which attempts to simulate an urban driving cycle.

**Gross vehicle weight rating (GVWR)**—The value specified by the manufacturer as the maximum design loaded weight of a vehicle (i.e., vehicle weight plus rated cargo capacity).

**Heavy-duty vehicle (HDV)**—Any motor vehicle rated at more than 8,500 pounds gross vehicle weight (GVWR) or that has a vehicle curb weight of more than 6,000 pounds or that has a basic vehicle frontal area in excess of 45 square feet. This excludes vehicles that will be classified as medium-duty passenger vehicles for the purposes of the Tier 2 emissions standards.

**Heavy-duty diesel vehicle (HDDV)**—An HDV using diesel fuel.

**Hydrocarbon (HC)**—Organic compounds containing various combinations of hydrogen and carbon. See Appendix B for details of how HC relates to other terms, such as volatile organic compounds (VOC), used to describe organic compounds.

**IM240**—The name for the emissions test used in some I/M programs including those in Arizona and Colorado. The IM240 is a *transient, loaded-mode* emissions test. "Loaded-mode" refers to the fact that the test is run on a treadmill-like device called a *dynamometer*, which simulates driving with the engine in gear. "Transient" refers to the fact that the car drives under a load that varies from second to second during the test. The "240" in IM240 indicates that the test lasts for 240 seconds. The IM240 is intended by EPA to be a shortened version of part of the FTP and to correlate well with the FTP.

**Light-duty vehicle (LDV)**—A passenger car or passenger car derivative capable of seating 12 or fewer passengers. All vehicles and trucks under 8,500 GVWR are included (this limit previously was 6,000 pounds). Small pick-up trucks, vans, and sport utility vehicles may be included.

**Loaded-mode emissions test**—An emissions test performed with the engine in gear.

**Malfunction indicator light (MIL)**—The instrument panel light used by the on-board diagnostic (OBD) system to notify the vehicle operator of an emissions related fault. The MIL is also known as the "service engine soon" or "check engine" lamp.

**Medium-duty passenger vehicle (MDPV)**—A new class of vehicles introduced with the Tier 2 emissions standards that includes sport utility vehicles and passenger vans rated at 8,5000 to 10,000 GVWR.

**Metropolitan Planning Organization (MPO)**—The organized entity designated by law with lead responsibilities for developing transportation plans and programs for urbanized areas with populations of 50,000 or more people. MPOs are established by agreement of the governor and units of general purpose local government, which together represent 75% of the affected population of an urbanized area.

**Model year**—Vehicles are certified for sale, marketed, and later registered as a certain model year that indicates the year a vehicle was produced and offered for sale. Model years typically began in September or October of the prior year and ran for roughly 12 months. In the last decade, certain vehicles have been introduced as a "pull-ahead" vehicle, appearing as early as January of the year.

**National low-emissions vehicle (NLEV)**—A vehicle that meets voluntary low-emissions tailpipe standards that are more stringent than can be mandated by EPA prior to model-year 2004. The NLEV program introduces low-emissions cars and light-duty trucks into the Northeast beginning in model-year 1999 and the rest of the country in model-year 2001.

**National Ambient Air Quality Standards (NAAQS)**—Standards set by EPA for the maximum levels of criteria air pollutants that can exist in the outdoor air without unacceptable effects on human health or the public welfare.

**Nonattainment area**—A geographic area in which the level of a criteria air pollutant is higher than the level allowed by the federal standards. A single geographic area may have acceptable levels of one criteria air pollutant but unacceptable levels of one or more other criteria; thus, an area can be both an attainment area and a nonattainment area at the same time.

**Nitrogen oxides (oxides of nitrogen, $NO_x$)**—A general term referring to nitric oxide (NO), and nitrogen dioxide ($NO_2$). Nitrogen oxides are formed when air is raised to high temperatures, such as during combustion or lightning, and are major contributors to ozone formation and acid deposition.

**On-board diagnostic (OBD) systems**—Devices incorporated into the computers of new motor vehicles to monitor the performance of the emission controls. The computer triggers a dashboard indicator light, referred to as a malfunction indicator light, when the controls malfunction, alerting the driver to seek maintenance for the vehicle. The system also communicates its findings to repair technicians by means of diagnostic trouble codes, which can be downloaded from the vehicle's computer. OBD systems do not measure emissions.

**On-board diagnostic generation one (OBDI) systems**—An on-board automotive diagnostic system required by the California Air Resources Board since 1988. The OBDI uses the microprocessor and sensors to monitor and control various engine system functions.

**On-board diagnostic generation two (OBDII) systems**—OBDII expands upon OBDI to include emissions system and sensor deterioration monitoring.

**Open-loop fuel control**—A system in which the air/fuel mixture is preset by design and contains no feedback correction signal to optimize fuel metering for emissions control (see also "Closed-loop fuel control").

**Oxygen Sensor**—A sensor placed in the exhaust that measures exhaust oxygen content. Typically, there are oxygen sensors before and after the catalytic converter.

**Oxygenated gasoline (oxyfuel)**—Gasoline containing oxygenates, typically methyl tertiary-butyl ether (MTBE) or ethanol, intended to reduce production of CO, a criteria air pollutant. In some parts of the country, CO emissions from cars makes a major contribution to pollution. In some of these areas, gasoline refiners must market oxygenated fuels, which typically contain 2-3% oxygen by weight.

**Oxygenates**—Compounds containing oxygen (alcohols and ethers) that are added to gasoline to increase its oxygen content. MTBE and ethanol are the most common oxygenates currently used, although a number of others are available.

**Ozone**—A reactive gas whose molecules contain three oxygen atoms. It is a product of photochemical processes involving sunlight and ozone precursors, such as HC and $NO_x$. Ozone exists in the upper atmosphere (stratospheric ozone) where it helps shield the earth from excessive ultraviolet rays, as well as in the lower atmosphere near the earth's surface (tropospheric ozone). Tropospheric ozone causes plant damage and adverse health effects and is a criteria air pollutant. Tropospheric ozone is a major component of smog.

**Particulate matter (PM)**—Any material, except uncombined water, that exists in the solid or liquid states in the atmosphere. The size of particulate matter can vary from coarse, wind-blown dust particles to fine particles directly emitted as combustion products or formed through secondary reactions in the atmosphere.

**Photochemical reaction**—A term referring to a chemical reaction brought about by the light of the sun. The formation of ozone from $NO_x$ and HC in the presence of sunlight involves photochemical reactions.

**Ping-pong**—Colloquial term to describe the case where a car fails its emissions test at a testing facility, is repaired at a repair facility, goes back to the testing facility for retesting, and fails again.

**PM-2.5**—A subset of particulate matter that includes fine particles with an aerodynamic diameter less than or equal to a nominal 2.5 micrometers. This fraction of particulate matter penetrates most deeply into the lungs and causes the majority of visibility reduction.

**PM-10**—A major air pollutant consisting of small particles with an aerodynamic diameter less than or equal to a nominal 10 micrometers (about one-seventh the diameter of a single human hair). Their small size allows them to make their way to the air sacs deep within the lungs where they may be deposited and result in adverse health effects. PM-10 also causes visibility reduction.

**Preconditioning**—Preconditioning refers to a set of steps followed to warm up a vehicle prior to the emission test. Cutpoints, which determine passing or failing for such a vehicle, are based on testing a fully warmed-up vehicle in which the emissions control equipment, including the catalytic converter, are hot and fully functional. If an owner drives a short distance to the test station or if the vehicle has to wait in the test station for a long time, the vehicle may not be fully warmed up. This may result in a false reading: a car that would have passed if fully warmed (i.e., fully preconditioned) would fail.

**Primary standard**—A NAAQS for criteria air pollutants based on health effects.

**Reformulated gasoline (RFG)**—Specifically formulated fuel blended such that, on average, the exhaust and evaporative emissions of VOCs and hazardous air pollutants (chiefly benzene, 1,3-butadiene, polycyclic aromatic HC, formaldehyde, and acetaldehyde) resulting from RFG use in motor vehicles might be significantly and consistently lower than such emissions resulting from use of conventional gasolines. The 1990 Clean Air Act Amendments requires sale of reformulated gasoline in the nine areas with the most severe ozone pollution problems. RFG contains, on average, a minimum of 2.0 weight percent oxygen.

**Remote sensing**—A method for measuring pollution levels in a vehicle's exhaust while the vehicle is traveling on the road. Remote-sensing systems use infrared absorption to measure HC and CO emissions relative to carbon dioxide. These systems typically operate by continuously projecting a beam of infrared radiation across a roadway and measuring the exhaust plume after a vehicle passes through the beam.

**Scan tool**—A hand-held computer that is plugged into a vehicle's data link connector allowing a technician to read diagnostic trouble codes, readiness status, and other information collected by the OBD system.

**Secondary particle**—Particulate matter that is formed in the atmosphere and generally composed of such species as ammonium ions or the products of atmospheric chemical reactions, such as nitrates, sulfates, and organic material. Secondary particles are distinguished from primary particles, which are emitted directly into the atmosphere.

**Secondary standard**—A NAAQS for criteria air pollutants based on environmental effects, such as damage to property, plants, and visibility.

**Speed-correction factor (SCF)**—Factors used in the MOBILE model to adjust emissions factors from the average speed used in the Federal Test Procedure (used to obtain emissions data) to other average speeds driven by vehicles in the geographical area being modeled.

**Supplemental Federal Test Procedure (SFTP)**—The SFTP is a certification test for measuring the tailpipe and evaporative emissions from new vehicles. Two driving cycles not represented in the FTP are a test cycle that simulates high-speed and high-acceleration driving (US06 cycle) and a test cycle that evaluates the effects of air-conditioner operation (SC03 cycle).

**State implementation plan (SIP)**—A detailed description of the programs a state will use to carry out its responsibilities under the Clean Air Act for complying with the NAAQS. SIPs are a collection of the programs used by a state to reduce air pollution. The Clean Air Act requires that EPA approve each SIP. The public is given opportunities to participate in the review and approval of SIPs.

**Steady-state emission test**—An emissions test performed under one stable operating condition, such as testing when a vehicle is at idle or under a constant engine load.

**Tampering**—The malfunctioning of one or more emissions-control devices due to either deliberate disablement or mechanical failure.

**Three-way catalytic converter**—A catalytic converter designed to both oxidize CO and HC and reduce $NO_x$ emissions from gasoline-fueled vehicles.

**Tier 0 vehicles**—Vehicles that meet Tier 0 tailpipe standards. For light-duty vehicles, these tailpipe standards began with model-year 1981 and were phased out in model-year 1995 for passenger cars and most light-duty trucks.

**Tier 1 vehicles**—Vehicles that meet Tier 1 tailpipe standards. For light-duty vehicles, these tailpipe standards began with model-year 1994.

**Tier 2 vehicles**—Vehicles that will meet Tier 2 tailpipe standards. For light-duty vehicles, these standards would not begin until model-year 2004.

**Transient emission test**—An emissions test performed under a load that varies from moment to moment during the test.

**Two-way catalytic converter**—A first-generation catalytic converter designed to oxidize CO and HC emissions from gasoline-fueled vehicles.

**Vehicle miles traveled (VMT)**—The number of miles driven by a fleet of vehicles over a set period of time, such as a day, month, or year.

**Zero emissions vehicle (ZEV)**—A vehicle that produces no emissions from the on-board source of power, e.g., an electric vehicle.

# Appendixes

# Appendix A

# Biographical Information on the Committee on Vehicle Emission Inspection and Maintenance Programs

**Ralph J. Cicerone** *(Chair)* is the chancellor of the University of California at Irvine and the Daniel G. Aldrich Professor in the Department of Earth System Science and the Department of Chemistry. He is also a member of the National Academy of Sciences. His areas of research include the study of atmospheric and human processes important in stratospheric ozone depletion and global climate change. Dr. Cicerone received his B.S. from the Massachusetts Institute of Technology and his M.S. and Ph.D. from the University of Illinois.

**David T. Allen** *(Vice-Chair)* is the Reese Professor in Chemical Engineering and the Director of the Center for Energy and Environmental Resources at the University of Texas at Austin. He conducts research in atmospheric chemistry, emissions inventory development, and air-quality modeling. Dr. Allen received his B.S. from Cornell University and his M.S. and Ph.D. from the California Institute of Technology.

**Matthew J. Barth** is an associate professor at the Center for Environmental Research and Technology of the College of Engineering at the University of California at Riverside. He is the manager of transportation systems research and is currently principal investigator on several transportation and emissions modeling programs, including the development of a comprehensive emissions model. He received his M.S. and Ph.D. degrees in electrical and computer engineering from the University of California at Santa Barbara.

**Hugh Ellis** is chair of the Department of Geography and Environmental Engineering at The Johns Hopkins University in Baltimore and holds a joint appointment in the Department of Environmental Health Sciences. His research interests focus on the development of uncertainty and risk-based approaches for environmental management, including the use of such techniques for assessing emissions-control policies. He received his B.S., M.S., and Ph.D. degrees in civil engineering from The University of Waterloo in Ontario, Canada.

**Gerald Gallagher** is president of J Gallagher and Associates. Previously, he served as manager of the Mobile Sources Program for the Air Pollution Control Division of the Colorado Department of Public Health and Environment. His responsibilities included the operation of a metrowide inspection and maintenance program, consisting of approximately 1.8 million inspections per year for gasoline and diesel vehicles. In addition, he was an assistant professor at Colorado State University, where he assisted in the formation of the National Center for Vehicle Emissions Control and Safety. Dr. Gallagher received his B.S. from Northern Illinois University, his M.E. from Colorado State University, and his Ph.D. from the University of Colorado.

**Deborah Gordon** is a transportation consultant. Previously, she was the director of the Project on Transportation and the Environment at the Yale School of Forestry and Environmental Studies in the university's Center for Transportation and the Environment, which provides technical and policy expertise on transportation policy to corporations, state agencies, nonprofit organizations, and the news media. She also served as the director of transportation and energy programs with the Union of Concerned Scientists, where she developed transportation policies such as the clean-car incentive program. She earned a B.S. in chemical engineering from the University of Colorado and an M.P.P. from the University of California at Berkeley.

**Robert A. Harley** is an associate professor in the Civil and Environmental Engineering Department of the University of California at Berkeley. He studies the sources, atmospheric transport, and photochemical reactions associated with air pollution with a special interest in the role of mobile sources (especially gasoline- and diesel-powered vehicles) in these issues. Dr. Harley directs research on air quality modeling, motor vehicle emissions characteristics, and the impact of reformulated gasolines on emissions. He received his Ph.D. in environmental engineering science from the California Institute of Technology.

**Harold Haskew** is president of Harold Haskew and Associates. Prior to that, Mr. Haskew spent 42 years at General Motors Corporation where he directed many automotive emissions testing programs and was involved with regulatory issues. His work at General Motors included comprehensive studies on vehicle emissions controls, the durability of control systems in actual use, and the ability of short-duration tests to identify problems in control systems. He holds a B.M.E. from the General Motors Institute.

**Douglas R. Lawson** is a principal scientist at the National Renewable Energy Laboratory (NREL) where he heads the Environmental Science and Health Effects Program. Before joining NREL, Dr. Lawson was the technical project manager for the Northern Front Range Study at Colorado State University, a program designed to identify the sources of urban air pollutants in the Denver metropolitan area. He has also been involved in programs to assess motor vehicle inspection and maintenance programs as well as those to identify and repair high-emitting vehicles. Dr. Lawson received his Ph.D. in chemical oceanography from Florida State University.

**Virginia McConnell** is a senior fellow in the Quality of the Environment Division of Resources for the Future (RFF). She is also a professor of economics at the University of Maryland, Baltimore County. Her recent work has centered on the evaluation of policies to reduce motor vehicle pollution, including the analysis of inspection and maintenance programs, old-car scrap programs, and emissions taxes. She has also analyzed the impact of environmental regulations on industry productivity and on facility-location decisions. She received her B.S. in economics from Smith College and her Ph.D. in economics from the University of Maryland.

**Alison K. Pollack** is a principal at ENVIRON Corporation, an environmental consulting firm. Her work is in the analysis of mobile source emissions data, the evaluation of mobile source control programs, and the development and evaluation of on-road and off-road mobile source emissions models. Ms. Pollack received her B.S. and M.S. degrees from Princeton University and the University of Wisconsin-Madison, respectively.

**Robert Slott** is a visiting engineer at Energy Laboratory of the Massachusetts Institute of Technology. Prior to that, Mr. Slott spent 34 years at Shell Oil Company. He retired as its technology planning director in 1997. His research interests include measuring the effectiveness of vehicle emissions-control strategies, including the assessment of inspection and maintenance programs. He earned his B.S., M.S., and Sc.D. in chemical engineering from the Massachusetts Institute of Technology.

# Appendix B

# Abbreviations and Names Used for Classifying Organic Compounds

| Common Abbreviation | Full Name | Definition |
|---|---|---|
| VOC[a] | Volatile organic compound | Organic compounds that are found in the gas phase at ambient conditions; might not include methane |
| ROG | Reactive organic gas | Organic compounds that are assumed to be reactive at urban (and possibly regional) scales; by definition, those organic compounds that are regulated because they lead to ozone formation; does not include methane; term used predominantly in California |
| NMHC | Nonmethane hydrocarbon | All hydrocarbons except methane; sometimes used to denote ROG |
| NMOC | Nonmethane organic compound | Organic compounds other than methane |
| RHC | Reactive hydrocarbon | All reactive hydrocarbons; also used to denote ROG |
| THC | Total hydrocarbon | All hydrocarbons, sometimes used to denote VOC |
| OMHCE | Organic material hydrocarbon equivalent | Organic compound mass minus oxygen mass |
| TOG | Total organic gas | Used interchangeably with VOC |

[a]Unless noted otherwise, HC is the term used in this report to represent the general class of gaseous organic compounds.
Source: Adapted from NRC (1999).

# Appendix C

# Some Statistical Issues in Inspection and Maintenance Evaluations

## VEHICLE EMISSIONS DISTRIBUTIONS

A few broken vehicles contribute a disproportionate share of the total emissions made up of exhaust hydrocarbon (HC), carbon monoxide (CO), and nitrogen oxide ($NO_x$) or evaporative HC emissions (including diurnal, running loss, liquid leaks, or hot-soak emissions). A vehicle can deteriorate in many ways, and different types of deterioration affect emissions differently. As discussed in Chapter 1 of this report, there is considerable correlation between exhaust HC and CO emissions in high-emitting vehicles, but little relationship between these and high $NO_x$ emissions. High evaporative emissions may or may not be correlated with high exhaust emissions (Pierson et al. 1999). High diurnal evaporative emitting vehicles are usually different from those with high hot-soak emissions.

Since most vehicles do not have high emissions, the distribution of emissions among vehicles for any single emission type are highly skewed and are best characterized by a log or gamma distribution (Zhang et al. 1994; Wenzel et al. 2000). Emissions distributions are more skewed for newer model-year vehicles than for their older counterparts, because only a few newer vehicles have broken fuel delivery or emissions-control equipment. HC and CO emissions distributions are more skewed than those of $NO_x$.

## SAMPLING METHODS AND BIAS

Special care must be taken to avoid selection bias. Since a small percentage of vehicles will emit a large percentage of the emissions, any sampling technique that decreases or enhances the percentage of these higher emitters may cause questionable conclusions to be drawn from the data. Every report describing an analysis of an inspection and maintenance (I/M) program that uses a sample of the vehicle fleet to estimate the benefits of the program should estimate the degree of selection bias in the sample. The methods for selecting the vehicles in the sample and the tests to determine if the sample is representative of the fleet should be described. An estimate of the magnitude of selection bias should also be made for any vehicle sample used to derive a correlation between an I/M test and the Federal Test Procedure (FTP) for the purpose of estimating the tons of pollutant per day reduced by the I/M program.

Mail solicitation of vehicles for laboratory testing has been practiced by the California Air Resources Board (CARB), the U.S. Environmental Protection Agency (EPA), and by auto manufacturers. Responses to mail solicitations have shown low voluntary acceptance by vehicle owners; CARB and EPA have typically experienced acceptance rates on the order of 10%. In the California I/M pilot study, when CARB threatened vehicle owners solicited by mail with loss of registration if they did not come in for testing, only a 60% acceptance rate was obtained.[1] The selection bias in mail solicitation sampling will be influenced by the rewards, penalties, and risks perceived by the recipient of the solicitation. If vehicle owners think that they might be penalized by the result of the tests they are asked to volunteer for, they will be less likely to agree to do so. If free inspections and repairs are offered for the vehicles to be tested, a disproportionate number of dirty vehicles might be included in the sample.

---

[1]The CARB acceptance rate of 60% is not 60% response rate of letters that were mailed out. Fifteen hundred solicitation letters were mailed out. Of the 1,500, 444 vehicles were dismissed, usually because (1) that the vehicle had previously received a Smog Check test, (2) that the addressee no longer owned the vehicle, or (3) the solicitation letter was returned as undeliverable. The " 60% response rate" is 60% of the (1,500-444) vehicles. Of the 1,500 letters mailed out, only 43% resulted in a recruited vehicle.

Higher acceptance rates have been obtained when vehicles were solicited directly rather than by mail. Recruitment of vehicles to be tested for multiday evaporative emissions testing solicited directly at an I/M lane resulted in a 90% acceptance in the Coordinating Research Council's (CRC) study of evaporative emissions. High acceptance rates were also obtained in the 1997-1999 California roadside tests, where vehicles were pulled over by police officers, asked if they would agree to be tested, and then tested at roadside. In a sample of the California roadside-test program, where vehicles were also measured by remote sensing as they left the roadside test area, a 92% acceptance rate was obtained. The remote-sensing results in this case showed no differences in the average HC and CO emissions for a model year between the vehicles' drivers who agreed to be tested and those who refused. An earlier roadside testing program, however, showed evidence of considerable bias because of higher emissions from vehicles whose owners refused to have them tested.[2]

Samples of vehicles taken from I/M lanes will not include vehicles that avoid being tested. These include both unregistered vehicles and vehicles registered in an area where I/M is not required but garaged and driven in the I/M area. If recruitment at I/M lanes is limited to vehicles arriving for their initial tests, not having had pre-test repairs, selection bias may exist, since vehicles that received pre-test repairs probably had higher emissions. Vehicles that are unsafe to test on a dynamometer would not be tested in an I/M program using loaded-mode testing.[3]

## FACTORS INFLUENCING VEHICLE EMISSIONS

Vehicle emissions are influenced by numerous factors other than I/M. When evaluating the effect of an I/M program, other factors that may be

---

[2]In an earlier Roadside Testing program in California, remote sensing showed that vehicles whose owners refused to allow testing had emissions more than twice those whose owners agreed to the roadside tests (Stedman et al. 1994).

[3]There is a group of vehicles (a relatively small fraction of the fleet) that cannot be tested on a two-wheel drive (2WD) dynamometer due to all-wheel drive (AWD) or non-switchable traction control. However, many centralized I/M programs are either using or considering the use of AWD dynamometers and therefore will be able to test these vehicles. The number of vehicles that are unsafe to test on a dynamometer is small enough so that it can be considered insignificant. Many of these are older (pre-1981) vehicles that are not subject to loade-mode testing.

partly responsible for emissions changes (either reducing or increasing them) need to be considered. To obtain the influence of the I/M program itself, these other factors should be shown either to have a low impact on the results, to be controlled, or to be randomized through sample selection.

Vehicle age and model year are important factors in vehicle emissions, but the most important factor is vehicle maintenance. Most analyses group vehicle data by model year, which is closely associated with vehicle technology. For example, the shift from carbureted to fuel-injected vehicles occurred over a period of a few years.

Since emissions deterioration rates have been decreasing due to improvements in vehicle design, the amount of emissions reduction attributable to an I/M program will be a function of the year during which the evaluation was made. When comparing evaluations of I/M programs in different years, change in vehicle technology must be taken into account. This includes vehicle design (engine design, fuel delivery system, and emission controls) and vehicle type (i.e., passenger car, light-duty truck), especially if different vehicle model years and different vehicle types within a model year were built to different regulatory emission standards.

The amount of vehicle use (miles driven per year) can also influence vehicle emissions. High-use vehicles (e.g., taxis) can be expected to have faster rates of deterioration than similar vehicles driven fewer miles.

Another important factor influencing vehicle emissions is driving mode (i.e., cold start, warm start, low load, high load, high acceleration or deceleration). In a cold start, the emissions control systems will not be operating at full capability. Under high load, many vehicles are designed to run fuel rich, causing very high CO emissions. During high acceleration or deceleration, some vehicles have high HC emissions.

Fuel quality also effects emissions. Laboratory tests using fuel different from that blended for local conditions can introduce bias into the data. Fuel composition parameters influencing emissions include volatility (especially for evaporative emissions), sulfur level, the presence of oxygenates (especially for older, carbureted vehicles), and other fuel reformulation, such as federal and California reformulated gasolines. Where there is a seasonal change in fuel composition (e.g., higher oxygenates and volatility in winter), comparisons of year-to-year changes in vehicle emissions should sample vehicles taken the same time of the year. In the wintertime, areas using oxygenated fuels may have a lower I/M test failure rate, because CO emissions are reduced as much as 10%. In this situation, the use of oxygenated fuels allows vehicles that normally would have failed to "pass the test" without being repaired.

Additionally, ambient conditions (temperature, altitude, and humidity) can have an impact on vehicle emissions as evidenced by the strong seasonal variation in the emissions from I/M and remote-sensing data.

Finally, the motorist socioeconomics can have an effect on vehicle emissions. Less affluent areas will have, on average, older vehicles. But age corrected vehicle emissions from a less affluent area still showed higher emissions (Stedman et al. 1994). Correlations have been found between average vehicle emissions and the zip code where the vehicle was registered (Singer and Harley 2000). Vehicles of the same model year and vehicle type registered in more affluent areas have lower emissions (Wenzel 1997).

## HUMAN BEHAVIORAL FACTORS

The introduction of a more severe I/M program can lead to the re-registration of vehicles into areas not requiring the new I/M program (Stedman et al. 1997; McClintock 1998). Some of these re-registered vehicles still drive in the I/M program area but are not subject to inspection.

The degree of enforcement affects the human behavior of avoiding the test. An evaluation of an I/M program should help in determining where additional enforcement and/or additional economic incentives would improve program benefits.

Fraud, such as clean piping, distorts program assessment based solely on I/M program records. Clean piping is a type of test fraud in which a technician tests a clean vehicle and attributes the result to the vehicle that is supposed to be tested to ensure that the vehicle passes. The inspection-lane data would indicate that the program is more effective than it actually is. The use of roadside pullover testing and/or remote-sensing measurements is not sensitive to test fraud and could help to identify testing stations that should be subject to covert audits to detect fraudulent behavior.

## NUMBER OF VEHICLES

I/M programs are designed to minimize the percentage of high-emitting vehicles. To tell whether such vehicles are becoming less prevalent in the fleet, sufficient numbers of vehicles need to be in the sample. Comparing two populations requires enough vehicles in each to have a valid comparison. If further subdivision of the population is necessary, additional vehicle emissions data are required.

A small sample size may produce too much uncertainty to adequately describe the average emissions reductions due to the I/M program. The size of the sample to use depends on the amount of confidence one wants in the results.[4]

The number of vehicles needed to characterize fleet emissions is also influenced by vehicle test-to-test variability. Some vehicles, especially some high-emitting ones, show considerable variation in emissions in repeated tests under the same conditions. The shape of the vehicle emissions distribution has consequences for how to choose vehicle samples for analysis.

Stratified sampling is a method of reducing the total number of vehicles sampled, while obtaining sufficient numbers of high-emitting vehicles. For this purpose more vehicles are selected from segments of the population that are expected to have more high-emitting vehicles. To keep the frequency of these vehicles in perspective, a parallel record of the frequency of the fleet segment in the total fleet has to be obtained.

A variety of stratified sampling methodologies have been used. EPA and CARB have used sampling strategies based on vehicle technology groupings and vehicle model year. California has used Radian/Eastern Research Group's high-emitter index to select vehicles for sending to test-only inspection stations. The CRC E-35 evaporative emissions study selected equal numbers of vehicles in three age groups corresponding to their evaporative emissions-control technologies.

---

[4]When Stedman et al. (1997) applied the step method in Denver, five daily averages were used to get an estimate of the effect of the enhanced I/M Program being introduced. With about 4,000 remote-sensing measurements per day (2,000 each for "enhanced I/M tested" and "not enhanced I/M tested"), the study found about a 7% ± 2-3% emissions reduction benefit, with 95% confidence. Because Stedman et al. ran the experiment halfway through the new biennial program, almost all other factors were randomized. The appropriate sample sizes in any specific test will depend on whether the significance of other factors (such as vehicle type, fuel, and socioeconomics) needs to be understood. Guidance should be sought from a statistician familiar with handling non-normal distributions.

## AVERAGE VALUES AND LOG TRANSFORMS

Some researchers take the log of (sometimes binned) vehicle emissions data to obtain a near normal distribution and then take the mean and the error limits of the log-transformed distribution. This reduces the weight (importance) of the high-emitting vehicles in the relationships (Pollack et al. 1999). The mean of a log-transformed sample is the geometric mean of the sample rather than the arithmetic mean. The total vehicle emissions introduced into the atmosphere are the sum of all the individual vehicle emissions or the arithmetic average of emissions per vehicle times the number of vehicles. The mean of a set of log-normally distributed vehicle emissions will always be less than the arithmetic average.

## TESTING NULL HYPOTHESES

If the sample is sufficiently large, it can be randomly divided into two sets, and the difference between the (model-year weighted) averages of the two sets of data should be zero plus or minus some value within an uncertainty range. Assumptions about the lack of influence of certain factors should be checked with a null hypothesis.

## CONFIDENCE LIMITS

Confidence limits of vehicle emissions in log or gamma distributions are asymmetric and can be generated using bootstrap analysis. A bootstrap approach is a Monte Carlo-style simulation technique used to estimate the confidence interval when errors are non-normally distributed (Chatterjee et al. 1997).

Normal statistics can be applied to the arithmetic averages of sufficiently large subsamples of non-normal distributions. The confidence limits, in this case symmetrical, apply to the means of the samples.

## CORRELATIONS

Pearson product correlation is not appropriate for log or gamma distributions because the $R^2$ values are overly influenced by the small, high emitting fraction. Scatter plots should be presented in linear space so the reader can visually assess the degree of correlation. Spearman rank correlation can be performed, however, to minimize the effect that high emitters have on vehicle emission distributions.

## ISSUES IN EMISSIONS OF I/M TEST DATA
## TO ESTIMATE I/M BENEFITS

The difference between initial fail and final pass results on the same vehicle tested in one cycle of the I/M program overstates the benefit of the I/M program because of regression to the mean.[5] Also, the deterioration of emissions until the next required test (the next test cycle) is not taken into account.

## COMPARISON OF TEST RESULTS AMONG PROGRAMS

I/M evaluation methods depend on comparing emissions from one vehicle fleet with another, or comparing emissions from one vehicle fleet at different times. Fleet emissions are dependent on the load that the vehicles are under during the test. In order to compare a test fleet with a reference fleet measured using different tests, a correlation equation is necessary. This equation is created from a third fleet (a "correlation fleet") that has experienced both tests. The test and reference fleets need to be free from selection bias and representative of the same population. The correlation fleet needs to be free from selection bias and representative of the same vehicle population, unless it can be shown that the correlation equation is not sensitive to potential differences between the correlation fleet and the test and reference fleets. The correlation equations should be derived from fleets subject to the same kind of test procedure. Significant differences between fleets may be caused by differences in any and all of the following: vehicle emission control and fuel system technologies, vehicle ages, vehicle types, inspection maintenance histories, socioeconomic owner histories. In addition, similar fuel and environmental conditions may be required (altitude, temperature, etc.) for measurement con-

---

[5]A description of the statistical concept of regression to the mean by W.M. Trochim, a professor in the Department of Policy Analysis and Management at Cornell University, is available on the web at http://trochim.human.cornell.edu/kb/regrmean. htm.

ditions for the test, reference, and environmental fleet emission measureme
However, fuel and environmental conditions are not taken into account in
pass/fail cutpoints when the scheduled I/M test is performed.